New Forms
of Governance for
Economic Development

OECD

ORGANISATION FOR ECONOMIC CO-OPERATION AND DEVELOPMENT

ORGANISATION FOR ECONOMIC CO-OPERATION AND DEVELOPMENT

Pursuant to Article 1 of the Convention signed in Paris on 14th December 1960, and which came into force on 30th September 1961, the Organisation for Economic Co-operation and Development (OECD) shall promote policies designed:

- to achieve the highest sustainable economic growth and employment and a rising standard of living in member countries, while maintaining financial stability, and thus to contribute to the development of the world economy;
- to contribute to sound economic expansion in member as well as non-member countries in the process of economic development; and
- to contribute to the expansion of world trade on a multilateral, non-discriminatory basis in accordance with international obligations.

The original member countries of the OECD are Austria, Belgium, Canada, Denmark, France, Germany, Greece, Iceland, Ireland, Italy, Luxembourg, the Netherlands, Norway, Portugal, Spain, Sweden, Switzerland, Turkey, the United Kingdom and the United States. The following countries became members subsequently through accession at the dates indicated hereafter: Japan (28th April 1964), Finland (28th January 1969), Australia (7th June 1971), New Zealand (29th May 1973), Mexico (18th May 1994), the Czech Republic (21st December 1995), Hungary (7th May 1996), Poland (22nd November 1996), Korea (12th December 1996) and the Slovak Republic (14th December 2000). The Commission of the European Communities takes part in the work of the OECD (Article 13 of the OECD Convention).

Publié en français sous le titre :
Les nouvelles formes de gouvernance et le développement économique

Cover photo: Prague, by Nathalie Buisson

Foreword

The concept of local governance has now made its way to the core of the debate on ways to improve the effectiveness of policies. Local governance is considered today a key determinant of the outcome of economic development strategies and action to improve the quality of life. Yet, only a few years ago, it was still a vague concept which left many practical questions unaddressed.

Part of the progress can be attributed to the work of the OECD's Co-operative Action Programme on Local Economic and Employment Development (LEED). Back in 1998, its Directing Committee launched an ambitious research agenda on local governance, released a seminal report on Local Management and held a high-level Conference in Venice on decentralisation. Major rewards have been reaped since, as we now know from Local Partnerships for Better Governance (2001) and Managing Decentralisation (2003) how to use partnership and decentralisation to improve local governance.

Further progress has been made on this agenda. This publication presents and analyses new forms of governance which have emerged for the pursuit of economic development strategies and the solution of socio-economic problems. It is based on a survey of the local governance experience of seven countries undertaken as part of the OECD Study on Local Partnerships, with the support of the European Commission (DG Employment and Social Affairs), a full participant in the LEED Directing Committee. This book is intended for use by government and its partners to set up mechanisms that can effectively promote an integrated and sustainable approach to economic development.

Sylvain Giguère, Deputy Head of the LEED Programme, designed this project and prepared this publication. Assistance was provided by Cécile Cordoliani, Sheelagh Delf, Nathalie Gosselin and Bevan B. Stein.

This book is published on the responsibility of the Secretary-General of the OECD.

Sergio Arzeni
Director, OECD Centre for Entrepreneurship
Head, OECD LEED Programme

Table of contents

ISBN 92-64-01530-2
New Forms of Governance for Economic Development
© OECD 2004

Chapter 1

Building New Forms of Governance for Economic and Employment Development

by

Sylvain Giguère,
Deputy Head of the LEED Programme, OECD

Local governance is in constant evolution as government, business and civil society experiment to find the optimum methods for them to address issues of common interest jointly. New forms of governance have emerged as stable models for pursuing economic development strategies at local and regional levels and solving socio-economic problems. By concentrating on endogenous development, regional strategic platforms, partnerships, open governments and other agents of change have succeeded in releasing the potential of their area thanks to better co-ordination, adaptation to local conditions and participation. This chapter examines their impact on local prosperity and the quality of life despite the barriers that they must overcome.

Increasing attention is being devoted to the governance of policy making. Is the level of government currently responsible for a given policy area the most appropriate one? Should other levels of government be involved? What role, if any, should civil society and business play? Which aspects of policies should be co-ordinated, which not? What type of information should be shared by government? How can the outcome of co-ordinated actions be evaluated? Are the frameworks covering public services' accountability adequate?

These and other questions are frequently asked by the actors in various policy domains. In some areas, such as economic development, there is now a consensus that action must be co-ordinated at the local level, and ideally also with related policy areas, to stimulate synergy, avoid conflicts, and make the best possible use of the information available. Improving local governance i.e., the way policies are co-ordinated, adapted to local conditions and oriented in partnership with civil society and business (see the definition in OECD, 2001a), has thus itself become a goal of government. It is now clear that improving local governance enhances the effectiveness of certain policies and takes full advantage of the resources and energy of business, civil society and the other levels of government in the pursuit of common objectives.

Less consensual are the ways to achieve this goal. Experiments in local governance have been conducted at a rapid pace in many countries over the past few years. The combined effects of local initiatives, national reforms and supranational frameworks (in the case of the European Union) have generated various models. Some of these have lasted and evolved, some not. The LEED Programme of OECD has itself contributed to continuous experimentation in this field with its analysis of the various models that have been developed over time. LEED's achievements include a report on Irish partnerships (1996), a study on the local management of policies (1998), the OECD Study on Local Partnerships (first results published in 2001) and two major studies on decentralisation, in 1999 and 2003.

It is now possible, within the local governance framework of OECD member countries, to identify a number of new forms which are emerging as stable models aimed at specific and clear tasks. They are presented in this chapter and examined in further detail later in this report. Some initial findings obtained for the two main general tools for improved governance, partnership and decentralisation, are set forth immediately below, followed by a review of the main obstacles inhibiting initiatives to improve local governance. The driving forces for improved local governance in the OECD today will then be discussed. The new forms of governance will be introduced, and the main issues they raise addressed. The chapter will conclude with an assessment of the prospects for the future.

Partnership performance

Between 1999 and 2003, the OECD conducted an in-depth study of area-based partnerships in which it examined the experience of 14 countries. The first results, released in 2001, revealed that the main impact of partnerships is to improve local governance. Three factors contributing to this outcome were identified. First, in all the countries surveyed, partnerships stimulate the uptake of public programmes in a way that is consistent with locally-shared priorities. Second, partnerships combine public programmes with local initiatives, and in so doing, support the development of these initiatives. Third, there are many instances in which partnerships have influenced the targeting of public programmes better to meet local needs. Partnerships may also be involved in other types of activity, but most of their impact on local governance is achieved through the impact of the three factors reviewed.

The involvement of partnerships in the delivery of services and programmes to the population appears to be comparatively weak. This comes as a surprise: most local partnerships seek to enhance their profile in this area and to deliver employment, social, training or business services, depending on their area of specialisation. Most partnerships undertake fund-raising activities towards both the public and private sectors with a view to reinforcing their capacity to develop services and projects. But the amount they obtain for such activities is in general fairly low compared to the resources of public institutions operating in the same fields (for example, the Irish partnerships' total programme budget corresponds to 3% of the outlays on active labour market policies delivered by the public employment service). From a local governance perspective this can be seen as a good thing since emphasis on service delivery by partnership-based organisations is often associated with conflictual relationships among the partners and a distribution of tasks inconsistent with the skills and competence that the various organisations can provide. Though partnerships fill policy gaps and bring benefits to the local community, some of the new services developed by partnerships may be delivered more effectively by the public services (possibly through delegation to the private and non-profit sectors). Moreover, delivery of services in parallel with the public sector reduces the scope for the latter to learn new techniques of working and improving its methods. The impact on governance is greatest when the partnership helps the partners, including the public services, to do a better job.

In sum, partnership is a valuable tool. It can have a significant impact on local governance, as long as it is seen by the partners as a way to improve their action, not as a substitute for action. There are, however, a number of obstacles to this. Effective partnership working is impeded by: a) a disconnection between national policy objectives and local goals. This can happen even when national ministries set the goals for partnerships and are represented in the partnerships; b) the limited administrative flexibility of many public programmes, including those which are relevant to local economic and employment development; c) weak accountability relationships, between the various partners, between the partnership and the public, and between the representatives and their constituency; and d) a tendency for partnership-based organisations to be process-driven as they seek to secure their continuity.

A series of recommendations has been made to overcome these obstacles. The recommendations aim to improve the policy management and accountability frameworks of the various partners, including central government, and to make them consistent with a partnership approach. This "strategy to improve governance through partnerships", has been endorsed by the LEED Directing Committee (see Box 1.1). As this survey will show, the strategy applies fully to the new forms of governance now being developed.

Managing decentralisation

Another tool widely used to improve local governance is decentralisation. Decentralisation can take the form of either devolution to a lower level of government (e.g. regional or local government) or "deconcentration" of the central government administration, i.e. transferring decision making to a lower tier within the same administrative structure. In both cases, decentralisation raises hard questions: How can decision-making power be passed on to a lower administrative tier or a sub-national entity while guaranteeing the same level of efficiency and transparency? How can more flexibility be provided while maintaining full accountability? The pressures to preserve full accountability for the use of public money often translate into few actual gains from decentralisation in terms of flexibility and capacity to meet local needs (OECD, 1998). This has led several governments to turn instead to partnerships as a safer way to improve local governance (even if, as shown by the OECD Study on Local Partnerships and other reports, partnership working is not exempt from accountability problems).

The OECD has looked at the problems associated with decentralisation and addressed in particular the critical trade-off between administrative flexibility and public accountability. Seeking to benefit from the advantages of both decentralisation and partnerships has required exploration of ways to reconcile accountability and flexibility. The most innovative were examined at the Warsaw Conference on "Decentralisation of Labour Market Policy and New

> ## Box 1.1. **A strategy to improve governance through partnerships**
>
> 1. *Make policy goals consistent at central level.* The creation of a network of partnerships should be accompanied by an exercise at central level to facilitate the necessary trade-offs between government departments (and social partners if needed) in order to achieve full consistency among national policy objectives in relation to the goals assigned to partnerships. Partnerships should not be accountable to one single central agency, but rather to all the partners needed to fulfill their mission. The partners should agree on the role to be given to partnerships in policy implementation and in improving governance.
>
> 2. *Adapt the strategic framework for the partnership to the needs of the partners.* Programming exercises should enable public service officers and local officials to achieve their own policy objectives through participation in the partnership strategy. This will encourage them to use the partnership as a tool to improve the quality of their own action locally. To foster a co-operative climate, the terms of the contribution of each partner to the implementation of the common strategy should be explicit and transparent. Services should normally be delivered by individual partners rather than by the partnership itself.
>
> 3. *Strengthen the accountability of partnerships.* Partners from all sectors (public services, social partners, the voluntary sector) should have a clear policy on the issues addressed by the partnerships. They should, accordingly, define mandates and reporting mechanisms for their delegates. Partners should agree on appropriate representation mechanisms for each sector, and on a clear distribution of responsibility when a partnership is involved in the implementation of a public programme. They should seek to separate the functions of strategic planning, project appraisal and technical assistance. These measures will ensure efficient co-ordination and secure partners' commitment.
>
> 4. *Provide flexibility in the management of public programmes.* The needs of local public service offices for more flexibility in the management of programmes should be so addressed as to ensure that their participation in the definition of a local joint strategy can be consistently followed up by involvement in its implementation. Partnerships should be involved in the targeting of public programmes related to common goals, while the responsibility for delivery should remain with public services.
>
> *Source:* OECD (2001a), Local Partnerships for Better Governance.

Forms of Governance: Tackling the Challenge of Accountability", held in March 2003 (results published in OECD, 2003).

A common thrust of some of the methods identified is the assignment of more responsibility to public service officers and regional authorities for establishing and running operational co-ordination mechanisms. One way of doing this is to require the local public service offices to review, jointly with the relevant local actors, the annual targets proposed for national programmes. The example of the Irish Community Employment Framework shows that this allows programmes to be adapted to local needs while delivering them within the public service structure, thereby fulfilling standard accountability requirements. In other experiments, governments have requested public services to set targets formulated in terms of local priorities, in co-operation with the local authorities. An example is offered by the United Kingdom where public service agreements are reached in combination with local strategic partnerships chaired by local authorities.

These reforms do not involve transfers of power to lower levels of government but seek to ensure that local concerns are taken into account in the implementation of government programmes. While the public service remains responsible for the delivery of programmes, this ensures that the programmes are better adapted to local needs and better co-ordinated with other measures. Thus partnerships are formed, but of a different type, as government moves away from a model led by civil society and its community-based organisations to a model in which responsibility lies mainly with civil servants and local or regional authorities.

Local governance barriers

The analysis of decentralised policies, new public service arrangements and partnerships across sectors and between government, business and civil society, makes it possible to outline some of the main barriers hindering government initiatives to improve local governance.

These obstacles are as follows:

- *Rigidity in target setting.* In setting targets for the implementation of the various policies, government administrations seek to ensure that national policy goals are met. Even when public services are decentralised to a network of local or regional offices enjoying some discretionary power, leeway to adjust targets to local concerns and measures taken in other policy fields is often limited. For example, local targets for labour market policy (*e.g.* number of job-seekers placed or being trained) are often set at central level in a way to achieve national goals for employment and unemployment.
- *The pursuit of efficiency.* Performance management methods designed to maximise output results are used to give public services incentives to

achieve annual targets and ensure that public resources are used in the most efficient way. For this purpose, in several policy fields, services may be outsourced to the private sector or delivered in competition with private and non-profit organisations. This promotes a relatively narrow approach to policy implementation.

- *Vertical accountability.* Public service officers are accountable to their internal administrative hierarchy and have no obligation to respond to requests from other policy areas or organisations at local level. In specific circumstances, decentralisation or tripartite management can broaden the set of policy objectives that are pursued locally.

- *Legitimacy.* Partnerships are formed in an attempt to overcome governance failures by calling on the help of civil society and business to meet local concerns better. However, the appointment of representatives of civil society and business is sometimes done on an arbitrary basis. Public sector officers, representing the state, may be reluctant to co-operate and share information with representatives of self-appointed non-government organisations (NGOs); or managers who volunteer to represent the business community. Federations of municipal authorities may also have difficulty in organising their representation in bodies of strategic importance.

- *Monitoring and evaluation.* The results of co-ordinated actions must be monitored and assessed within suitable performance management frameworks which make full allowance for shared objectives, governance outcomes and multiple accountability relationships. Little progress has been made so far on the evaluation agenda. Public services are reluctant to participate in joint initiatives if no record is kept of their contribution and if partnerships produce outcomes of a type that is ill-adapted to their accountability framework.

Finding solutions to these problems is currently a high priority on government agendas. Governments acknowledge that uniting forces can aid local and regional areas to achieve a sustainable improvement in their competitiveness, social cohesion and quality of life. New forms of governance are being built to this end.

Three driving forces for improving local governance

The present study is based on a set of experiments carried out in OECD member and non member countries to improve local governance. The experience of seven countries was analysed: Belgium (Walloon Region), the Czech Republic, Mexico, Norway, Slovenia, Spain and Sweden.

The survey of these countries has led to the identification of three main policy goals as part of the rationale for improved local governance.

Regional competitiveness

The shift from traditional regional development policies, aimed at reducing disparities and based on infrastructures and heavy industrial investment, to endogenous development, drawing on local knowledge, skills and competitive advantages, has emphasised the concept of network. Three networking circles play a complementary role in fostering regional competitiveness. First, the network among firms (cluster). Promoting co-operation between firms stimulates innovations in the development of products and processes as firms take advantage of synergies. Second, there is the network linking production and research. The establishment of links between production, education and research bolsters the learning process since it favours the development, the application and the distribution of knowledge. This is the rationale for promoting the development of so-called local innovation systems. Finally there is the network between production, research and public actors (public services, local authorities and other agencies). Broadening co-operation to public services and local and regional authorities fuels further this motor of innovation and competitiveness as it contributes to the building of an integrated strategy, which ensures that the conditions for co-operation are fulfilled, that the investment decisions taken are sustainable, and that public services adequately meet local needs as part of the strategy implemented.

Setting up these networking circles in a coherent manner is no easy task. The economic development field offers some specific challenges to the local governance framework. The field is often crowded by a number of initiatives led by various organisations (business organisations, local authorities, economic development agencies), themselves poorly co-ordinated. The various tiers of government (local, regional) may independently pursue their own strategies for the economic development of the local area, and these may not be fully consistent with one another. As a result, efforts in the areas of foreign direct investment, endogenous development and spatial planning, for example, may not be consistent with one another, let alone co-ordinated with the programmes and activities implemented in the fields of R&D, employment, skills development and education. This explains why several governments have promoted the creation of regional partnerships to bring coherence to the economic development field and to design strategies aimed to stimulate regional competitiveness.

Efficient labour markets

Improving local governance has an impact on the overall effectiveness of labour market policy. It is widely acknowledged that efforts to co-ordinate policies with economic development strategies and social inclusion initiatives, to adapt them to local conditions and to involve representatives of

NEW FORMS OF GOVERNANCE FOR ECONOMIC DEVELOPMENT – ISBN 92-64-01530-2 – © OECD 2004

neighbouring policy areas, business and civil society in the orientation of measures, bring significant benefits. They are likely to enhance labour market outcomes in the long term as the superior quantity and quality of the information brought to bear in the implementation of programmes and enhanced overall synergy make their effects felt.

Labour market programmes are more likely to be effective when they take into account the local characteristics of the target groups and seek to dovetail them with local labour market needs (Martin and Grubb, 2001). Information provided by local employers and representatives of the target groups helps to guide labour market programmes as well as reducing the substitution and the displacement effects (respectively, non-subsidised workers and activities displaced by subsidised ones) and deadweight losses (jobs that would have been created anyway) that are associated with active labour market policies. Business organisations, trade unions and community-based organisations often provide services that supplement those of the public employment service, such as vocational training, placement and re-integration services, and joint steering is required to maximise complementarity while avoiding duplication (OECD, 1998). The delivery of employment services must also take account of existing infrastructure (and gaps in it), public transport and municipal services. Training programmes must meet business demands for skills that change rapidly and should be adjusted ahead of forthcoming local investments. Furthermore, helping businesses to access these programmes is conducive to upgrading the skills of low-qualified workers (Research Institute for Small and Emerging Business, 2004), now a priority for labour market policy in many countries.

The relationship between local governance and the effectiveness of labour market policy explains why many countries have now adopted an active approach to the improvement of local governance and taken firm steps towards decentralisation and partnership (Giguère, 2003). Their governments seek better co-ordination between labour market policy and other policies in the belief that it can be implemented in the way that best meets businesses' needs and contributes to social cohesion. However, taking a genuinely strategic approach to employment and labour markets reveals the presence of a real challenge as will be seen later.

Building social capacity

Civil society makes an important contribution to the struggle against poverty and social exclusion through dedicated non-profit organisations and local initiatives. Many governments seek to confer a more powerful role on these organisations in strategic planning exercises, looking to them for inputs to both the design and the implementation of local development strategies and assigning them a central role in the promotion of local initiatives and the delivery of some services to the population. Many governments now form partnerships with the non-profit sector for the delivery of services which were traditionally delivered by public agencies, such as employment and social services.

In economies in transition and countries whose citizens have only recently come to enjoy full democratic rights, nurturing the development of an organised civil society is both a priority and a prerequisite for the development of a non-profit sector capable of assuming responsibility for the delivery of services to the population and the promotion of local initiatives. As will be shown by this survey, the simultaneous construction of a democratic society that is both representative and participatory is a difficult task.

Models emerging

The above somewhat simplified picture of the main thrusts for improving local governance omits a number of concerns that have also contributed to shape current initiatives in this area. Building the institutional capacity for implementing the financial assistance programmes of the European Union (EU) is one of them, and it proves to be particularly significant in the new Member states of the EU, including those surveyed in this book (the Czech Republic and Slovenia), as well as countries expected to join the Union at a later stage. Another factor is the need to modernise the public employment service. Several countries are currently reforming these services to improve their performance and to render their administrative structure more accountable and more responsive to local needs. This is an important aspect of the initiatives to improve governance that have been taken in the Walloon Region of Belgium. Nevertheless the three main stylised motivations identified above can be considered as the main driving forces underpinning action to improve local governance, for they are consistent with those highlighted for the first seven countries to participate in the OECD Study on Local Partnerships (OECD, 2001a).

These initiatives have generated a number of new forms of governance. Experimentation with them started years ago, and several countries have now a long experience of the management of governance structures. Although the area is constantly evolving, adapting to changes in policies, state reforms of administrative structures and new supra-national arrangements, some models can now be considered as fundamentally stable, despite differences between countries and notwithstanding on-going modifications of their normal functioning. The present 7-country survey extends the knowledge gained from those previously reviewed and makes it possible to identify and analyse the new forms of governance. They will be discussed under four main headings: *i)* regional strategic platforms; *ii)* area-based partnerships; *iii)* open governments; and *iv)* agents of change.

a) Regional strategic platforms

The most robust trend in local governance today is clearly the establishment of regional strategic platforms. Many countries and regions, after experimenting for years with various institutional arrangements, have either turned to or reinforced this model to pursue more effectively the goal of regional competitiveness and co-ordinate economic development actions on the ground. The tasks of these platforms are: *i)* to foster co-operation among the main organisations involved in economic development (*e.g.* agencies, business organisations, regional authorities) and neighbouring policy fields (*e.g.* employment, education, tourism); *ii)* to design, and possibly implement, a strategy for sustainable economic development; and, often *iii)* to stimulate innovation through building clusters of firms and establishing links between enterprises and the research and education sectors, among others.

These platforms are most often set up at the level of administrative regions. There are two main reasons for this: *i)* to secure sufficient critical mass, both in terms of size and population, to be able to influence major economic development activities, such as attracting foreign direct investment and providing infrastructure to support high-technology industrial activities; and *ii)* to gain enough legitimacy to play a role in these economic activities; this legitimacy is often underpinned by the existence of regional administrative boundaries and support from regional authorities. In Norway and Sweden, platforms have been established in the regions or counties (*Fylke* in Norwegian, *Län* in Swedish), in which elected county councils share public responsibility with the central government, represented by a governor and a regional administration.

A platform may be made responsible for implementing the economic development strategy that it contributed to design. However, unless it directly supervises a regional development agency, the platform is more likely to play an indirect role in operational matters, concentrating instead on the strategic aspects of economic development, though it may also be involved in the delivery of some specific projects. Implementing the economic development strategy is often the responsibility of a dedicated regional development agency, sometimes a separate public-private partnership[1] (PPP).

Regional platforms usually concentrate on stimulating endogenous development (fostering entrepreneurship, assisting the start-up and development of SMEs and the clustering of firms, promoting innovation and indigenous investment). They have sought with various degrees of success to involve civil society and other local actors in finding solutions to social and employment problems. Their influence on measures to attract inward investment and provide industrial infrastructure is sometimes weaker, especially if another regional body is responsible for these tasks. In Sweden, the main actor for economic development at regional level is the county administration, which draws support from national agencies: NUTEK to promote industrial development, VINNOVA to promote local innovation systems, and ALMI to encourage entrepreneurship and SMEs. Among them, only the county administration and ALMI are typically members of regional platforms (regional growth agreements). Other partners include the county council, the public employment service (AMS), employer associations, trade unions and the local university if any. Thus the degree of influence of the platforms on economic matters depends on the relationship developed with the county administration and some influential state agencies.

The development of regional strategic platforms has raised a number of issues regarding in particular: i) evaluation; ii) optimal size; iii) breadth of approach to and scope of activities; and iv) links with labour market policy and workforce development activities. They are examined in turn below.

The evaluation issue

It is always difficult to identify what outcomes are to be directly attributed to the work of a regional strategic platform. Each organisation that is a member of the platform performs its own tasks, and its results may be similar to those that would have been achieved in the absence of a platform. In Norway, some of the projects that have been conducted by the platforms (the labour market councils of Oppland and Hedmark) would in any event have been carried out by the county council, which has played a leading role in the work of the platforms (see Chapter by Geddes). In the Swedish county of Uppsala, at the forefront of the initiatives to connect industry with research and education so as to achieve the optimal application and distribution of knowledge, much of the conceptual work had been done by a working group under the auspices of the county administration before the regional platform was set up (see Chapter by Morgan and Sol).

Certainly, not everything that is reported by platforms, or any other sort of partnership, should be considered as a direct outcome of platform activities. Conversely, it would be equally wrong to assume that a platform has no impact when no outcome is registered or reported. At a minimum, platforms allow information to be shared and knowledge to be disseminated, and they contribute to broaden the scope and extend the perspective of economic development. At a maximum, they enhance the long-term returns of economic development activities with their focus on endogenous development and they create the conditions required for the emergence of synergies and more efficient allocation of the resources available for local

NEW FORMS OF GOVERNANCE FOR ECONOMIC DEVELOPMENT – ISBN 92-64-01530-2 – © OECD 2004

development. At both extremes of this spectrum, impacts are difficult to measure, especially in that they may in good part only materialise in the long term.

But isn't it costly to operate a platform? The positive aspect of strategic platforms is that, in general, their benefits can be considered as a net gain. Partnerships normally require a modest budget to cover their operating costs, the budget for individual activities being funded by the partner organisations themselves or allocated on a project selection basis (see OECD, 2001a, for more details on the costs of operation of partnerships and the funding of their activities). As a rough average, the operating costs of a partnership (not directly responsible for policy implementation) are of the order of 150 000 EUR annually.

Partnerships may also generate transaction costs. The time needed to make decision may be longer within a partnership than it might be otherwise. Discussions and decisions may be biased because of weak accountability relationships: between the partners and their representatives; between the partners themselves; and between the partnership and the public. Other factors of bias include asymmetrical information among the partners and the tendency for some partnerships to go beyond their mandate. While longer time for decision making is an understandable side effect, poor accountability and biased decisions are symptoms of failed governance arrangements which should not be tolerated. The "strategy to improve governance through partnerships", outlined above, aims to ensure that partnership working contribute to enhance governance, and applying it should minimise transaction costs. In particular, it is up to the partners to decide what the limits to the mandate of the partnership are, how the various sectors should be represented and what information should be prepared and distributed.

The fundamental evaluation problem for partnerships is that evaluating the result of joint actions calls for the development of a dedicated set of outcome indicators, in addition to those which capture the results of the actions carried out separately by the members, for the specific purpose of evaluating the contribution of the partnership proper. In other words, if partnership working yields greater synergy, better co-ordinated actions, reduced duplication, or more sustained results, these are the outcomes that should be monitored to assess the performance of partnerships (Giguère, 2002). They can be referred to as "governance indicators", and ideally should be established by the partners themselves when they create the partnership and agree on the benefits they expect from working in partnership. Greffe identifies in OECD (2003) a number of governance indicators for the employment service working in partnership with other organisations in a decentralised framework.

Critical mass and the size of the region

In addition to the challenges associated with horizontal co-operation, partnerships and platforms also face the problem of vertical co-ordination. More precisely, they have difficulty in influencing the way government funding is allocated to their area. In principle, or so governments say, regional development strategies aim to guide the implementation of national policies. Yet central administrations have not always established proper mechanisms or selection procedures for correlating the allocation of funds with an assessment of the strategies and projects that are proposed at local or regional level. As a result, funds are allocated through less structured channels. This may lead to the development of a role of lobbyist for the platforms to influence the allocation of funds, which understandably encourages platforms to involve all the main actors of a region to give the proposals put forward to the central government more weight, and to make them as inclusive as possible. It also contributes to an enlargement of the territory covered by the platforms intended to increase their critical mass.

In Slovenia, regional development strategies are put forward by regional development agencies. These agencies are generally more specialised in the delivery of services to enterprises, and local actors feel that the existing structures are too weak to influence the targeting and implementation of overall national policy at regional level, to resolve co-ordination failures or remedy policy gaps. This has led to proposals for the creation of inclusive regional councils to increase bargaining power, with simultaneous debate as to what should be the optimal size of the regions. Current opinion is that they should probably be reduced from the existing 12 regions to around five (with an average population per region rising from 167 000 to approximately 400 000). In Sweden a similar debate took place recently. The number of regions was reduced from 24 to 21, raising their average population from 417 000 to 476 000.

This phenomenon is part of a larger trend. In Flanders, the *streekplatformen* (district platforms) in 17 regions (average population 347 000) proved too small to reach critical mass, and the number of member municipalities has been declining in recent years. Following the OECD recommendation (2001a) to strengthen the links between economic development and labour market policy at sub-regional level, the government decided to merge the *streekplatformen* with the sub-regional employment committees (STCs) and streamline the number of bodies to around 13 (average population 454 000). In Austria, where territorial employment pacts were initially set up at various levels (groups of districts and *Länder*) during the experimental phase (1997-1999), consolidation has been implemented at the *Land* level for the period 2000-2006 (average population 900 000).

A broader approach

As noted above, regional strategic platforms are mainly concerned with economic development overall, but in reality they concentrate on endogenous development (with a possible involvement in addressing socio-economic issues and problems, *e.g.* employment, social inclusion, education, health, environment). The ability of the regional platforms to take a genuinely integrated approach to local development varies widely. Many partnerships focus on business development, leaving aside aspects such as skills, housing and transport, which are critical to economic development. In many cases, this position is correlated with a weak capacity to take a strategic approach: many of the partnerships that are strongly oriented to the promotion of the development of the economy have been more involved in delivering services to the business community, a task that can admittedly be carried out efficiently by specialised consultant services, rather than in drawing up and pursuing strategic orientations for the development of the region.

Four reasons have been advanced to explain the narrow economic focus of many platforms:

- *Constituency.* In some cases the economic focus is directly linked to the expectations of the partners and tied to the composition of the board. In the Mexican state of Sinaloa, for example, the economic council of the state (CODESIN) is a partnership between the administration and the business community. This membership gives the organisation specific tasks for the economic development of the State. As a result, CODESIN concentrates on promoting an economic development strategy whose features are endogenously supported and sustainable growth. In the Spanish province of Almería (Andalusia), sector-based patterns of co-operation on tourism and water management have been developed in parallel, and the lack of a strategic, common approach has been identified as a major impediment to successful sustainable development (see Chapter by Mosley). Similar situations have been found in the United States, where partnerships are formed to promote the particular interests of predominant sectors in the local economy (Eberts and Erikcek, 2001).

- *Funding rules.* Under certain national programmes, a narrow focus may be a consequence of the rules imposed by the principal sources of funding available to partnerships. The territorial pacts operating under the Italian legislation applicable at the end of the 1990s and the beginning of the 2000s had authority to propose only projects of business development (for 70% of the funding) and infrastructures (30%). Projects in other areas (*e.g.* training of the labour force) were not eligible. Other dispositions obtain under EU-funded pacts, and the current rules applying to the new "integrated territorial projects" are also different.

- *Professional skills.* The failure to take a strategic or integrated approach can also reveal weaknesses in professional skills and the absence of networking activities among similar structures. Researchers in the field have for many years deplored the lack of proper skills for local development and stressed the need to develop appropriate training programmes for practitioners and local officials (see for example Chapter by Ó Cinnéide and Keane). The networking of partnerships allows information on strategic planning to be disseminated, and the exchange of experience also contributes to the reinforcement of skills at local level (see Chapter by Stewart). It is worth mentioning that networking of partnerships is now current practice in several countries. Countries with the longest standing arrangements include Austria (Austrian Co-ordinating Office for Territorial Employment Pacts), Belgium (Co-ordinating Office of Sub-regional Employment Committees within the Ministry of the Flemish Community) and Ireland (Area Development Management and the organisation "Planet") (see OECD, 2001a). These considerations have further led to the creation of the OECD LEED Forum on Partnerships and Local Governance, funded by Austria, to broaden the exchange of experience on an international scale.

- *Administrative obstacles.* In some other cases, the absence of an integrated approach reflects the fact that some partners experience administrative difficulties hindering active participation in collective exercises of strategic planning. These difficulties may be linked to an incompatibility of policy objectives set at national level, and to some rigidity in the management of programmes. The particular case of the employment services is examined below. In general, this problem may be solved, as the "strategy to improve governance through partnerships" recommends, if the main partners, including central government and its relevant agencies, explicitly agree on a set of actions that can be best carried out at regional level by the platforms, after which the partners would adjust their policy objectives and management frameworks appropriately.

Co-ordination with labour market policy

Labour market policy, or workforce development activities, is one of the key instruments used by government to stimulate local economic and employment development. Labour market policy comprises a wide array of tools, from job subsidies to vocational training and measures to promote self-employment, all of which can contribute to the development of productive capacities. Employment policy channels substantial resources to the local level. It is implemented through country-wide networks of government offices and, in some cases, private/non-profit organisations, which can join other organisations in pursuing common objectives. Eighteen OECD countries devote at least one per cent of GDP to labour market policy (both active and passive measures); for Denmark, the proportion is five per cent. In depressed areas, workforce programmes generate a particularly useful inflow of resources, which may be used to reinforce efforts to revitalise the local economy and foster endogenous development. The employment administration also provides a range of services locally, such as labour market information, which can play an important role in the design of integrated development strategies.

Thus labour market policy is potentially a powerful tool for economic development. However, the extent to which it actually plays a role depends on a number of institutional features which determine the flexibility of policy instruments, the behaviour of the local employment administration and the capacity for other actors and organisations (economic development agencies, local authorities, employer associations, community-based organisations) to interact with the employment services in the design and implementation of programmes. The section on local governance barriers above has identified the main factors which inhibit active participation by the public sector in collective strategic planning exercises. A wide range of institutional features can affect the capacity of employment and labour authorities in this regard. They include (non exhaustively): i) the degree of decentralisation; ii) the degree of administrative flexibility; iii) management by objectives vs. management by programmes; iv) the structure of funding mechanisms; v) the characteristics of the accountability relationships within the labour administration; vi) third party delivery; vii) the role of tripartite arrangements ; viii) integrated vs. segmented employment services; and ix) the linkages between employment services and training (see OECD, 1998 and 1999 for more details on the local management of employment policy).

These characteristics of the national policy and administrative framework normally apply to the entire territory of a country. This does not mean that the extent to which labour market policy contributes to local development is uniform. Agents adapt their behaviour to the existing rules and, as shown by numerous examples of local initiative, take steps to overcome administrative obstacles. As a result, the nature of the interactions varies from area to area, with different outcomes in terms of local development.

This issue is crucial for both the conduct of economic development activities and the effectiveness of labour market policies. Further work on it will be carried out by OECD to find ways to harmonise these two policy areas at local and regional level (see Box 1.2).

b) Area-based partnerships

Area–based partnerships are a second stable form of local governance that has been developed in part to address the issue raised above concerning

Box 1.2. **Integrating labour market policy and economic development: a new OECD initiative**

A new project will be carried out by OECD LEED in 2005-2007 on "Integrating Employment, Skills and Economic Development". The proposal emerged from the OECD Conference "Decentralisation and New Forms of Governance: Tackling the Challenge of Accountability" (Warsaw, March 2003). It was subsequently put forward by Poland to the LEED Directing Committee at its 42nd session (Cuernavaca, Mexico, June 2003). The project was approved as part of the Orientations of the 2006-2010 Mandate of the LEED Programme, which were outlined at the 43rd session (Trento, December 2003) and adopted at the 44th session (Copenhagen, June 2004).

The study will aim to identify the ways to co-ordinate labour market policy and economic development strategies designed at local and regional levels. In particular, the work will seek to answer the following questions:

● How can labour market policy best contribute to local development and feed economic growth? What are the changes needed in policy and administrative frameworks at national (regional) level?

● How can local employment administrations best contribute to local efforts for economic development? How can both areas cross-fertilise to meet business needs while providing sustainable solutions to the problems of the disadvantaged on the labour market (social exclusion, poor job retention, low skills)?

● How can labour market information and the expertise of local employment services best contribute to the design of effective local integrated development strategies?

● What are the best governance mechanisms to guarantee co-operation and co-ordination between the actors responsible for employment policy and economic development (and other relevant areas) at local and regional levels?

The project will examine the experience of a group of selected countries. In each country, the project will examine: a) the general policy and administrative framework for labour market policy and economic development; b) the strategies for economic development designed at local and regional levels and the local orientations followed by labour market policy; and c) the governance mechanisms used to link labour market policy and economic development at local and regional level.

The analysis will devote particular attention to the following topics, which were highlighted by the Warsaw conference: i) the examination of mechanisms for employment services to agree on local targets in a cross-cutting perspective; ii) ways to reconcile labour market goals with the concerns of local authorities and economic development agencies; iii) the financial instruments conducive to horizontal co-operation; iv) the supply of professional and occupational skills at local level and the ways to build up the capacity of civil society; v) ways to reinforce trust and augment social capital; and vi) the methods and indicators pertinent to monitoring and evaluation of governance improvements.

the weak connection between labour market authorities and local development actors. Area-based partnerships share some similar tasks with the regional strategic platforms, in particular as regards fostering co-operation and designing and implementing a strategy, but the partnerships differ from them in two main ways: they typically concentrate on addressing the socio-economic problems of their area, rather then seeking to encompass economic development considerations; and they cover an area smaller than an administrative region, i.e. a sub-regional or local area.

This well-known approach was first tried out in distressed areas in North America in the 1980s and was then adopted as a more systematic tool to remedy policy gaps and find answers to problems of long-term unemployment, rural under-development and urban decay in Ireland and the United Kingdom in the 1990s. In the mid-1990s, the European Union saw it as a way to reduce employment and development disparities and for this purpose, to stimulate the allocation of financial resources to local projects throughout the Union. The partnership model given effect as part of this initiative (which received specific funding during a limited period – 1997-1999), the "Territorial Employment Pact", is still in place in several countries and regions of the Union.

As mentioned above, area-based partnerships rarely seek to encompass economic development strategy, except in rural areas. In most cases, economic development strategy falls within the purview of another organisation, often an economic development agency, but which may also be a member of the partnership. Efforts to achieve co-ordination often focus instead on the employment services, training institutions, social welfare organisations and local authorities, with varying success. Extensive analysis of area-based partnerships can be found in OECD (2001a).

The present survey includes an excellent example of the implementation of an area-based partnership. The Territorial Employment Pact (TEP) of Vallès Occidental in the province of Barcelona in Catalonia pursues a sophisticated integrated strategy and has succeeded in obtaining a genuine commitment from the social partners and local authorities in the area. The partnership, born during the experimental phase of the European Union's TEP initiative, concentrates on the linkages between employment and economic development, supports social inclusion projects, serves as a lobby at regional level and acts as a forum in which the main actors (at the comarca level, which covers a group of municipalities) can address and solve local governance problems. Catalonia has a long tradition of co-operation between the regional government and the social partners, and has taken steps to extend this model to other areas of the region. There now exist 21 partnerships in total. Catalonia, together with Austria, areas of Finland, France and Greece, and the south of Italy, is among the regions in which the EU experiment has taken root. The EU initiative may also have contributed to strengthen partnerships that were set up before it was put in place, such as the area-based partnerships in Ireland. Partnerships of a similar type exist in other European countries as well as in Australia, Canada and the United States.

Localness and the limits to the pursuit of economic development

The size of area-based partnerships makes them well-suited to address social and employment issues. The territory they cover often corresponds to local labour markets comprising either a group of medium-sized municipalities or a larger urban centre with its neighbouring satellite zones. This makes it possible to develop effective relationships with community-based organisations and to interact with the target groups of various employment and social assistance measures, which is central to the work of organisations involved in socio-economic issues. The establishment of good relations with chambers of commerce, representatives of employers, elected local officials and officers working in sectors such as employment or tourism is also crucial for the identification of development opportunities in their area. Support from the regional government, except for the financing of projects, and the specification of administrative boundaries, do not play a major role in these matters.

While economic development is normally not their main goal, area-based partnerships have sometimes sought to extend their agenda and to take a broader role in stimulating the economic development of their area. In many cases, the critical mass issue has been raised and undermined these attempts: as mentioned above, the municipalities in Flanders' *Streekplatformen* reduced their commitment until a local governance reform streamlined and merged them with sub-regional employment committees. While many Irish area-based partnerships have traditionally pursued business development as one of their half dozen objectives (within a strategy mainly oriented towards social and employment issues), the government in 2000 created County/City Development Boards and assigned responsibility to them for the design and implementation of an economic, social and cultural development strategy covering their area. The area-based partnerships have been invited to provide inputs to these boards, considered as the *de facto* strategic platforms for their area. In Québec, a 2003 reform of local and regional development structures assigned responsibility to elected local officials in each sub-region (*Municipalité régionale de comté*) for finding the most suitable structure for the pursuit of economic development. The government had previously promoted the establishment of local development centres (*Centre local de développement, CLD*) taking the form of partnerships embracing institutions, social partners, representatives of civil society and local authorities to design economic development strategies. The current *CLD* configuration, i.e. involving civil society groups, is expected by local analysts to survive in around half the sub-regions, predominantly rural areas, where no particular priority attaches to attracting inward investment or providing industrial infrastructures and where the partnerships have proved particularly successful.

Thus only in very specific circumstances do area-based partnerships manage to obtain a firm mandate on economic development from the local authorities. Italy's experience supports the suggestion that only the most innovative partnerships in rural or weakly industrialised areas, which concentrate on endogenous development, will succeed in pursuing an economic development strategy (Melo, 2001).

The capacity building issue

Area-based partnerships are expected to draw as much as possible on their local nature and focus to play a strong role within the local community. In particular they may, with the assistance of local non-government organisations, help local communities to participate in public schemes, counsel them and provide technical assistance, help public service to reach disadvantaged groups, and bolster the development of community services and businesses. Conversely, governments expect area-based partnerships to be a forum in which to meet representatives of civil society and the local community. Governments recognise that the expertise and knowledge possessed by the representatives of civil society help adapt policies to local conditions and identify synergies and opportunities for local development.

A major difficulty here concerns the identification of "representatives". There is no clear understanding or agreement on the proper way to appoint civil society representatives. NGOs are often self appointed, and will presumably represent the interests of their members, and not those of the broader local community. This can bias discussions and decisions. Some countries provide for elections. This may represent a step forward but does not guarantee accountability as such. Full accountability of civil society representatives requires the definition of a mandate for representatives, the use of reporting and feedback mechanisms, and the dissemination of results to the civil society constituency at large (OECD, 2001a). This situation reinforces the dubious attitude of public services and local authorities toward sharing information and decision-making power. As a result, partnership-based organisations often develop their own services instead of helping public organisations to improve theirs. An unproductive competition may be the result, with few positive outcomes for either the local community or the effectiveness of the programmes delivered.

Whether to avoid this situation or to remedy it, area-based partnerships must devote efforts to build the capacity of local communities. These efforts must seek to improve the dissemination of information on the partnership mechanisms available, propose mechanisms for the participation of the local community that are acceptable to other partners, implement the proper selection mechanisms, ensure that mandates are defined by the constituencies, and ensure that the representatives report to them.

c) Open government

A third current tendency in local governance is to stimulate interaction between government and civil society and harmonise representative and participatory democracy. The approach is to create as extensive a direct interface as possible between government and civil society (i.e. without the filter of platform or partnership). The aim is to disseminate information as widely as possible on the views, plans and projects of local and regional governments and to receive feedback and inputs that can help to modulate intervention in the way that maximises impact and participation.

The traditional method of involving civil society is to set up consultative mechanisms, such as public hearings.[2] Various types of consultative mechanisms have been put in place recently to secure feedback from the social partners and groups of the population on projects led by local and regional authorities and public services, and to obtain input into the process of designing strategies. Under the Fox administration, Mexico has sought to foster participatory development and to involve civil society in the orientation of the country's development: the federal government conducted consultations with civil society in the preparation of both the 2001-2006 National Development Plan and the Vision for the Development of Mexico in 2020-25. To support these efforts, the government has decentralised resources and encouraged local and regional governments to regenerate consultative structures that were used as early as the 1980s to plan economic development at both local and state levels (COPLADEMUN and COPLADES, respectively). Similar structures are found in the Czech Republic at the local level, where municipalities are keen to show their openness and transparency, and to obtain suggestions from citizens on urban projects. As various reports show, participation is often weak in these forums as partners feel that the initiative lies mainly with the local authorities and that no strategic decision is to be made within such bodies (see Chapter on the Czech Republic by De Rynck and on Mexico by Ó Cinnéide and Keane).

For similar reasons, the members of tripartite organisations used to conduct labour market policy, such as the sub-regional employment committees in Wallonia used to have a mere consultative role. To strengthen this role, the Walloon regional government has integrated the committees within the structure of the public employment service (FOREM), to make them a regional unit of the employment service (see Chapter by Greffe). While it is too early to assess the results of this administrative reform, it is worth noting that Denmark and Flanders have taken different avenues to attain similar goals. To revitalise their tripartite boards, reforms in these countries have introduced new partners: local and regional authorities in the case of Denmark, and representatives of civil society (and one representative from municipalities) in the case of Flanders (OECD, 2001a)[3].

Beyond consultation: "participatory governments"

Can participatory democracy avoid being an empty concept? How can civil society, organised in groups and communities, take an active part in, and provide helpful inputs to the directions to be taken by the development of their area while keeping decision-making efficient and policy making effective?

Experience shows that fostering participatory democracy and creating operational channels between civil society and decision-making bodies constitute a difficult challenge, even more so when representative democracy is to be rebuilt after a long period of totalitarianism, as in the case of the economies in transition. But it may be in these very countries, laboratories of the advanced economies for the creation of democratic mechanisms, that most can be learned today on the effective ways to involve civil society.

Within a decade after its shift from communism to the market economy, the Czech Republic, like other economies in transition, has moved to reform its public administration and governance structure. The avenue followed by the Czech Republic was to reduce the powers of the districts (an administrative sub-regional level) and to create new elected self-governing regions. Given the strength of the pressures not to add to the fiscal burden of the population, the regions were given power to co-ordinate, but comparatively limited spending power. Accordingly, the main responsibility of the new regional governments is to design and implement regional development strategies, a task somewhat similar to those performed by the regional strategic platforms examined in this report. They are responsible for proposing new ways to implement national policies and to put forward new projects to be funded by national or local sources that are both relevant and available, as well as new co-ordinated approaches for local authorities.

To achieve these tasks successfully, and to achieve a significant impact in their region, the new self-governments must tackle two challenges. First, they must secure the commitment of public services and government agencies. National departments may carry on implementing their measures from the central level and through their network of local offices according to their own criteria and norms, since they are not legally bound by the regional strategies. Second, as regional assemblies and administrations have their own legitimacy to build, they must earn respect from the regional actors with whom they interact: non-government organisations, regional development agencies, social partners and local authorities. It is thus in the interest of the regional governments to be as all-embracing as possible in the design and implementation of regional strategies, and to report to the regional actors in the most effective and transparent way.

Although limited spending power can be interpreted as a sign of weakness for a level of government, the obligation to build consensus can be a source of strength for local governance, especially at the intermediary regional level, where democracy is in crisis in several OECD areas. Only the future will tell if this mix of representative and participatory democracy can prove an effective way to build an integrated approach to economic development and foster both regional competitiveness and social cohesion.

d) Agents of change

The vitality of local initiatives is considered by many as a pre-condition for the success of local strategies and the achievement of local prosperity. The United States has long shown the way with its *civic entrepreneurs* and community leaders able to mobilise resources around projects of common interest, drawing on local assets and synergies to maximise impact on the local economy. Little involved in strategic activities (they are "policy takers", not policy makers), these agents of change have nonetheless a positive impact on the health of local governance inasmuch as they stimulate debate and innovation.

Many governments today support this approach to the promotion of economic and employment development as a complement to the work of regional development agencies, strategic platforms and area-based partnerships. In Belgium, the Walloon government has set up local development agencies (*Agences de développement local*) in a large number of small municipalities, and town-centre management units (*Missions centre-ville*) in municipalities of more than 30 000 inhabitants. The task of these partnership-based bodies is to identify, support and promote projects of local development and job creation. They provide technical support and help in identifying funding sources.

As Greffe points out in Chapter 8, the nature of the actions performed by these organisations varies significantly from one area to another, as does their accountability framework, with some bodies more dependent on the local authorities than others. The issue of professional skills, addressed above for area-based partnerships, is fully relevant in the case of these small and flexible organisations, inasmuch as the success of their action depends on the capacity of a few agents recruited locally. It is thus of crucial importance to associate strict training and networking provisions with this sort of measure to ensure a minimum and comparable degree of effectiveness throughout the country as well as a degree of uniformity in the methods used. Indicators to monitor and assess the performance of the agents must also be put in place when their activities begin.

Dynamic delivery models

Many governments have paid attention to the delivery side of the policy implementation process. They have introduced non-public-sector actors who can be considered as agents of change in various circumstances, using innovative ways to approach the public and on occasion to combine various services provided by the private and the non-profit sector. The rationale behind these reforms has mainly been the need to improve efficiency and streamline costs. Initially, this led to a proliferation of public-private partnerships to operate regional development agencies, the privatisation of employment services, and the conclusion of contracts for NGOs to take in hand the delivery of social programmes. More recently, it has been realised that re-thinking the service delivery structure has potential to improve the way programmes are tailored to local needs and reach target groups. Accordingly, quality and community support have then been added to performance in the criteria used to select and assess providers of employment services (as for example in the second phase of implementation of the Job Network in Australia. See OECD, 2003). This has contributed to assigning an enhanced role to non-profit enterprises and community-based organisations in the service delivery structure. Their use of their own connections with local groups and their expertise in the local economy could modify the culture of service delivery.

Grouping services together and unifying gateways to access to public services for some target groups (entrepreneurs, job-seekers) has also made it easier to tailor the programmes to local needs. The Walloon government has recently set up *Maisons de l'emploi*, *Cités des métiers* and *Espaces resources emploi* in order to facilitate access to and uptake of employment, social and training services by all users, with a focus on disadvantaged groups. One-stop agencies are now the norm for the delivery of services to entrepreneurs and job-seekers in OECD countries. This trend has been inspired by local initiatives in various locations and boosted by the Workforce Investment Act, which launched the "one-stop career centres" in the United States in 1998.

These initiatives can be seen as providing support to improvements in the governance framework although the reforms do not carry any particular strategic overtones, in terms of policy co-ordination for example. The linkage of staff of various organisations and the delivery of services jointly with other organisations provide opportunities to adjust the measures and the approaches to the public as a more interactive relationship develops with users. However, these improvements should not be used to mask failures of the broader governance framework. In some policy areas, various government departments and agencies deliver programmes and services with a degree of confusion, duplication and waste of resources. This is the case of the employment services in a number of countries, where a lack of integration still prevails, inhibiting the smooth implementation of programmes. In France, for instance, the employment area embraces government offices for employment and training (*Directions départementales du travail, de l'emploi et de la formation professionnelle*), offices of the national employment agency (ANPE) and unemployment insurance offices (*Assedic*). An array of organisations provides other services, such as the regional governments (*Conseil régional*) and there are also some training organisations. This situation has been deplored as highly inefficient in a recent government report (Marimbert, 2004). In both France and Belgium, the lack of integration between the delivery of active (employment-promoting) and passive (income support) measures has often been criticized.

Conclusions

Governments are devoting increasing efforts to identify the governance forms most suitable to their institutional structure and most effective in pursuing integrated development strategies. Learning from the early experience of partnerships led by civil society, they are seeking to set up structures that are more stable and that can assume broader and heavier duties in terms of policy co-ordination and strategic planning. As a result, more responsibility is being handed over to local and regional authorities and to public service officers in managing platforms, partnerships and other framework agreements.

In this context, regional strategic platforms are emerging as the main instrument for coherent planning and organisation of the economic development activities of an area. While these platforms focus on fostering endogenous development, based on local competitive advantages, assets, skills and knowledge, their critical mass may allow them to take up a role in inward investment and industrial infrastructure activities, subject to the institutional context and the will to participate of their membership. Depending on their membership, they may be able to extend their strategic approach to solve socio-economic problems of their areas and to take a genuinely integrated approach to economic and employment development.

No strategic platform can be considered as the perfect model. As this chapter has shown (and the chapters that follow provide further detailed evidence) platforms have not yet released their potential as they encounter various problems associated with the accountability relationships, the evaluation of results and the capacity to adopt a strategic, integrated approach. They nevertheless represent a valuable and promising tool. The analysis confirms the validity of the recommendations made as part of the "strategy to improve governance through partnerships", which can be put to use to enhance the effectiveness of the platforms.

In particular, it is of crucial importance that the main partners of regional strategic platforms, including central government and its relevant agencies, realise that they cannot ask platforms to do things that they are not prepared to do themselves. Consequently, they must make sure that their policy objectives are compatible with the mission of the platforms. Partners at central level should agree on what can best be done at regional level and what they expect regional platforms to achieve on their behalf. Similarly they should state clearly what the limits of the platforms should be. They should discuss with national representatives of other partners, namely civil society, business and local authorities, what the role of each partner is in steering the platforms. They should establish representation and reporting mechanisms for each sector that are acceptable to all. Finally they should set up a common set of indicators that will fulfil each partner's needs in terms of satisfying accountability requirements.

Sufficient critical mass is necessary for the effective pursuit of an economic development strategy, although innovative and effective platforms in smaller or predominantly rural regions may have a considerable role to play in their area if they concentrate on endogenous development. Smaller partnerships have advantages with regard to addressing socio-economic problems as they usually have closer relationships with the relevant local actors, including representatives of community-based groups and employer associations. Indeed, the main strength of these area-based partnerships lies in this closeness. While these partnerships may not have the most appropriate structure for driving economic development in their area, this aspect can make them a major source of expertise for identifying opportunities for local development, and enable them to make a key contribution to the solution of difficult issues.

There may be some degree of complementarity and an optimal distribution of tasks between larger strategic platforms, at the level of regions, and smaller area-based partnerships at a more local level. Such regional/local articulation may be the way to tap the input provided by civil society while driving economic development most effectively.

Whatever arrangement is deemed best, it will have to address the lack of co-ordination between economic development activities and labour market policy, a critical governance failure which impedes local development. For this reason, the LEED Committee is launching a new activity for 2005-2007 to identify optimum ways to co-ordinate labour market policy with economic development strategies designed at the local and regional levels. Clearly, human resource and skills development is a key area to be dealt with in partnerships at local and regional level: Business needs change constantly, and local prosperity is built on knowledge and skills.

Regional governments can help in this process of co-ordination. Recent innovations suggest that they can reinvent themselves as co-ordinators for the economic and social development of their area and tailor national policies more closely to local needs. There is an opportunity for them to play a role as a regional catalyst for innovation, with potentially significant impacts on the lives of their citizens.

Similarly healthy for local governance are "agents of change" and dynamic delivery models, which help to connect policies with citizens' needs and to foster innovation locally. However, these models should not be allowed to mask any governance failures that may exist or prevent the correction of imbalances that impede local development. And agents of change should be seen as what they are, and not claim a strategic role that they are not in a position to discharge.

The supply of professional skills is common issue for all forms of governance to address. Decision-making is growingly being decentralised to the local level and the decisions to be made are becoming more complex. In an integrated economy, internationalising local SMEs and attracting global knowledge flows are now common objectives of local strategies, whose implementation calls for increasingly sophisticated expertise. Efforts to improve the development of expertise at local level to support local development constitute a wise investment.

A rich menu of new but tried and tested forms of governance is available to address economic development in optimum fashion. Some of the new forms will suit the governance framework of a given country better than others, in the light of its institutional characteristics and the needs expressed. Some may also be combined to become mutually reinforcing, for maximum impact on local prosperity and the quality of life.

Notes

1. There is sometimes confusion between the concepts of PPPs and of local or area-based partnerships. PPPs concern the delegation of power from the public sector to a private (or non-profit) contractor for the delivery of a service (*e.g.* assistance to business development, health care) or the management of infrastructures (*e.g.* roads, bridges). Their main expected impact is on the efficiency of service delivery and programme management, not on local governance as such. Local partnerships or regional strategic platforms are completely different organisations, in that they are not ruled by contract and normally do not concern

the implementation of programmes. Their vocation is rather of a strategic nature, intrinsically related to the characteristics of the geographical area concerned (e.g. social, employment, environmental).

2. The OECD has done specific work on the ways to engage citizens in policy making. More information on the methods used to open governments can be found in OECD (2001b).

3. More work on social dialogue at local and regional levels is to be carried out by the LEED Programme over its next Mandate 2006-2010.

Bibliography

Eberts, R. and Erikcek, G., (2001) "The Role of Partnerships in Economic Development and Labour Markets in the United States", in *Local Partnerships for Better Governance*, OECD, Paris.

Giguère, S. (2003), "Managing Decentralisation and New Forms of Governance", in OECD (2003), *Managing Decentralisation. A New Role for Labour Market Policy*, OECD, Paris.

Giguère, S. (2002), "Enhancing Governance through Partnerships", in T. Bovaird, E. Löffler and S. Parrado-Díez (eds): *Developing Local Governance Networks in Europe*, Nomos Publishers, Baden-Baden.

Greffe, X. (2003), "Stimulating the Emergence of Agents of Change", in OECD (2003), *Managing Decentralisation. A New Role for Labour Market Policy*, OECD, Paris.

Marimbert, J. (2004), Rapport au ministre du Travail sur le rapprochement des services de l'emploi, 14 janvier 2004.

Martin, J.P. and Grubb, D. (2001), "What Works and for Whom: a Review of OECD Countries: Experience with Active Labour Market Policies", Working Paper 2001:14, IFAU (Office of Labour Market Policy Evaluation), Stockholm, Sweden.

Melo, A. (2001), "A New Approach to Economic Development in Sicily: Planning in Partnership", in *Local Partnerships for Better Governance*, OECD, Paris.

OECD (2003), *Managing Decentralisation. A New Role for Labour Market Policy*, OECD, Paris.

OECD (2001a), *Local Partnerships for Better Governance*, OECD, Paris.

OECD (2001b), *Citizens as Partners: Information, Consultation and Public Participation in Policy Making*, OECD, Paris.

OECD (1999), *Decentralising Employment Policy: New Trends and Challenges*, OECD, Paris.

OECD (1998), *Local Management for More Effective Employment Policies*, OECD Paris.

Research Institute for Small and Emerging Businesses (2004), "Connecting the Workforce Investment System to Small and Emerging Businesses", Report prepared for the US Department of Labor, Washington.

ISBN 92-64-01530-2
New Forms of Governance for Economic Development
© OECD 2004

Chapter 2

Sweden: Fostering Regional Competitiveness and Governance through Partnerships

by

Brian Morgan,
Cardiff Business School, and Els Sol, University of Amsterdam

Sweden has chosen to promote regional competitiveness based on endogenous development through regional strategic platforms. Its rich experience illustrates well the difficulty to develop effective co-ordination mechanisms with government agencies, to link economic development and labour market policy at regional level and to identify suitable governance indicators. Comparison is made between two regions: Uppsala, well-positioned in high-tech sectors and experienced in connecting business and research; and Västerbotten, a Northern region which faces greater challenges in terms of economic diversification and promoting entrepreneurship.

Throughout the twentieth century the Swedish government has championed the principles of social partnership, and these have been strongly embedded into collective, tripartite national agreements. Because of this long history of corporatism in Sweden, it is somewhat surprising to find the authorities now seeking to improve governance by creating new area-based partnerships. This conundrum can be partly explained by considering the relationship between central government and the regions. There is a sharp contrast between the strength of the institutions at the centre and the relative weakness of institutions operating at the regional level. For this reason alone, a study of the operation of the new partnership arrangements in Sweden is both timely and useful.

This report explores the contribution of partnerships to local governance and to economic and employment development in Sweden from the perspective of fostering competitive regions. Local governance can be defined as the way actors from the public, private and voluntary sectors identify and implement solutions to local problems and unmet needs. It refers to the capacity to co-ordinate policies and adapt them to local conditions, within the framework of integrated strategic planning (OECD, 2001).

The analysis is based mainly on the experience of two counties (*Län*): Uppsala in the central/eastern part of Sweden and Västerbotten in the north. The "*Län*" represents the regional or intermediate division of public administration in Sweden, comprising the regional State authorities, the county councils and the associations of municipalities. The county of Uppsala aims to be competitive on the world stage through its clustering and technology-transfer approach, and the county of Västerbotten is an example of a depressed region promoting diversification and entrepreneurship.

As part of its new regional industrial policy, the Swedish government in 1998 invited the regions to create new area-based partnerships – regional growth agreements (RGAs). The partnerships were to be led by the county administration but they were to involve other partner organisations such as the universities, county labour boards, chambers of commerce and the ALMI Business Partners and other private sector partners. The RGAs were tasked with ensuring the active involvement of these groups in developing and implementing the "new industrial policy" at the county level.

The aims of the partnerships were to improve economic performance and to create a more equitable distribution of the benefits of economic growth across the regions. These RGAs were expected to achieve this aim largely by improving policy co-ordination at the intermediate level:

> "More efficient co-ordination and collaboration among sectors and actors (…) is the aim of the growth agreements. (…) The intention is to increase local and regional influence on national policy and to allow state resources (…) to be used more flexibly" (Ministry of Industry, Employment and Communications, 1997).

The political rationale for the RGAs was the need to address the perception of an uncoordinated regional development process within which the regional and local authorities had overlapping functions and responsibilities. The RGAs presented both national and regional policy makers with major challenges and opportunities, not least in the area of the effective utilisation of the European Union's Structural Funds.

A driving force: the EU

Prior to its accession to the European Union (EU) in 1995, regional governance in Sweden had not been strongly developed. In contrast, the regional dimension in most other EU countries was stronger and the regions had devolved powers and more critical mass. Consequently, the Swedish economy lacked the sort of regional structures needed to implement the EU's Structural Fund programmes effectively.

The achievement of the Structural Funds are characterised by certain partnership forms. The main focus of the Structural Funds partnerships is the decentralisation of decision-making and competencies to sub-national government and to social partners. This means that new inclusive partnership formats are required to be set up which can tailor programmes to local needs. Greater inclusion within decentralised partnership forms are championed because they improve partnership legitimacy and enhance regional level identification with the Structural Funds themselves. "Partnership needs to be understood as being rooted in and conditioned by the prevailing context of progressive decentralisation, as well as being a force for decentralisation itself. This process of decentralisation is a key contextual feature which both conditions partnership and is conditioned by the overlaying of the partnership" (European Union, 2000).

With 21 county administrations, 289 municipalities and a number of state agencies operating at the regional level, it was inevitable that the central government would need to take the lead in developing the partnerships needed to implement the Structural Funds and focusing them on regional development.

At the time that the first Structural Fund partnerships were being formed in the mid-1990s, the Swedish employer organisations withdrew from all central policy bodies but often maintained representation in local and regional bodies, *e.g.* Structural Fund bodies. As a result, with the significant exception of the Objective 4 programme, the partnerships to implement the Structural Funds were initially State-selected, administrative organisations. They eventually became more decentralised and partner oriented as the Structural Funds programme evolved.

So although in a weakened position at the national level, the social partnership model was to some extent reinvented at the regional level by the Structural Funds programme. Essentially, the RGAs evolved from these new regional partnership arrangements and, in line with the EU agenda, they quickly became programme-driven.

Harmonising economic development and labour market policy

The twin goals of economic policy in Sweden are to increase growth and employment. With the RGAs focused on economic growth, the other key pillar of economic policy has been the approach of the labour market administration (*Arbetsmarknadsverket*, AMV) to unemployment. At both the regional and national levels the AMV plays a key role in promoting employment and implementing labour market policy. The AMV consists of the Swedish national labour market board (*Arbetsmarknadsstyrelsen*, AMS), 21 county labour boards and 350 local employment offices. The main objective of the AMS currently is to ensure the efficiency of the labour market, as a condition for sustained economic growth and price stability. Hence it promotes geographical mobility of workers to better match supply and demand. In a regional development perspective, with lagging regions losing population, this may lead to some potential policy conflicts.

A central objective of this study is to analyse the policy inter-relationships between developing the RGAs and reforming the AMV. Specifically, are the RGAs helping the AMV (and other public actors) to take a broader approach to policy development and adapt policy implementation to local conditions? After all, the AMV is the largest state agency and has the biggest budget at the regional level. One way that the AMV could contribute to regional competitiveness is by developing more targeted demand-side labour market policies, specifically adapted to the needs of SMEs, such as training for clusters of firms.

Therefore, its involvement and interaction with the RGA partnership could be a key element in the success of the new economic development policy, including its regional dimension. AMS endorsement of the RGA process would be an important step in creating a regional framework in which the regional authorities can work together to pursue consistent objectives that help implement and co-ordinate national policies and foster competitive regions.

Good local governance and effective partnerships are ways to resolve potential policy conflicts. One of the aspects examined in this study is whether RGAs in Sweden can improve the trade-off between the (sometimes conflicting) goals of stimulating economic growth (including greater labour market efficiency) and supporting lagging regions (including helping the unemployed develop their skills and contribute to endogenous development in their disadvantaged region). At present the role of the numerous institutions involved in economic policy and labour market efficiency tend to overlap and there is an acknowledged need for better coordination between the various actors involved in regional development.

National and regional context in Sweden

Economic situation

Sweden has developed a successful "mixed" economy with a high standard of living based on high-tech industries, a skilled workforce and an extensive welfare system. Its main strengths lie in sectors such as engineering and ICT (which account for over 50% of both output and exports) but it also has significant concentrations in traditional sectors like timber, hydropower and iron ore. It has excellent internal and external communications as befits an economy heavily oriented toward foreign trade. In recent years, however, this favourable picture has been clouded by rising unemployment and a gradual loss of competitiveness in international markets. Since 1980 Sweden has slipped down the OECD's league table of GDP per head, from fifth to 15th place and, before the economic upturn in the late nineties, unemployment was close to 10%.

Following the economic downturn in the 1990s, the government's traditional commitment to full employment and the welfare state began to be questioned. Also the economic policy regime changed sharply in 1995 with Sweden's accession to the EU. Sweden began harmonising its economic policies with those of the EU but it remains reluctant to join the Euro zone. Internally, steps have been taken to reduce civil service employment and trim back social-welfare programmes. The tax system has been reformed with income tax reductions being financed by increases in direct taxation. It also began to privatise some state industries, such as the telecommunications and electricity networks. In the labour market, where 80% of workers are unionised – the largest percentage of unionised workers of any industrial nation – moves have been made in the direction of increased flexibility.

The economic climate in Sweden today is more subdued than it was in 2000. Only a few years ago, there was great enthusiasm for the new economy and Sweden was one of the most vibrant centres of ICT activity outside Silicon Valley. With a high concentration of Internet and mobile phone usage (around 70%), international companies used Sweden as a testing-ground for many new telecom products. Ericsson, one of Sweden's largest companies became a dominant player in the market. But business confidence in future activity has recently fallen to its lowest in ten years. The ICT downturn has taken its toll and Ericsson's profits, have fallen sharply, hitting the stock market, reducing exports, and amongst others causing the krona to fall sharply during 2001.

However, the SME sector remains strong (of Sweden's 625 000 firms, only 740 employ more than 250 people) and there is still plenty of potential in the Swedish economy. It continues to be a world leader in the ICT sector and R&D spending remains high. The exuberance for the digital revolution has waned but Sweden is still at the forefront of the development of new sectors like, biotechnology, which are particularly strong in Uppsala – one of the regions that will be studied in detail.

An unwanted by-product of the strong economic growth during the ICT boom may have been the postponement of some of the structural reforms and tax reductions that are needed to strengthen Sweden's long-term competitiveness. The old tripartite agreement has changed and the traditional relationship between the social democrat government and big business has shifted. Most of Sweden's large multinational companies were set up decades ago and many are moving their headquarters abroad. Hence the current emphasis of economic policy is on encouraging entrepreneurial efforts and generating new companies through new forms of partnership at the regional level.

As mentioned in introduction, the twin goals of economic policy in Sweden are to increase growth and employment. Stable public finances and low inflation are seen as prerequisites for achieving these goals. After the economic upheavals of recent years, it is now acknowledged that Swedish labour market policy has to operate within a stable macroeconomic policy framework. The labour market administration is now being reformulated to

Table 2.1. **Selected economic indicators, Sweden, 2000 and 2001**

	2000	2001
GDP growth (%)	3.6	2.7
Price inflation (%)	1.3	1.5
Wage inflation (%)	3.0	2.5
Unemployment (%)	4.7	3.9
Employment ratio (%)	77.2	78.1
Public sector finances (% GDP)	4.1	3.6
Exchange rate (trade weighted 1990 = 100)	79.6	75.8

Source: Statistics Sweden.

place increased emphasis on creating the right conditions for enterprise and growth. Essentially this means developing a flexible labour market that will promote efficiency, contribute to keeping inflationary pressures at a low level, and produce a business climate that supports the creation of new firms and the growth of existing businesses.

The Swedish labour market has developed more favourably in the past few years – the largest increase in employment being attributable to the service sector – and unemployment has fallen greatly. While the population grew steadily throughout the 1990s the employment rate has been in decline since 1992, turning upwards only in 1998. In the last few years Sweden has pursued a strong top-down political goal of lowering unemployment and raising the employment rate. Specifically the government has adopted the target of re-reaching the 80% employment rate and of reducing the unemployment rate to less than 4% – this target has been achieved recently. However, significant differences remain in unemployment rates between groups. Among the young and among ethnic minorities, open unemployment is twice to three times higher than average. Also there are regional differences. Open unemployment in growth regions was 3% in 2000, while in poorly developed regions 7% (Government of Sweden, 2001).

While the government acknowledges that the prerequisites for an efficient and flexible labour market are different in different parts of the country, labour market policy is seen as a national policy and a national responsibility in order to avoid locking-in effects and to grant equal rights and obligations for citizens in different parts of the country (*idem*). As a national policy, labour market policy also has a regional dimension. To develop the regional dimension in line with regional priorities and to create better sector co-ordination along with a more efficient use of resources the central government has recently initiated the RGAs.

Regional governance

With the RGA initiative, the central government – inspired by the success of the EU Structural Fund Programmes – has entrusted the regional authorities with the task of formulating regional development strategies based on the priorities and measures agreed by regional partnerships. In a short space of time the RGAs have become the foremost instrument of Swedish regional industrial policy. They were introduced by the Ministry of Industry, Employment and Communications – as innovative instruments for the purpose of joint problem solving and policy making – in a government bill in 1998.[1] The initiative is being driven from the centre and by 2000 growth agreements were created in all 21 political-administrative regions of Sweden and were being implemented in a first three-year round.

No additional financial resources are being provided to support the RGAs. Financial resources are limited to the already available public resources at the central and regional government's disposal for economic development purposes – including some of the financial resources allocated within labour market policy and under the control of county labour boards and the EU Structural Funds. In practice national resources are circumscribed by regulations and other limitations that often rule out their usage within the RGA framework, as will be explained below.

Partnership between the public and private actors is believed to be fundamental for pooling resources earmarked for regional economic and industrial development. In order to better match the public and private sphere in the regions the involvement of business interests and their needs are at the core of development strategies. "The participation of the private business community is considered to be a prerequisite for the success of the programmes. Regional public actors are encouraged to enter into discussions with representatives of local and regional business communities to ensure that their views and needs are integrated into the action programmes" (Ministry of Industry, Employment and Communications, 1997).

Key responsibility for RGAs in the region is given to the county administrative board, a state organ. Other core public actors involved in the partnerships are county labour boards, county councils and the municipalities. Competencies of each organisation are listed further on.

The RGA initiative changes the public-private balance in the Swedish regions (Svensson, 2001). The emphasis on business involvement and the belief in public-private partnerships as a strategy for arranging development work was new at the regional level. The adoption of the partnership principle from the EU Structural Funds has forced each region to search for broad support and involvement in the RGA process and to find ways of involving business interests in the process.

The emphasis placed on stimulating local partnerships within the EU structural funds programmes has had the desirable spin-off of improving governance (or the way society collectively solves its problems and meets its needs) in Sweden as in other countries (OECD, 2001). To improve governance, governments throughout the OECD have created and supported networks of area-based partnerships. These partnerships have facilitated consultation, co-operation and co-ordination. The introduction of the RGAs can be seen as a step to strengthen these partnerships. In this section we sketch the perceptions, interests and resources of these actors.

NEW FORMS OF GOVERNANCE FOR ECONOMIC DEVELOPMENT – ISBN 92-64-01530-2 – © OECD 2004

Government departments and agencies

The Ministry of Industry, Employment and Communications has a broad field of responsibility in the area of regional policy, which encompasses industrial policy and RGAs as well as labour market policy, including employment training and unemployment benefits. In the Ministry there are different secretariats with responsibilities for RGAs, labour market policy and regional policy. At least four agencies under the umbrella of these different secretariats are involved in the implementation of RGAs; besides the national labour market board (see below), these are VINNOVA, ITPS and NUTEK.

VINNOVA is the Swedish agency for developing innovation systems. VINNOVA promotes and finances the development of innovation systems at the regional level accentuating the co-operation between the government, business and the universities (the so-called "triple helix"). ITPS, the Swedish Institute for Growth Policy Studies, is closely involved with the new industrial policy and monitors the RGAs. NUTEK is the Swedish agency for industrial development and regional policy; it is also active in the RGA process together with its regional tool, ALMI.

ALMI is a national agency with a regional structure that aims to stimulate the growth and development of the SME sector. All 21 regional ALMI companies are owned by the ALMI parent company (51%) and by the county council in which they are located (49%). This ties ALMI's organisation strongly to the regional level while providing full national coverage. ALMI manages a fund of approximately SEK 4 000 million (EUR 447 million) that is used for making loans to Swedish SMEs.

Apart from ITPS the role of the other national actors in the RGAs remains somewhat blurred. For example, it is unclear whether they are steering the process or predominantly providing the RGAs with information. At this stage the national agencies do not appear to have an agreed set of clear objectives amongst themselves regarding the RGA process. For example, ALMI is closely involved in some RGAs to the extent that it makes specific funding commitments whilst in others it has a more arms length relationship.

One of the keys to successful partnerships to foster competitive regions is an ongoing dialogue between the different policy areas within the central authorities. Interviews in Sweden revealed collaboration difficulties and lack of communication between and within government offices at the national level. These views are confirmed in a national study of cooperation between national and local actors in Sweden in the context of the European Employment Strategy (Statskontoret, 2002). Employers and trade unions complain about too much bureaucracy and lack of mutual information between the four agencies in the Ministry of Industry, Employment and Communications relevant for developing the RGAs.

Regional and local government

The primary units of local and regional government are county administrative boards, the municipalities and the county councils. The county councils (*landsting*) and municipalities are governed by the Local Government Act of 1991, which set out their respective jurisdictions and powers. The counties are primarily a central government administrative division at the regional level. In the county councils the assembly is the decision making body. It consists of an odd number of elected members depending on the size of the population. For example, in areas with more than 200 000 residents entitled to vote there have to be at least 71 elected members.

Executive functions are held by the county executive board. The municipalities are organised in similar fashion and have at least 41 members in areas with more than 12 000 residents entitled to vote. The executive boards of both the county councils and the municipalities appoint their own chairmen but these individuals do not exercise functions on behalf of the state.

However, there are units of state administration at the county level that do act on behalf of the state at the regional level and these are called the county administrative boards. These boards are responsible for both planning and administration and at the head of these boards are the county governors who are appointed by the central government. The county administrative boards have 14 members appointed by the government on the advice of the county councils. They exercise supervision over the municipalities, reviewing their appeal processes, but primarily the functions of the county administrative boards are focused on social and physical planning as well as regional policy (Council of Europe, 1999).

Another important role for the county administrative boards relates to their position as the representatives of government agencies. Not all agencies have established regional departments and in this situation the county administrative boards perform the functions of the agencies in their respective counties. Where the agencies have established regional organisations they are called county boards – as with the *Riksdag* which has established county labour boards.

Trade unions and employer associations

At the regional level actors are capable of establishing more frequent contacts and tend to be more committed to the regional cause; as such they can often generate the mutual trust necessary to build a well-functioning policy network. In these networks trade unions and employer associations can serve as intermediaries for public authorities to establish contact with individual actors, such as SMEs and unemployed, in the regional labour market – contacts that are of important for the successful implementation of economic policy. Regional representatives of trade unions are often in a position to benefit from this form of regional governance by influencing the strategic orientation of policies and the implementation of programmes and by gaining access to public funds.

Trade union representatives as well as employer associations such as the Federation of Private Enterprises and the Swedish Employer's Confederation and chambers of commerce and also individual companies have become involved in the RGAs. Sometimes these actors are involved in the management and supervision of the process, but predominantly in the operative working committees that generate suggestions for viable measures and projects. Trade unionists complain about the county administrative boards not letting them participate in the inner circle of the core actors. The inclusiveness of the regional partnerships in terms of the business sector differs from region to region.

An indication of the importance of the role of these intermediary organisations in the RGAs is provided in the following table which provides a comparison between regions with "active" and "passive" involvement of business associations and private enterprises. Individual private enterprises tend to be more active in RGAs where intermediary business organisations are actively involved (see row 1 of Table 2.2).

Table 2.2. **Involvement of business associations and private enterprises in RGAs, Sweden**

Individual firms	Business associations		
	Active role	Passive role	Total
Active role	5	1	6
Passive role	12	3	15
Total	17	4	21

Source: Svensson (2001).

Trade unions and business associations can bring different kinds of resources into the network: linkages with their members and broader networks, knowledge of the regional labour market and financial resources. According to experts in the field only non-financial resources are being contributed to the RGAs.

The labour market administration

The core actor in the RGA with the biggest purse is the AMV. In 2000 the total estimated AMV budget amounted to SEK 60.1 billion, and their labour market programmes amounted to SEK 16.8 billion. Approximately 40% of the budget of the RGAs is brought in by AMV. As a background to their role in the RGAs we first briefly outline the Swedish labour market administration and policy.

Organisation. The overall responsibility for labour market policy rests with the Swedish parliament (Riksdag) and the government. They decide upon national directions for the Ministry of Industry, Employment and Communications who is entrusted with the responsibility for labour market policy. Under the Ministry, the AMV implements labour market policy on behalf of the cabinet. Overriding annual targets for labour market policy are established in Riksdag resolutions on the government's budget bill. After this bill has passed the government allocates funding for the AMV and for labour market policy programmes and states the goals for their utilisation. Since the second half of the nineties the government defines national quantitative targets specified for labour market programmes.

Within AMV, the AMS (national labour market board) oversees the 21 county labour boards that supervise the public employment service offices. AMS is responsible for managing, co-ordinating and developing labour market policy to comply with the guidelines set by the Riksdag and the cabinet as well as for establishing goals and guidelines for the county labour boards and for following up and evaluating the results of their activities. The Riksdag leaves limited room for AMS board to issue instructions by itself. On the other hand, within the national directions AMS is free to set priorities and is autonomously responsible for the operative performance. After AMS has defined the county operational targets and the allocation of funding to the county labour boards, the requirement concerning the number of persons taking part in labour market programmes is distributed by AMS according to the allocation of funding. The county labour board allocates resources and monitors activities at county level to employment offices. The public employment offices which are located in nearly all the municipalities are responsible for providing assistance to job seekers and employers. Employment offices are engaged in providing information about job openings, placement services for job seekers and employers and employment counselling services.

Centralisation. For two reasons the Riksdag and Swedish cabinet decided to reform labour market policy and modernise AMV services. The first reason is the low employment rate. While the population grew steadily, the share of the employed labour force has been in decline since 1992, turning upwards only since 1998. Currently the Swedish government is pursuing the goal of lowering the unemployment rate to less than 4%. The second reason is the wish of re-reaching the 80% employment rate by 2004. These national political decisions have had direct implications on programming and related activities by the AMS. The national policy mix designed by national government is very much focused on active labour market policies to achieve these goals.

This mostly labour supply policy is translated into short-term objectives and targets for the implementation of policies which leaves leave little room at the regional level for involvement in regional growth policies. Notwithstanding the fact that a large share of AMS funds is allocated to training measures aimed to meet employers' demand for skills, hence contributing to enhancing competitiveness in regions, there are few opportunities for regional AMV actors to engage in innovative package deals within the RGAs. This may be particularly harmful for disadvantaged regions where the need for strategic and integrated development projects based on local skills, knowledge and competitive advantages is relatively more pressing than the skills shortage issue. Thus, due the limited discretionary room that is provided to the regional public employment service to help facilitate, coordinate and support business-driven and community-driven partnerships with demand side services improving the competitiveness of their region, AMV is sometimes regarded as a difficult partner for the RGAs.

Currently the devolved powers of the county labour boards are under further pressure from both AMS and national politics. From 1 January 2002 the county labour offices are being placed under the stricter control of AMS and the boards no longer exist as separate accounting bodies, but as advisory bodies.

Problems with decentralisation. Decentralisation of decision-making in labour market policy makes it possible to use local information to the fullest but may also impinge on the fulfilment of national objectives. A main problem with decentralising labour market policy in Sweden seems to be that institutional reforms that devolve power to the regions can easily get into conflict with the Swedish tradition of labour market policy as a centralised and integrated part of national economic policy. Also negative experiences in the nineties with decentralisation strongly influences the current strategic orientation taken by AMS.

In the beginning of the nineties AMS could not come up with an answer to the growth of structural unemployment. The economic crisis strongly affected the municipalities who were directly confronted with the problems facing the unemployed and wanted to become more actively engaged in programme delivery. Eventually the central government decided to involve the municipalities in various labour market programmes, *e.g.* in activities for young people and in education of unemployed adults. In 1997 local employment service committees were established in which the municipalities had a majority. The municipalities favoured a very broad policy mix and labour market policy became a melting pot of social, educational and regional policy. The term "labour market policy" became hazy and no one really knew what it meant (Behrentz, Delander and Niklasson, 2001). Mutual trust between AMS and the municipalities was low. In addition, AMS had problems with the scale of municipalities. In their view, local labour market areas comprise more than just one municipality and AMS wanted to facilitate co-operation and perspective to grow *across* municipal boundaries in order to involve the labour market parties to a greater extent. After the upturn of the economy when labour shortages quickly arose, AMS was incapable of reacting with sufficient speed or purpose because the capacity to influence the key players had been taken away. In order to respond to the mismatch in the labour market and to avoid the potentially inflationary consequences, AMS focused its attention on regaining power.

In "The Swedish Labour Market Administration in the 21st Century" (1999), AMS describes its current tactics: concentrate on core tasks of labour market policy and centrally organise and utilise resources from a macro-economic perspective. In the perception of AMS, the labour market administration has grown more complicated and has been weakened as a result of too little target-oriented programmes, uncertainties caused by alterations to the directorates of county labour boards and local employment service committees with a municipal majority. During the recent period several county labour boards had demonstrated deficiencies in their budgetary control, regulatory systems have not been complied with and policy decisions had deviated from existing rules. The national audit office noted a contradiction between responsibility of the AMS for these shortcomings and the powers available to AMS to rectify them. As a precondition for overcoming these problems, AMS asked for clear-cut responsibilities and powers as well as precise management procedures in order to "efficiently implement labour market policy and control of resource utilisation". As a result, AMS has regained power at the expense of the regional and local actors. Central AMS has entered the RGA as a partner but as was indicated in our interviews not wholeheartedly. Regional actors as well as regional AMV employees in charge report little involvement in strategic planning and rigid national rules that make co-operation between AMV and other regional partners troublesome.

Municipalities

The position of the municipalities is not as strong as it was before 2002, as far as labour market policy is concerned. As part of the reforms initiated by AMS, the local employment service committees are being changed by the central government into boards where municipalities no longer have a decisive role to play. Despite this, the role of the municipalities will remain dominant in the public sphere, as they still retain many other powers and responsibilities. The relatively strong position of the municipalities contrasts with the lack of power at county level and highlights the need at the regional level for policy co-ordination, transparency and accountability.

Municipalities have a variety of different interests in the RGA process. They realise that the RGAs can provide closer linkages with private actors, who determine the functioning of the local and regional labour market and can foster economic development. But the municipalities also have control over major resources such as social assistance funds. In the past municipal policy has been ineffective due to compartmentalisation, i.e. a lack of co-ordination and integration between social assistance policy and economic policy. The RGAs offer a mechanism that will help bridge the gap between the delivery of social and economic policies.

The municipalities and the elected county councils question the current leading role in the RGAs of the county administrative board, which, as the representative of the central state in regional economic development, could be seen to be undermining local democratic control. In the public sphere questions are raised like: How will this new pattern of governance affect the relationship with representative democracy? Can these regional partnerships be effective without implementing regional reforms that define the formal competence at the regional level more explicitly? (see also Svensson and Östhol, 2001).

Recently the government has taken initiatives to strengthen the role of the municipalities and the elected county council in regional policy. United municipalities and county councils will assume now responsibility for regional development.[2]

Reforming regional governance

The fragmented nature of the regional structure in Sweden becomes apparent when the responsibilities of the 21 county administrations and 289 municipalities (with varying degrees of autonomy and administrative power) are set alongside the responsibilities of the large number of state agencies operating at the regional level. During the last twenty years there has been a significant transfer of responsibility by the state to organisations at the intermediate level but there has been little corresponding reform of the structure of governance. The inevitable consequence has been poor policy co-ordination and overlapping responsibilities.

In recent years there have been several attempts to reform and refocus the organisations involved in delivery at the regional level. The most recent, "The Organisation of Regional Governance" (1997), followed the government's tacit acceptance of an earlier report by a parliamentary commission entitled "Regional Future" (1995). This set out proposals for new regional organisations.

The main recommendation was the transfer of the responsibility for regional economic development from the state agencies and administrative boards to the county councils. There was also the suggestion of more radical reforms that could replace the existing 24 counties with 7 or 11 new regions. Some minor movement in this direction has already taken place with the result that the number of counties has been reduced to 21. A further reform of the structure of governance is planned in 2002 with the creation of municipal co-operation bodies – comprising of municipalities and county councils – in all regions starting in 2003, to lead the RGA process as of 2004.[3]

The debate in favour of strengthening the regional level of government was bolstered by reference to the increasingly important regional dimension that underpinned EU policies – particularly the Structural Funds programme. Prior to joining the European Union in 1995, regional governance in Sweden had not been strongly developed and the Swedish regions were much smaller than those in other European countries. For example, Swedish counties are relatively small (21 counties and a population of 9 million) compared with the 22 regions of France (population 60 million), or the 10 Länder of Germany (population 85 million) or the 9 Länder of Austria (population 10 million). Not only do these regions have more critical mass, but they also have more devolved powers and more control over larger budgets.

Another argument in favour of strengthening regional organisations focused on the globalisation of production and the importance of regional competitiveness in gaining access to global markets. It was felt that the benefits of regional networks and clusters, benefits that have been increasingly identified as the key drivers of regional growth, could not be easily generated at the local level. They require strategic organisations able to address broader geographical areas and more complex market structures than those contained in individual Swedish counties. These global issues were at the heart of the EU's drive to raise competitiveness – particularly in the "less favoured regions" – through its Structural Funds programmes. It was soon apparent that the Swedish economy lacked the strong regional structures and organisations needed to effectively implement the comprehensive programmes being proposed under the Structural Funds umbrella.

Things were also changing at the national level in Sweden. By the early 1990s, the old style tripartite social partnerships were coming under pressure across Europe but particularly in Sweden. The Swedish employer organisations were questioning their role in areas that they felt should be the prerogative of government. Their withdrawal from social partnerships then led to a diminished role for the unions. This trend (referred to as "retreating corporatism") was gaining speed at the same time that the first EU Structural Fund partnerships were being formed. With tripartite, corporatist arrangements waning with the distinguished exception of "the pilot" Objective 4, the central

NEW FORMS OF GOVERNANCE FOR ECONOMIC DEVELOPMENT – ISBN 92-64-01530-2 – © OECD 2004

government had to take the lead in developing the Structural Funds partnerships. Initially they were centrally-selected administrative organisations with little or no role for social partners. Subsequently, under pressure from Europe, they became more decentralised with the social partners playing a more active role in regional development through involvement in project selection and programme delivery at the local level.

So although, at the national level, the social partnership model appeared to be seriously weakened during the 1990s, the Structural Funds seems to have reinvented, decentralised and strengthened partnership arrangements in Sweden at the regional level. It is not surprising therefore that the Swedish government freely admits that, in general, the new industrial policies that are being introduced, and the RGAs in particular, "have been inspired by the EU".

Because local partnerships are by definition modelled upon local and regional conditions, the nature of the goals, motivations, contexts, forms and modes of operation can differ from region to region. These differences influence policy efficiency. Therefore to evaluate the effectiveness of policies one has to trace, in each region, the tensions that have occurred, the solutions that have been sought and the impact on measurable policy goals like employment and new firm formation. Economic conditions and opportunities differ across Sweden. The structure and organisation of the RGAs in Uppsala and Västerbotten (the two counties surveyed as part of this study) vary significantly, as does the involvement of the local, regional and national organisations in these two RGAs. Uppsala is a region creating a competitive edge for itself in the global economy through the development of an innovative clustering and technology-transfer strategy; Västerbotten is an example of a more peripheral region promoting diversification and entrepreneurship in response to the challenges facing its staple industries. A more detailed analysis of the practical issues involved in the RGA process is developed in the next section.

Regional growth agreements in practice

Uppsala

Uppsala is one of Sweden's most dynamic regions with a unique science community, made up of companies, institutions and universities, located in the prosperous central region of Sweden, adjacent to the capital city region of Stockholm. Regional partnership arrangements in Uppsala were first developed in 1984 with the formation of STUNS (Foundation for Collaboration between the Universities in Uppsala, Business and Society). The partnership was formed between the county administrative board, the county council, the universities, the chamber of commerce and the municipality. The objective was to stimulate growth and the development of business activity by

Map of Sweden

identifying, initiating and running various projects – especially in sectors related to biotechnology and material technology.

The county administrative board initiated the first county economic strategy in 1995 called "The Strategy for Development in Uppsala County to 2010". The steering group (*Utvecklingsradet*) established theme groups for different subjects, including: i) increasing co-operation between the Universities and SMEs; and ii) developing entrepreneurship. These groups identified activities and projects to be developed, and a working committee (the LIBER group) was set up to carry out the work. The group consists of ten members, four from the county administrative board with the vice-governor as chair. The rest of the group consists of the directors for the county labour board, the county council, the Association of Local Authorities, the chamber of commerce and ALMI Business Partners.

By the end of 1996 around 90% of the activities in the strategy had been started but the momentum waned. In August 1998 the process had to be restarted with new theme groups for growth focused on: i) integration and multicultural developments; and ii) growing companies, particularly biotech but also rural companies.

Two further groups were set up to form a joint organisation in the region to market business opportunities to potential inward investors and to create a "vision" for the county. A final version of the strategy was produced in December 2000 called "The Strategy for Growth in Uppsala County 2010+". This set some challenging objectives for the county to become the top county in Sweden in terms of economic growth and one of the leading regions in Europe within the biotechnology, IT and material technology sectors.

To achieve these goals the strategy would focus on regional and local business services to encourage indigenous firms to take advantage of the region's potential for growth. This would require the full participation of the private sector to successfully carry out the measures.

The invitation to develop a RGA came in 1998 when work to develop the economic strategy was already underway. Therefore the theme groups were tasked with preparing pilot cases that could be easily developed as projects within the growth agreement. In this sense, the RGA in Uppsala county is based on the broad partnership from the earlier strategy work. The LIBER group became the core members while the theme groups made up the broader partnership in which other organisations were invited to participate.

Various methods have been tried to formulate a coherent set of measures under the RGA using SWOT analysis (strengths, weaknesses, opportunities and threats). The partnership focused discussion on strategic matters to identify concrete measures that could stimulate growth in the region. The maxim for the RGA has been that it is better to realise a few good projects than to build an over ambitious programme which will be difficult to deliver.

Consequently the RGA for Uppsala county focused on three areas, derived largely from the earlier strategy work:

● Infrastructural support for business development.

● Entrepreneurship and development of SMEs.

● Social integration.

Specific projects were identified within these three areas for inclusion in the RGA totalling more than SEK 100 million per year but it proved impossible to raise this level of finance. The steering group was given the task of slimming the RGA down to a more realistic amount of about SEK 20 million per year. Following considerable discussions on priorities the group has sanctioned 21 projects costing a little over SEK 21 million per year.

Prioritisation was essential because the budget for the Uppsala RGA is small in relation to other counties and there are few subsides from the central government or financial support from the EU. The budget has to be financed largely from the regional state organisations, from the municipalities, some small contributions from the EU (Objective 4) and co-financing from private companies.

However, the success of the partnership approach can be gauged from the fact that in the first year (2000) of operation the real allocation of money into the projects was more than SEK 38 million compared with the original SEK 21 million calculated in the budget for the RGA. This is largely the result of the partnership process that had been created during the work on the earlier strategy and the understanding that had developed within the group that the RGA was probably the best instrument for delivering an integrated group of projects.

One of the success stories is the Campus Uppsala project (discussed in detail below) which has succeeded in attracting SEK 3 billion of venture capital, both Swedish and international into biotechnology companies in Uppsala. The other projects within the RGA have not yet produced results on this scale but the "integration measures" are having an impact on shortening the induction process for immigrants and refugees into the Swedish society. This is an important goal because many current employees will soon be retired and there is a need to recruit new employees into the labour market – both to the public and private sectors. Pursuing the objective of integration therefore is seen as helping to tackle the issue of labour shortage.

Delivery of RGA projects is delegated to smaller partnerships for each project consisting largely of the funding bodies – mostly only a few people are involved together with the project leader and decisions are made informally. However, the funding bodies eventually make their own formal decisions on the amount of money they will contribute to the project. These smaller partnerships are the real drivers of project delivery.

The area of integration offers a good example. The policy is based on the principle that having a job is the key to successful integration into society. So the core of the model is integration through employment to address the problem of labour shortage. The key elements in achieving job integration are supply-sided factors: i) language, i.e. a good working knowledge of Swedish;

and *ii)* an understanding of labour market culture, *i.e.* a working knowledge of the rules of the Swedish labour market. In contrast to initiatives in other EU countries, the programme is *for* non-Nordic participants but is not delivered *by* them: *e.g.* very few non-Nordic actors appear to be involved in the organisation or implementation of the model.

To ensure that activities are in line with the objectives of the model, the small steering group has at its disposal some project funds. However, each member in the partnership (each authority) is responsible for its own accounting so that bureaucracy is kept to a minimum. During 2000 about SEK 6 million was spent on different integration projects and activities with the money coming largely from the different partners' ordinary budgets. In addition, some EU Social Funds were available.

The project has been running for only a short period of time and has already levered in some additional funding but it is probably too soon to tell whether this approach will succeed in achieving the actual integration of non-Nordic participants into the regular labour market.

Västerbotten

Västerbotten is located in the less prosperous northern region of Sweden. The county is the second largest in Sweden with 12% of Sweden's total area – the same size as Denmark – but with only 260 000 inhabitants (3% of Sweden's population). More than two-thirds live in the coastal cities, making the interior region sparsely populated with a density as low as one person per square kilometre.

The county accepted the invitation to design and negotiate a RGA in 1998. Local and regional development activity has centred around the RGA and these actions have been closely integrated with the EU Structural Funds programme for the region. The growth agreement has been prepared by a broad partnership composed of representatives from business and commerce, the municipalities in the region, the county council, the universities, employer organisations, unions, regional organisations and national government regional offices. The county administration has been responsible for co-ordinating the work.

The aims of the growth agreement for 2000-2002 are:

- to achieve the same level of economic development as other comparable regions in Sweden and Europe so that full employment can be attained;
- establish more firms and the expand existing ones through a high level of competence within the firms and well-qualified, skilled workers; and
- broaden access to international markets.

The programme is composed of five investment or achievement areas:

- *Education and R&D.* The three universities within the region are one of the region's most important growth factors. Courses are being developed tailored to business needs and focused on IT and new technology. This is not just a one way process, knowledge possessed by businesses is also be transferred to HEIs to facilitate co-operation and the development of networks at national and international levels.

- *Technology development*. This is taking place close to firms with the aim of improving business opportunities and ensuring that the output of the region's R&D institutions can be commercialised by existing or new firms. This will require access to good information and communication infrastructure at a reasonable price so this measure will focus on creating a cost-neutral IT net for the whole region.

- *International markets*. The aim is to maximise Västerbotten's strategic position in Northern Europe as an entry point to the Barents and Baltic Sea regions and to encourage firms to increase their activities in new markets outside Sweden.

- *Business development*. The region's economic structure is dominated by SMEs. Companies will be offered better services and more effective use of resources: "one-stop shops" will allow firms access to decision-makers. Growth will be championed through expanding existing businesses and setting up new firms.

- *Quality of life*. A rich and stimulating range of cultural and leisure activities will be supported to improve the region's attractiveness and competitive position.

The cost for these measures is about SEK 925 million in 2000. Finance will mainly come from the public purse – national government, the municipalities, the county council, Umeå University, ALMI, the Foundation for Technology Transfer and EU funds – plus a number of private financiers. It is expected that the EU, through Objective 1 funding, will contribute SEK 156 million towards the financing of the RGA.

The content of the RGA is now well anchored amongst the region's stakeholders and there is broad support for the process. Around 40 organisations have signed the agreement and undertake to contribute to its implementation, both financially and through the provision of the necessary skills and competence. The next regional growth agreement is planned for the period 2003-2007. Together the two agreements will be executed under the umbrella of the EU's Objective 1 programme 2000-2006 for the larger region of Norrland, consisting of Norrbotten and Västerbotten counties.[4] In many respects the RGAs in the two counties have formed the foundations of the current Objective 1 programme.

Regional development activity under the RGA has made a considerable impact on Västerbotten county as a learning process – helped by experience with the ESF programmes – improving relations among a large number of local and regional partnerships. It has also successfully involved business interests in the regional partnership through a bottom-up mobilisation of resources. One example is the development of the Route 12 Alliance discussed below. Other examples include the Tärnaby/Hemavan area, in co-operation with local business groups, creating airport, tourism facilities, and attracting new companies to the area and the education-project "Akadmi Norr" is an example of bottom-up mobilisation of resources to introduce ICT "distance" teaching into the inland area.

The interaction between local actors and the embeddedness of the governance structure into social networks in Västerbotten has definitely helped to reveal new needs and to provide innovative responses to these needs. But the innovation process has generated costs such as the costs of undertaking feasibility studies and of experimenting with new projects. The mobilisation of the relevant actors of the region is costly in terms of information, consultation and building a consensus on local development strategies.

A comparison

At SEK 925 million, the RGA in Västerbotten is much more ambitious than the Uppsala agreement and involves capital infrastructure projects alongside the development of better business support services. In Uppsala the budget for the whole RGA was originally only SEK 21 million, focused largely on improving the business support services

Not surprisingly, compared with the Uppsala region, Västerbotten has developed a greater number of projects but, inevitably, it has been unable to give as much attention to the rapid implementation of these projects. Local business people involved in Västerbotten's RGA complain about spending too much time in collective conferences during the first two years of the Agreement, and are now anxious to see all the plans brought to fruition. However, in terms of participative democracy, the involvement of citizens in the governance structure can be considered a positive step forward and is often a prerequisite for the success of local strategies. In this sense Västerbotten's RGA has been very successful. No less than 200 actors have participated in the partnership from public bodies, business associations and trade unions, universities and companies – all of whom have helped in preparing the RGA.

Differences in the scale of the two RGAs also have implications for strength of the partnerships. For example, the initial objectives of the Uppsala project were less ambitious than those set out in the Västerbotten RGA. This in turn meant that the preliminary discussions leading up to the RGA in Västerbotten were much wider, more inclusive and, to some extent, achieved greater involvement of private sector actors. This can be partly explained by the greater amount of funding that was potentially available for project development but the greater breadth of the partnership in Västerbotten did provide a certain amount of legitimacy to the RGA process. Also, the task that was facing the partnership in Västerbotten was much clearer than that facing the Uppsala RGA: the task was simply how to formulate an effective regional development strategy that could also form the basis for accessing and implementing the EU Objective 1 programme. Previous involvement in EU programmes meant that a successful partnership was speedily put together in the northern region and it was able to retain its focus over a three year development process.

The RGA processes in both Uppsala and Västerbotten can be seen as attempts to introduce new forms of legitimacy and accountability at the regional level that, to some extent, evade control and manipulation by local democratic institutions. It can be expected that private sector involvement in the RGA process is likely to be more forthcoming where local party politics is not allowed to dominate the discussions. Since the new regional partnership in Västerbotten has greater control over public funds compared with Uppsala, it is not surprising that discussions over accountability are more common in the former RGA. But to prevent accountability being undermined, there is a need for strong monitoring and reporting mechanisms to be put in place that also address the issue of performance measurement. At this early stage in the RGA process both regions appear still to be grappling with this issue.

Both the Uppsala and Västerbotten case studies show that the balance between private and collective interests is not easy to achieve. Especially the integration of a large number of public partners that, on the one side, can improve the cost effectiveness of the RGA, but on the other hand can increase the costs of negotiation and co-ordination. To the extent that the administrative and bureaucratic organisation expands in greater proportion than the number of viable projects then this can lead to reduced flexibility and increased costs. In the initial stages of developing the RGA and achieving inclusivity it is difficult to get the balance the right.

To look at these issues in greater detail we investigated four separate projects, three of them undertaken within the two RGAs and one outside RGA. This last project is chosen as an example of how projects of regional importance can develop separately but in tandem with the RGA process.

Campus Uppsala

The Uppsala region underpins Sweden's claim to be one of the most advanced countries in terms of scientific output (in terms of patents per head of population and scientific publications) and, building on this regional strength, Campus Uppsala has successfully blended together scientific and entrepreneurial cultures.

Campus Uppsala is managed by the STUNS foundation whose long-term goal is to create a dynamic and attractive environment for innovative companies and entrepreneurs. It is based on the premise that successful companies need to establish effective and extensive networks through which they can fully utilise the creative talents of their employees in the development of new products and processes.

The Uppsala Science Park is the biggest in the region with over 150 R&D companies and 1 200 employees. It is an ideal environment for developing new ideas and this is bolstered by the unique Swedish legal system that permits scientists to retain the patent rights on their own research. This means that the legal system is very favourably positioned for encouraging academic spinouts. The other key element has been the development of synergies between this patented research and the venture capitalists. The upshot is that the system created on Campus Uppsala specifically encourages scientists to patent and develop their own inventions.

The ethos of Campus Uppsala is that successful regional development has to be based on knowledge and the ease with which new ideas can be exchanged and developed into new products and processes. Diversity in the innovation process is also a key aspect, hence collaboration is encouraged between entrepreneurs, scientists, lawyers, social scientists and other professionals.

Some very big companies – like AstraZeneca and Pharmacia – have been founded and nurtured in the region. This is a good example of the role of large enterprises acting as catalysts for the creation and implementation of effective partnerships. For example, Pharmacia has been very important for the success of some of the more innovative aspects of Campus Uppsala. Having grown to be a significant employer in the region it decided to move some large departments out and to spinoff some of its local operations. This action acted as a catalyst for the biotech boom by channelling resources into start-up companies, new projects and new products. These developments have created a regional growth pole that combines to best effect academic strengths with business acumen, an entrepreneurial spirit and financial risk capital.

Its competitive edge comes from its ability to generate investment driven technology transfer. This helps it attract new firms and to grow existing firms. The quality of life within the area and other lifestyle issues have made a significant contribution to the success of the project – the age bracket of most entrepreneurs is between 25 and 35.

The Campus assets are: i) a critical mass in terms of infrastructure technology and ii) a dedicated and supportive partnership in STUNS. But STUNS has been around a long time and the general feeling is that although the RGA has been helpful, the RGA itself has not had very significant impact on the project.

In reality Campus Uppsala and STUNS act like a very specialised inward investment agency, offering mobile companies the possibility of sharing in the unique atmosphere of the Campus and the region. They apply development concept oriented towards high tech industries with extensive research operations. The goal is to attract 100 new establishments (each employing over 100 people) and also to attract or grow a similar number of smaller businesses, each employing around 30 people. The key to this will be careful infrastructure development to absorb the growth in population in an environmentally friendly way alongside a long-term strategy to highlight current assets and competencies.

The graphic industry in Uppsala (outside RGA)

In the Uppsala metropolitan labour market a major bottleneck is the shortage of labour available to traditional SMEs. New innovative industries with high-tech appeal make it hard for local traditional firms to compete and attract the scarce youth population to their enterprises. Individual firms have difficulty in reversing their image. They lack time, networking skills and finance to invest in the development of attractive career patterns and learning opportunities in order to convince young people to make other choices in the transition from school to work. As local public SME support policies are fragmented and restricted, reflecting compartmentalisation at national level, it is hard to bridge the differences in attitude and culture. The role of the local office of the public employment service in getting young people to work in these traditional sectors appears to be limited.

Under the umbrella of the RGA, local employers in co-operation with local trade unions recently started a vocational training project in the graphic industry through the regional committees for educational and skill development. In this project local employers co-operate with the Graphic Education Centre (GEC), a public company in which Uppsala Community is the major shareholder. The regional committees are composed of the county administrative board, county council, municipalities, local public employment service office, ALMI and private training firms, employees and industry. The aims of the project are to safeguard staffing of the industry in the long run by offering "life cycle proof" career patterns and help to create a new perspective on traditional industries.

The actors expect to achieve this aim largely by delineating a collective strategy of pooling resources. They offer the young at school and during their "trial and error" period in the beginning of their careers all kinds of facilities to get them to know the working conditions and career possibilities in the sector. Local SMEs set up innovative vocational training facilities in co-operation with local high schools and universities using facilities such as the Internet and organise introduction programmes to individual firms. These introductory programmes are combined with "learn and work" projects to highlight the "life cycle" career patterns that the sector wants to offer in an attempt to solve long term labour shortages. Major actors of the RGA are involved in this project and it is a good example how local actions can help pool resources in order to address cross-sector labour market problems. Traditional schools can learn from the experience of the GEC in dealing with companies. Projects like this could successfully develop further under the umbrella of the RGA in close cooperation with the schools and local companies.

Mining project in Västerbotten

One of the larger projects in the RGA is a geo-scientific mining initiative – called Georange Vision – that aims to utilise an existing business activity to achieve a structural transformation of the labour market. Its primary objective is to create new employment in the region by organising education, research activities, excursions, seminars etc. around the heart of a programme of area mining. The region will be used for geo-scientific education and research. The project focuses on creating better opportunities for finding more ore bodies faster, on increasing protective environmental knowledge through new research and on increasing the understanding and knowledge about the importance of geo-science for continued economic growth in the region.

The Georange non-profit organisation acts as a research broker between proposed projects and different organisations (inland and abroad) and combines and basic research suggestions from different organisations (industry, universities, official organisations) into larger multidisciplinary and scientifically sound projects that could help attract industry into the area. Most of the municipalities have accepted the common goal of development of the region through the mining industry. Trade unions and business associations are members of the non-profit organisation. The total financing is SEK 30 million per year for the first two years. A large amount, SEK 23.8 million, is financed through EU Structural Funds.

Route 12 in Västerbotten

In 1999 as part of the process underpinning the RGA, a number of partners began developing trans-national projects in co-operation with Norway and Finland. The aim was to create a development corridor that extended from the coast of Norway, through Västerbotten, and onto Osterbotten in Finland. The "E12 Alliance" was formed to develop the project as a platform for co-ordinated development and as an engine of growth in line with the general outlines of EU Structural Fund (Objective 1) programme.

The regional objective was to create new links between the coastal area of Umeå and the inland mountain areas. It was felt that the E12 offered opportunities for better urban co-operation and networks, tourism and exporting from Norway through to Helsinki and the Baltic States. In this sense the E12 project was seen as a means for stimulating both county development and international co-operation. To achieve this E12 Alliance investigated various avenues for inter-regional co-operation and for accessing various funding mechanisms:

● Regional/national co-operation could use the Objective 1 programme.

● Cross-border inter-regional co-operation could use the Interreg III A (EU).

● Trans-national co-operation could utilise Interreg III B (EU).

The key to progressing the E12 Alliance as a well-managed regional development project was the ability to apply for sufficient funds and other resources within the framework of the RGA and the EU Structural Fund programme. This enabled the county council and its partners to become active members in the E12 Alliance along with regions in Finland and Norway. This element of the project is now being further developed within the framework of Interreg III B.

The overarching objective is to create new communications corridors and border crossings that encourage transport along east-west access routes rather than the more traditional north-south corridors. The significance of an increase in these east-west links is being built increasingly into the county's future development strategy.[5] "The challenge is to find suitable 'cross links' between the northern regions that can stimulate trade and commerce, as well as environmental efforts. Although NGO contacts and administrative work contribute to the building up of networks, it is efforts of trade and industry that ultimately play the decisive role."

The E12 Alliance provides a good example of how the transport infrastructure can be used as an important instrument for regional development planning. The Alliance is aware that the prospect of receiving investment aid from both the national government and the EU Structural Funds is going to have a significant impact on the development of transport routes in peripheral areas for several years ahead. The Alliance has created public-private partnerships to highlight the need for a comprehensive transport network that will create the conditions needed for regional growth.

However, if the east-west communications network and transportation infrastructure are to become important instruments for the county's development then a new integrated partnership model must replace the traditional "single project" approach. More than 30 large inter-related development projects are under way along the route and the main intention of this co-ordinated development plan is for the partners jointly to carry out these projects over the next decade. The large number of projects confirms the importance of the RGAs in creating a co-ordinated approach to infrastructure development and the Alliance is now developing further proposals to reinforce the economic impact of the route.

Some conclusions from the case studies

These four case studies indicate the benefits of taking a co-ordinated and cross-sector approach to development. For example, the Georange Vision project and the Route 12 Alliance hope to achieve both economic and social cohesion in a geographically isolated area with development projects that will address the region's skills and infrastructure deficits. The Campus Uppsala and Graphics Industry projects, through the RGA, have attempted to develop a synchronised view of the labour market that addresses the mismatch between vacancies and unemployment in a vibrant, central region with a plethora of high-tech industries. The graphics project shows that more traditional sectors like the graphical industrial sector which as yet are not included in the actual RGA have growth potential. Many of the programmes and measures in Västerbotten have been developed in line with the guidelines of the EU Structural Fund programme, to ensure that wherever possible, the funding of the projects can be accommodated within the framework of the RGA and alongside other funding mechanisms. However, projects within the Uppsala RGA have less opportunity to access outside funding and therefore the whole programme is inevitably less ambitious.

The strength of the RGA process is demonstrated wherever the measures making up the agreement can be developed within an inter-related single programme, rather than divided up into constituent parts. To achieve this the RGA has to create a professional administration to implement the agreement, focused on achieving co-operation for all development work within the region. Perhaps because of the difference in the resources available to the two regions, the Västerbotten programme has succeeded in putting in place a specialised body to oversee the development of an ambitious programme. In turn the regional and national authorities must co-operate in order to provide the necessary joint funding of the measures within the RGA. This often requires attracting Structural Fund support and providing access to central budgets of organisations such as the AMS and ALMI.

Another difference between the regions is the way in which the partnerships have succeeded in involving the national government agencies in the RGA process. For example, although ALMI is a partner in the Uppsala RGA (which is almost entirely focused on business development) it does not appear to have committed its own resources to the RGA process. Whereas, in Västerbotten, there was a genuine commitment from ALMI to become an active partner and they had agreed to allocate a significant share of its funds through RGA projects. The AMS appeared to have only weak involvement in the RGA process in terms of participation in the strategic planning exercise and the proposal of new projects. It is worth noting that its financial contribution to projects designed by the RGA can nevertheless be significant. For instance, in Västerbotten, the county labour board and the employment offices provided around 10% of the funds needed to carry out the various projects.

These significant disparities in the degree of involvement of government agencies in the RGA process is not easy to explain. The county administrative boards have been charged with the task of developing the RGAs and they are also supposed to perform (or at least to oversee) the functions of the government agencies (like ALMI and AMS) in their respective counties – especially where the agency does not have a regional department. So the administrative support for the active involvement of all agencies in the RGA process would appear to be in place as indeed are the main building blocks for the introduction of "new" regional policies in tune with the latest thinking.

Competitive regions and the RGAs

Theory and practice

The rapid contraction of more traditional industries in a number of OECD countries, including Sweden, has resulted in lower economic activity rates in some regions and a workforce without the necessary skills to adapt to changing circumstances. At the same time the growth in high value-added service sector activities, the "knowledge economy" and the "lightening" of many processes and occupations requires a new kind of regional policy to address these developments. In the past regional policies have been far too focused on hard infrastructural projects, rather than the development of people.

A major lesson learned from innovation activities in the last decade or so is that while the environment for innovation and productivity growth requires stable and sound macroeconomic policies, the real impetus comes from the microeconomic level – especially from clusters and networks of firms. Clusters (i.e. geographically proximate groups of interconnected companies and associated institutions in a particular field) thrive where there is a high-quality microeconomic business environment. Firms cluster together to take advantage of the "external economies" available in the region to local firms operating in related sectors – such as the availability of specialised skills. In the new global economy, developing the supply of these local "raw materials", in terms, human capital, new entrepreneurs and a skilled workforce lies at the very heart of developing a robust regional economy.

This growing emphasis on *people* rather than buildings has been shaped to some extent by recent developments in modern growth theory. Instead of emphasising factor inputs such as capital in which exogenous technology shocks drive the production process and lead to rapid increases in total factor productivity, the new theories of growth stress that increases in productivity occur only gradually through a learning process as new products and processes are introduced along the supply chain. This leads to an innovation process that is not just about inventions but about the generation, development, application and distribution of knowledge.

To emphasise this distinction, the new growth theorists make technological progress *endogenous* by linking it more closely to investment decisions about human capital and skills development. They emphasise the spillover effects from R&D and technical knowledge, especially where regional networks of firms are important in forging supply chain links. Economic clusters, regional networks and supplier associations are examples of regional activity that help internalise (*i.e.* reduce) the risks associated with new product development. The main contribution of clusters and networks is to help harness these external economies by encouraging vertical and horizontal links between independent firms. These reciprocal and cooperative links facilitate risk sharing and encourage joint product and process development.[6]

The new endogenous growth theories and the introduction of networking activity make a big difference to the analysis of the innovation process. It is no longer sensible to view innovations as taking place in isolated firms with large R&D departments, but rather as a complex process of knowledge flows that are heavily influenced by the dynamics of regional networks. The success of networking is based firmly on the view that firms learn most from other firms, and that this interactive, inter-firm learning is a key ingredient of the innovation process.

New policies

In response to these challenges, a new kind of regional policy is emerging across the OECD in which the emphasis is changing from basic infrastructure provision to institutional innovation and the development of cross-sector networks that facilitate collective learning (Morgan, 1997; Morgan and Henderson, 2002). These new policies on regional innovation provide the foundations for ambitious attempts to build up (and to re-build) social capital, particularly in more disadvantaged regions, by developing the "soft infrastructure" that underpins partnership arrangements. The RGAs are best viewed as experiments that are in tune with this new regional policy: the positive attributes of the RGAs stem from their ability to formulate effective network arrangements and to develop practical problem-solving approaches to delivering regional development. Through local consultation and practical knowledge of local conditions, they are able to provide area based solutions and integrated policy-making.

In developing regional partnerships, two efficiency conditions could prove to be vital to the success of the RGAs. The first is the importance of active business involvement to efficiently manage both state employment and regional growth policies as businesses are best placed to identify labour shortages and skill deficiencies in the regions. Second is the political environment in which partnerships have to operate. This environmental structure of relations between national governmental units and political organisations as well as the ability of regional partnerships to resolve conflicts between community and other organisations can make the difference between failure and success.

Trust is the key issue in partnership formation. To be successful in this endeavour the RGAs need to focus on the nurturing of trust, a relationship that can only be developed gradually over a significant period of time. This emphasises the need to shift away from the present impatient political evaluation criteria, that demands almost instantaneous results from any form of public intervention. The RGAs will need time to broker the informal alliances and partnerships that are needed across their regions in order to provide effective support for collective actions. Their objective should be to generate within the partnerships a willingness to collaborate in order to build the critical institutional capacity needed to achieve economic regeneration.

An integrated approach to regional policy

In order to build on existing strategies for achieving high sustainable growth and high employment, the central authorities need to concentrate more on the regions, identifying both their potential for growth and the barriers. Thanks partly to EU programmes there now exists decentralisation of funding and policy but governance structures are still largely national.

Aware that centrally-based decision-makers tend to have little direct experience of regional problems, the government seems to have set up the RGAs as a precursor to introducing institutional reforms at the regional level. The RGAs were initially set up to gain a better understanding of the options available at the local level and to give local communities more control over the factors that impact on their livelihoods. One of the most important benefits of the RGAs was supposed to be their ability to develop the local economy, based on support for existing indigenous businesses, and the skills needed to support a flexible labour market.

The differences and tensions within and between regions – e.g. urban vs. rural issues and unemployment in old low-productivity sectors vs. areas with labour shortages – have convinced the state authorities that problems such as unemployment and social exclusion often have a number of interrelated causes that are better dealt with at the regional level. However, to the extent that the new regional policy focuses on strengthening the power of the disadvantaged regions (still suffering from the decline in traditional industries) the plans are still controversial and cannot count automatically on broad national political support. None of the larger political parties in parliament seem willing to support the case for strengthening regional governance structures. Despite the greater role ascribed to the regions by the EU, the consensus of national politicians appears to be in favour of greater decentralisation through a strengthening of the municipalities.

However, the complex issues that need to be tackled require diverse solutions that are more broadly based than those under the control a single municipality, so again the regional level is the preferred delivery mechanism. It is not just a matter of "top down" vs. "bottom up". The resolution of multifaceted economic problems requires a combination of flexible local responses that can be more effectively co-ordinated through a regional partnership. Although the municipalities have been central to the implementation of many of the projects, they acknowledge the significant role of the RGA in initiating, co-ordinating and developing projects to the point where they can deliver measurable outputs.

Challenges for the RGA process

The creation of new forms of governance like the RGAs can induce some atavistic human desires like reinventing the wheel, empire building, power struggles, etc. To avoid these mistakes the RGAs need to work closely interregionally with national partners like the AMS in an iterative and inclusive fashion and intraregionally, they need to build robust horizontal working methods and flat management structures that enable the project committees to interact in a creative and effective manner with the AMS and other state organisations.

On the internal challenge it is clear that the project committees will need to develop innovative cross-functional working methods if the RGAs are to deliver added value and become more than the sum of their parts. If the RGAs can address the above priorities in an iterative and inclusive manner we feel they are likely to impact positively on the growth process. Ultimately what the

RGAs do is important but, even more important, is what the RGAs enable others, like the AMS, to do for themselves.

To be effective the new regional policies will need to address two traditional weaknesses in economic regeneration processes:

- the knowledge gap; and
- the institutional deficit.

The knowledge gap refers to the fact that there is a dearth of information on the sectoral performance of local, private sector SMEs and of their development needs. Consequently, it is difficult to develop proactive business support services and work-based training programmes that are tailored to the needs of indigenous firms. One of the biggest problems is the lack of investment by companies in "on-the-job" training. The key requirement is that training must be adapted to the skill needs of the future and hence it must be designed and implemented in close co-operation with the business sector. To become more proactive the RGAs will need to improve not only the information flow to SMEs but also improve the information flow about SME needs to partner organisations, like the AMS, in economic development.

To achieve this it may be necessary for the RGAs to create a new stratified, representative database of manufacturing and service sector firms that is targeted at relevant sectors, such as "tradable producer services" i.e. those services that add value to the manufacturing sector and can enhance the competitiveness of the region. Much data already exists in Sweden on small firms and is being utilised by ALMI to good effect. But the aim should be to use the close links that the RGAs are forging with the private sector to develop a new relational database that can be used to identify and target local firms who are growing (i.e. those firms that can have a real impact on regional growth) and also firms who are currently facing difficulties but have the potential to grow if better targeted and focused support is made available. This information is a vital pre-requisite for the development of innovative programmes that can effectively assist local firms to achieve their growth prospects and maximise their contribution to regional regeneration.

In this respect, the institutional deficit refers to the lack of a partnership approach to developing institutional mechanisms that can focus regional development policies on the needs of private sector firms and to promote a radical rationalisation of the business support services and labour market initiatives delivered to SMEs. From the view point of the private sector, the institutional deficit is paradoxically characterised by the multitude of institutions currently involved in delivering various forms of business and labour market development programmes to indigenous firms. To remedy this it will be necessary to more fully integrate the economic development aspects of regional development with the labour market policy of the AMS. Indeed the one thing that would probably do more than anything else to signal success of the RGA process and to generate regional growth would be the rationalisation of the organisations involved in economic development and the labour market. A successful strategy for indigenous growth will require the RGAs to integrate these economic development organisations into effective regional partnerships.[7]

Private sector participation

The authorities are also aware that if integrated plans are to be developed from below and co-ordinated within a decentralised regional planning framework, with little control from the centre, then the success of the programmes will be market dependent and require the full support of the private sector.

Hence, the aim of the RGAs is to involve local and regional organisations from both the public and private sector in developing innovative projects that offer local solutions. To do this effectively they will need to carry out a certain amount of experimentation and this will inevitably involve the risk of failure. The RGA process is all about increasing the ability of the regions to respond locally to address local issues. To date efforts have been pragmatic and purposeful but not very innovative. Prior to the introduction of the RGAs, the implementation of projects to resolve community problems was largely uncoordinated. There is now a more favourable attitude towards co-operation and networking, and more organisations are involved directly in strategic planning. The RGA, by involving the private sector, has had the practical effect of encouraging greater community involvement in the economic development process.

However, despite private sector participation, the RGAs have not yet succeeded in raising the innovative capacity of partnerships, especially in terms of encouraging new forms of business organisation – such as explicit and contractual public-private partnerships (PPPs) in which investment capital is jointly supplied and development risks are shared. There is also more to be done in terms of connecting business and research, and in connecting the solutions to social problems with economic development issues. Again contractual PPPs might offer a solution. The main function of the RGAs should be to devise the most effective blueprint that offers innovative solutions to these connected problems but at the same time helps speed up the regional development process.

A key project within the Uppsala RGA has pioneered ways of linking together the business and research agendas. For example, Campus Uppsala has created a dynamic environment for innovative companies and encouraged extensive collaboration between entrepreneurs and scientists.

Successful companies like AstraZeneca and Pharmacia have used the project to support their business growth. Through Campus Uppsala, they have established effective networks and developed wide-ranging partnerships to sustain product and process innovation.

One of the most important gains from the RGA in Västerbotten has been the extent to which the concept of partnership has gained acceptance by a wide range of actors. The partnership approach adopted by the region to prepare the 2000-2006 Objective 1 programme document, in which all the municipalities and many private sector actors were actively engaged, created a more co-ordinated and democratic approach to regional development than had previously been the case. Previously, economic development and the application of the EU Structural Funds had been largely focused on sectoral measures. This time, there is a clear move towards integrated development but it is not obvious whether the RGA process itself has had a positive impact or whether the county's involvement in the EU Structural Fund process has paid dividends.

Support and steering

One of the main weaknesses of the RGA process (that has been highlighted from the outset) is that the partnerships were not provided with sufficient resources to develop new initiatives. No new funding was made available and the funding provided for the pilot programmes was spread too thinly. National steering of the RGA process has been weak and there has not been the devolution of powers needed for local partnerships to engage in a search for innovative solutions. There is a need to agree and clarify the role of the RGA partnerships before the next stage of development.

The funding issue is important but increased resources alone will not pay dividends unless the partnerships are encouraged to identify original solutions and explore new approaches. In this sense the organisational weaknesses of the RGAs may be more problematic for the long term than the funding issue. For example, the objectives and purpose of the RGAs were not set out with sufficient clarity at the outset, there were no formal mandates for the participation of members and the reporting procedures remain weak. This lack of clarity has strained relations with democratically elected local government and caused some confusion across the programme as a whole. The informal character of the decision-making process "makes it difficult to hold members responsible and to insist on public control".

Evaluation

In terms of evaluation we must be aware of the dangers of judging the RGAs (which should aim to raise the long-term innovation capacity of the region) by the standards of the old regional policies (which were focused on short-term job creation). Since innovation and improved organisational relationships hold the key to successful partnerships, more attention needs to be given to "process evaluation" as against regular "output-based" evaluations. Process evaluations could focus on measuring improvements in network formation, information flows, institutional linkages, institutional innovation and capacity building [or what OECD (2001) describe as "governance outcomes"]. However, this will not obviate the need to develop more concrete, output based indicators to assess *longer-term* changes in the capacity of the private sector to innovate and grow. These would include benchmarking the RGAs on the number of employees achieving new skills, the amount of investment in workplace training, other targeted expenditures, like R&D expenditure, the number of new products and processes developed, patents filed, etc. Inevitably, at this early stage, the RGAs have made reasonable progress with respect to process indicators but more limited headway with the longer term output indicators.

The distinction between process (or governance outcomes) and outputs (or policy results) is important in order to avoid a premature abandonment of the RGAs because they fail to meet the (traditional) output-based measures in the short term. The evaluation must state clearly that more innovation in regional policy making is to be commended but that, in the short term, it will not necessarily lead to the creation of more jobs.

If jobs are the objective stated for the RGAs then the new innovation-oriented strategies that they develop will need to be supported by the job-creating programmes of the AMS and the Structural Funds. The RGAs are in place to help the regions to become more innovative and more cohesive. The RGAs clearly have their limits in terms of fostering employment and growth. They have direct control over fairly limited resources. At present the programmes are small-scale, low-budget experiments which have yet to be fully mainstreamed even in the regions which have pioneered them.

The tangible and quantifiable outputs from an evaluation process in terms of governance outcomes will necessarily take time to materialise. However, since an important factor in the success of interactive, cross-sector networks is the establishment of good working relations between the private sector (especially the individual entrepreneur) and other public sector actors (such as civil servants) a good short-term indicator for the RGA process will be the extent to which the key participants, especially the private sector firms, remain involved in the process and find it rewarding. This on-going involvement can be easily measured and used to monitor the value of the RGAs as it signals the collective commitment of the regional stakeholders to the regeneration process – even though many of the benefits of the RGA process may remain less tangible and difficult to measure.

Flexibility

Promoting significant change will require the RGAs to pay more attention to using cross-sector networks to harness more resources and to get the AMS and other partners to agree to introduce greater flexibility into their mainstream programmes. The important point is that the RGAs must remain flexible enough to be used to pilot new structures and to develop mechanisms that help build the institutional capacity of their regions, through which local agents can begin to develop joint solutions to common problems.

The problem is that traditional regional policies have engendered an expectation that peripheral regions, like Västerbotten, have to look outside their area (essentially to the State and to organisations like the AMS) for solutions to their internal problems. The objective of the RGAs should be to internalise the policy process of the AMS to make it more accountable to the regional partnership and thereby create ownership of the solutions. The AMS needs to become more flexible at the regional level and able to directly participate in regional projects that foster endogenous development, growth and competitiveness. A positive way forward would be for the AMS to earmark, say, 20% of its budget, for regionally-allocated funds that are targeted in support of regional competitiveness, through strategic and integrated development projects based on local skills, knowledge and competitive advantages designed in partnerships. In the disadvantaged regions, this would help AMS to move further away from seeing its role as one of offering short term regional assistance in the form of job subsidies.

The RGAs in this sense can be seen as small regional experiments based upon a new and more innovative form of governance that focuses and targets the expenditure of State organisations at the regional level. They should be seen as experiential attempts to foster interactive, bottom-up, network-based solutions, aimed at diversifying the economic structure of their regions rather than relying on the purely top-down assistance provided by the traditional Swedish model of development delivered through organisations like the national labour market boards. The top-down approach cannot be expected to bring together and organise effective regional partnerships to stimulate innovation and economic regeneration. There are too many externalities involved. Therefore, the RGA process should not become involved in the debate about the scale of state intervention in the regions (e.g. the size of regional subsidies, etc.). The RGAs should concern themselves with the type of state intervention that will allow local solutions to evolve; i.e. the objective should be to create an effective framework for interaction between state organisations like the AMS and region partners that generate, internal, network solutions to traditional problems.

The efficiency of employment services

The basic functions of the public employment services provided by the AMS are to advance labour market functionality to match labour demand and supply and as part of its distributional task, to place the disadvantaged in employment. Under current conditions of rapid social change where both the demand and the supply can gain new forms in quite a short period of time, these labour market issues have to be resolved in new ways (Beck, 2000). Modern policies used to be characterised by a strong role for state corporatism, covering welfare state interventions where the balance between labour demand and supply was clear and predictable. These policies no longer fit with the changes in (labour) markets and society.

The ICT revolution and the dominance of global markets have led to "the densely woven institutional structure", being broken up and to a decline in the supremacy of the nation state in relation to the implementation of centralised labour market policies. Instead, global, regional and local markets have become interconnected and boundaries have become blurred. As a consequence, labour demand and supply relations in Sweden have become more complex, creating new problems of predicting future market developments. Against this background the AMS in Sweden has continued to pursue a strong top-down political goal of lowering unemployment and raising the employment rate based very much on a supply-oriented approach. In doing so AMS has not invested much resource into accommodating developments on the demand side of the labour market but concentrated instead on activating labour market reserves. It has left other sectors of the labour market to private sector participants, interfering only when necessary or when asked to do so by central organisations of the state.

The role of national agencies

The co-ordinating role of the national agencies in the RGA process has been ambiguous. They seem to have focused on providing information to the project partnerships but their role in guiding or providing funding to the RGAs appears to have been minimal. Also the agencies have not developed a clear set of objectives either with the co-ordinating ministry (Industry, Employment and Communications) or amongst themselves regarding the RGA process. For example, ALMI and the AMS are closely involved in some RGAs to the extent that they have developed specific funding commitments to individual projects in Västerbotten but there is little evidence of such a commitment in Uppsala.

To allow for the structured longer-term development of the RGAs the national agencies will need to ensure that the objectives they set for their regional administrations are consistent with the goals assigned to RGAs. There is also a need to agree the rules of engagement between the regional organisation of the national agencies and the RGAs, especially since the county administrative boards and the county councils are involved in both delivering the regional programme of the agencies and in co-ordinating the RGAs. There is a clear need for them to establish together how they plan to participate in processes at the regional level.

There are various options that could be considered in terms of steering the RGAs and providing technical help but the overarching objective should be to provide guidelines at county level for their regional arms to adapt the national targets that have been set for certain programmes to the priorities agreed in RGAs. This is not a one-way process. The national agencies will be in a better position to achieve their targets if they can establish better working arrangements with the RGA partnerships at regional level.

The involvement of the AMS in the RGAs will be an important test case of the ability of the national agencies to form meaningful relationships with deliverers of other programmes that impact upon their sphere of influence. For example, closer links between the AMS and the regional partnership is vital because, through their ability to link together the various public and private partners, the RGAs are well positioned to integrate labour market policy into economic development strategies. They are also well informed about demand and supply conditions in the broader regional context and are hence able to positively influence both sides of the local labour market.

In this context it needs to be noted that although the RGAs have devoted some efforts to longer-term planning and to developing an integrated approach to labour market issues their activities to date have consisted largely of a series of uncoordinated projects that address short-term unemployment problems rather than link the activities of the AMS directly to regional needs. The reforms of the AMS system that are currently being discussed will need to take this issue into account, i.e. can a restructured AMS be focused on longer-term goals that are more closely embedded into regional economic development?

Where matching problems exist between current vacancies and the skills or geographical location of the unemployed they can have negative effects on regional growth and employment. Labour market policy should offer the most effective solution but the current focus of AMS is on national political issues and the macroeconomic perspective: restricting official unemployment figures to less than 4% and ensuring labour market efficiency to promote economic growth and price stability. At the moment AMS appears to be under pressure due to the perception that its active labour market policies are not working as effectively as they might, i.e. they appear to be too focused on measures to raise employment (Calmfors, Forslund and Hemström, 2002). The question is the extent to which these traditional labour market policies work in favour of the unemployed and the extent to which they can be refocused to act as a catalyst for regional growth.

In pursuing this strategy the AMS focuses on promoting geographical and skills mobility but – from a regional development perspective – it pays too little attention to the need to take an integrated approach to endogenous development. This is particularly important in terms of encouraging new firm development and in helping to promote an entrepreneurial culture amongst the unemployed. In focusing more on new sources of employment growth and in increasing the contacts with local firms labour market policy will become better integrated into the objectives of the regional partnership and the AMS will be better placed to reinforce the regional dimension of its organisation. Reinforcing the regional dimension could increase the efficiency of AMS and thereby indirectly help achieve national goals.

This may require the central authorities like the government and the Parliament to develop future labour market interventions by issueing instructions for AMS in some innovative directions. For example, the larger element of the AMS budget could remain allocated to achieving macroeconomic goals but a proportion of the programme budget could be allocated to help implement regional priorities. This would be consistent with a bottom-up approach to programme implementation and would offer better solutions to regional and local problems such as the marginalisation of older workers, the decreasing population in certain regions and related social problems. Since these are real problems that are difficult to solve under present arrangements it may be a good opportunity to allow the county labour boards to place up to 20% of their programme funds at the disposal of the RGAs, i.e. allow specific programmes related to the objectives pursued by RGAs to be targeted by RGAs themselves.

The aim of this strategy would be to ensure that innovative programmes are developed and implemented in line with the regional strategy being pursued by the partnership. The benefits to the central AMS would be that this process could help develop bridges between labour market policy interventions on the one hand and economic development and social regeneration actions on the other. It could thereby facilitate transitions into employment or self-employment for "outsiders" as well as "insiders".

To sum up, conditions for success in RGA networks are likely to differ from those in traditional hierarchic structures. In these embryonic partnership networks conditions for success will be linked to their ability to make effective decisions about complex issues. This will require: a) a clear conception of the RGA process; b) clear tasks, roles and responsibilities of the participating organisations and actors; c) the presence of measurable objectives and targets to be achieved; d) an incentive structure in which success and failure hit back on the participating organisations and generate or broaden the available resources through common investment in regional policy; and, finally, *e*) the independent measurement of actual results (Eberts and Erickcek, 2001).

Links with the Centre

To this end there is a need for greater collaboration between the central ministries and departments concerned with economic development and those involved in setting labour market policy. A key way forward will be for them to assimilate their respective policies with regard to the development of the RGAs. Greater direction from the centre will be required concerning the future roles of the RGAs and the restructured AMS. An inter-ministry collaborative structure that allows for greater consultation between departments on the development of new initiatives could serve this purpose.

Greater direction from the centre could also reinforce the RGAs co-ordinating function at the *local* level and help develop stronger and more tangible and durable links with the municipalities and the local population. To strengthen the RGA process mechanisms will need to be developed that encourages more consultation with local citizens – the unemployed, the self-employed and employees – about their labour market needs and how these needs can be better addressed within the new partnership model compared with the more traditional policy instruments favoured by the AMS. The discussions between the AMS and the RGAs should focus on new plans and priorities for the local labour market in terms of the educational and life-long learning needs of the area and how these can be better attuned to the needs of business.

At the national level policies have shifted from an emphasis on welfare to a focus on growth and this has to be translated at the regional level into policies more adapted to the needs of those organisations that create growth. In other words, the RGAs should seek to create a balance between the skills needs of the business sector and the needs of the individual. For labour market policy, this could mean using the RGAs newly formed links with private sector firms to design and implement labour market initiatives more in line with the needs of employers, and not focused too rigidly on the needs of job-seekers. At a time when, for demographic reasons, the number of job seekers is expected to decline, labour market policy must become more focused on meeting the needs of business in every region. To achieve this it will also need to become more flexible with an increased ability to respond quickly to the changing demand for labour and the need for new skills.

In order to accommodate this process we recommend an experiment incorporating the county labour boards more firmly into the RGA structure. Up

NEW FORMS OF GOVERNANCE FOR ECONOMIC DEVELOPMENT – ISBN 92-64-01530-2 – © OECD 2004

until now county labour boards have operated within the framework of the national rules set by AMS. As the RGAs focus their development efforts more and more on capacity building there is more need for the AMS to enter into partnership arrangements. One way forward would be to make the county labour boards a key constituent part of the RGA process, with their budgets allocated in line with the priorities and measures identified by the RGA board. In addition, the administrative budgets and personnel of the county labour boards could also be placed in support of the RGA process. By making county labour boards a key part of the RGAs, the public and private actors in the labour market would be brought more in balance with each other and thus provide the legitimisation needed for greater involvement from the business community.

To support the above projects and measures we recommend VINNOVA, NUTEK and ALMI be encouraged to develop specific "service agreements" with the RGAs for the delivery of specific inputs, such as the number of small firms helped by Almi in the project areas, or the number of SMEs given innovation support by VINNOVA etc. In return for which VINNOVA, NUTEK and ALMI get the opportunity to lever some additional funding from the county labour board budgets to support their own objectives. For example, the AMS could begin the process by providing support to the development of NUTEK's regional industrial cluster initiatives.

National co-ordination

One of the problems has been the fragmentation of policies relevant to the RGAs from within the various ministries, and this has to be multiplied across all the RGA regions, which are all different and which in turn makes it difficult for regional actors to pursue a consistent strategy. For example, there has been some divergence on aims between the centre and the regions: the Ministry for Industry, Employment and Communications has prioritised the achievement of certain objectives such as increasing employment, creating new businesses and involving the business sector in decisions, but regional actors have placed more emphasis on promoting co-operation among public sector organisations and identifying integrated solutions to complex problems.

In this sense there has been a fixation with practical short-term goals rather than addressing more strategic issues such as developing new approaches to tackling economic inactivity and integrating these into broader regional and national programmes. The monitoring and reporting requirements of the Objective 1 programme in the North may have pushed the partnerships in Västerbotten in the direction of attaining short-term measurable outputs rather than creating better forms of governance.

The main criticism at the local level has been reserved for the central role given to the county administration. The strength of any partnership comes from harnessing the different viewpoints of the partners particularly creating an atmosphere where the public and private sectors can debate openly with each other. However, the lead role of the county administration has led to the charge of a lack independence and flexibility – the partnerships have been criticised for operating as an extension of the central bureaucracy. Meaningful participation in partnerships requires the partners to feel that they have ownership of the process and that their views will be taken into account. This may require significantly more democratisation of decision-making than is presently the case at the regional level.

If too many of the measures are controlled from the centre then it becomes more difficult for local partners to develop ownership of the process and therefore difficult to encourage the level of co-operation needed for successful and innovative programmes to be implemented. However, strong support from the centre is a necessary precondition for establishing sustainable partnership arrangements. It is important to get the balance right. The lack of central leadership in the RGA process has led to the wide variety of different delivery mechanisms across the regions. The diversity of RGA partnerships is a proof that there is no simple delivery method that will ensure the success of local initiatives. Moreover, while the active participation of all the regional stakeholders is a necessary condition, it is not sufficient. There must be the willingness to take risks and develop new approaches.

The role of the RGAs in policy co-ordination

The RGAs must avoid becoming focused on only one aspect of regional development, say delivery mechanisms. If the RGAs are restricted to delivering a narrow set of services, with the broader co-ordinating functions being left say, to the county boards, then this would limit the potential of the RGAs to influence policy and to develop regional strategies. They will need to break down outmoded divisions between the design and delivery of regional policies and draw together regional actors around a flexible, more integrated, "joined-up", interactive policy agenda that designs and delivers policies that are better tailored to local needs.

This highlights the requirement for regional policies to integrate the skills agenda with the business development agenda and to integrate workforce training with innovation initiatives. The RGAs should seek to upgrade the physical capital of the region and the human capital embodied in the workforces of private sector companies *in tandem* rather than separately. This will require close working arrangements between the RGAs, the AMS and private sector firms. The current lack of co-ordination and interfacing between key intermediaries and the business sector means the RGAs and the AMS are not fulfilling this role as effectively as they might

To be effective, therefore, the RGA experiments need to be extended to include influence over the budgets of state organisations, and ratcheted up in terms of scale and resources. In this context it is likely that the RGAs will be able to provide some lessons for the Ministry in terms of governance structures and policy-making processes. Politicians at the centre and officials in state organisations too often see themselves as quite exempt from learning from new ideas developed in the regional hinterland. However, the Ministry needs to maximise the strategic benefits from the RGA process by publicising and also encouraging the emulation of the interactive governance structures that the RGAs are pioneering.

Ultimately the effectiveness of the multi-layered governance systems that operate in Sweden will depend on real interaction between policy makers and deliverers at each level of government and on the willingness of regional and national actors to respect the capabilities of each other. In other words the successful evolution of the RGAs will depend on how well they succeed in building inter-dependent policy and delivery mechanisms within their regions i.e. learning networks that help resolve the tension between the traditional hierarchical conventions of the state (including organisations like the AMS) and the new flatter, inclusive structures of the regional partnerships.

Conclusion

Against the backdrop of the new regional policies that are emerging across the OECD, the RGA process is best viewed as an experiment that is in tune with this new policy agenda: the RGAs highlight the importance of effective network formation, informal alliances and partnerships in providing operational support for collective actions. Alongside institutional capacity raising, the key role for the RGAs will be to provide active backing for existing businesses, help develop new firms and deliver the skills needed to underpin a flexible labour market. In order to focus the RGAs on helping indigenous firms to grow, we make the following specific recommendations:

1. It was suggested that one alternative to developing the RGA process is to strengthen the role of the municipalities. We do not feel that this is a viable option. Although the municipalities have played a significant role in implementing local projects, the RGA partnerships have been influential across a much broader front and have been pivotal in initiating and co-ordinating policies as well as developing projects that can deliver measurable outputs. Political parties at the centre need to acknowledge this by supporting the case for stronger regional governance structures. We

recommend enhancing the RGA process in terms of democratic accountability rather than strengthening the role of the municipalities.

2. In the spirit of developing a practical, problem-solving approach to business development we recommend that the RGAs should use the close links that they are forging with the private sector to develop a new relational database to identify potential growth companies. Such information will be a vital pre-requisite for the development of innovative programmes to effectively assist local firms.

3. In this context we also recommend that streamlining the plethora of institutions delivering and duplicating business support services to indigenous firms should be a top priority of the RGA. One-stop-shops are the way forward.

4. To succeed the RGAs must work closely with external partners like the AMS, VINNOVA, NUTEK and ALMI in order to build flat management structures that encourage interaction with other state organisations and the municipalities. We recommend that they concentrate on integrating these economic development organisations into effective regional partnerships with the private sector. A practical outcome of this would be greater community involvement in the regional development process.

5. The funding provided for the pilot RGA programmes was sparsely allocated and one of the remaining weaknesses of the RGA process is the lack of sufficient resources to develop new initiatives. This weakness has been compounded by inadequate leadership form the centre. The informal character of the decision-making process and the lack of devolved powers are likely to make it difficult to hold members accountable for performance. The role of the RGA partnerships in the devolution process is in urgent need of clarification before the next stage of regional development is put in train. To some extent the organisational weaknesses of the RGAs are more likely to undermine the process in the longer term than the lack of funding. Therefore we recommend firmer direction from the centre in terms of a clearer role for the RGAs with devolved powers being introduced alongside more explicit funding arrangements.

6. The key to the RGAs developing stronger links with external partners will require the successful integration of the AMS into the regional innovation process. The AMS currently pursues a top-down, fairly short-term agenda in the labour market, based firmly upon supply-side policies, whereas there is a growing need to focus on longer-term goals that can stimulate innovation and be more closely linked to business development needs. AMS policies need to be refocused to promote an entrepreneurial culture and to act as a catalyst for new firm development and the growth of indigenous firms. New policies and priorities for the local labour market should focus

on meeting the skills needs of the area by adjusting or customising these skills in line with the needs of local businesses. This new focus on issues that impact on regional growth will require the regional dimension of the AMS to be strengthened. We recommend that this be put in place – preferably through a significant proportion of the programme budget of the county labour boards being allocated to implementing RGA projects.

7. The aim of any reforms should be to develop closer links between labour market policy interventions on the one hand and economic development and social regeneration actions on the other. This in turn will require greater collaboration and dialogue between the central ministries concerned with economic development and those involved in setting labour market policy. These discussions could usefully focus on utilising the RGAs newly formed links with private sector firms to devise new initiatives for the labour market that are better attuned to employers' needs. We recommend that collaborative actions at ministerial level be put in train to refocus national and regional policies by increasingly switching the emphasis from welfare to growth: the centre should identify and support regional organisations with the capacity to foster growth and competitiveness.

8. Following global developments in the "knowledge economy" there is a growing requirement for regional policies to integrate the skills agenda with the business development agenda and also to integrate workforce training with innovation initiatives. In general, the innovation process is not about research activities taking place in remote technology labs in individual firms. Instead it refers to the multifaceted knowledge flows that are generated within regional networks, i.e. firms learn most from other firms. We recommend the RGAs should develop close networking arrangements between the AMS, VINNOVA, NUTEK (and other state organisations) and those private sector firms in the region that have the capacity to have a significant impact on economic regeneration and growth. The RGAs should become the key network facilitators for their regions.

9. To initiate successfully significant change in the current regional structure, the RGAs will need to use their key resource – their cross sector networks that encompass both private and public partners – to harness more resources by getting their partners to introduce more regional flexibility into their mainstream programmes. This will require developing an effective framework for interaction between state and regional organisations in order to generate, internal, network solutions to traditional problems. We recommend that the RGAs should create local ownership of national initiatives by encouraging state organisations like the AMS to become more involved and more accountable to the regional partnership.

10. Because of the increased importance of finding local, internal solutions to traditional problems, we have emphasised the need to place greater weight on "process evaluation" compared with "output-based" evaluations during this embryonic stage of the RGAs. Increased organisational capacity to deliver an innovative programme holds the key to the successful future development of the RGA partnerships. There are currently a wide variety of different delivery mechanisms across the regions. We recommend that the various RGA experiments are urgently monitored, evaluated and benchmarked to measure the impact that the RGAs have had on influencing regional policy and developing regional strategies and to inform the next stage of the regional innovation process.

11. In addition to informing the next stage of the RGA experiment, greater use of process evaluation will also be important to prevent the RGAs being narrowly restricted to delivering local projects without being actively involved in the broader policy issues. In our view the whole purpose of the RGAs is to help the regions to become more innovative and more cohesive. Therefore, instead of reinventing the archaic divisions between the design and delivery of regional policies we recommend that these artificial barriers be removed by using the co-ordinating function of the RGAs to develop integrated solutions.

To conclude, the successful evolution of the RGAs will require them to build effective, streamlined, inter-dependent policy and delivery mechanisms within their regions. In our view these could form the basis of new regional learning networks that will help integrate the conventional hierarchical practices of the Swedish state with the broader more inclusive structures that the new partnerships now have the opportunity to create.

Notes

1. Regeringens proposition 1997/98/62 (see Government of Sweden, 2001).

2. Prop. 2001/02: 07 Regional Samenverkan och statlig länsförvaltning.

3. Prop. 2001/02: 07 Regional Samenverkan och statlig länsförvaltning.

4. www.ac.lst.se.

5. "Kaspnet Progress Report", December 2000.

6. The Nutek report, "Innovative Clusters in Sweden", provides an excellent starting point for developing a cluster policy to underpin the Regional Growth Agreements. The report highlights the characteristics of a dozen or so regional clusters, including the biotech cluster in Umeå and the woodworking cluster in inland Västerbotten.

7. See the interim recommendations in the Central Sweden RITTS (2001) report: "1) Provide simpler and more transparent support to firms. 2) Achieve maximum results from public investments by concentrating on sectors and companies with strong growth potential."

Bibliography

Beck, U. (2000), *The Brave New World of Work*, Polity Press, Cambridge.

Behrentz, L., Delander, L. and Niklasson, H. (2001), "Towards Intensified Local Level Co-operation in the Design and Implementation of Labour Market Policies: an Evaluation of Some Swedish Experiments and Reforms", in: De Koning, J. and Mosley, H. (eds), *Active Labour Market Policy and Unemployment*, Edward Elgar.

Calmfors, L., Forslund, A. and Hemström, M. (2002), "Does Active Labour Market Policy Work? Lessons from Swedish Experiences", Working Paper, IFAU, Stockholm.

Council of Europe (1999), "Structure and Operation of Local and Regional Democracy: Sweden", Council of Europe Publishing, Strasbourg.

Eberts, R.W. and Erickcek, G. (2001), "The Role of Partnerships in Economic Development and Labour Markets in the United States" in OECD (2001), *Local Partnerships for Better Governance*, Paris.

European Union (2000), "Partnership under the Structural Fund Objectives: Forms, Outcomes, Effects and Benefits", Brussels.

Government of Sweden (2001), "Action Plan for Employment", Stockholm.

Johanneson, J. (2001), "On the Efficiency of Placement Service and Programme Placement at the Public Employment Services in Sweden", Discussion Paper, WZB, Berlin.

Ministry of Industry, Employment and Communications (1997), "Regional Industrial Policy and Agreements for the Promotion of Regional Growth", Stockholm.

Morgan, K. (1997), "The Learning Region: Institutions, Innovation and Regional Renewal", in *Regional Studies,* Vol. 3, No. 5.

Morgan, K. and Henderson, D. (2002), "Regions as Laboratories: the Rise of Regional Experimentalism in Europe", in Gertler, M. and Wolfe, D. (eds), *Innovation and Social Learning*, Palgrave.

OECD (2001), *Local Partnerships for Better Governance*, OECD, Paris.

Statskontoret (Agency for Administrative Development) (2002), "Collaboration between policy areas. Study for the Swedish national evaluation of the European Employment Strategy", Stockholm.

Svensson, B. (2001), "Partnerships for Growth: the Public-Private Balance in Regional Industrial Policy", in *International Review of Sociology*, Vol. 11, No. 1.

Svensson, B. and Östhol, A. (2001), "From Government to Governance: Regional Partnerships in Sweden", in: *Regional and Federal Studies*, Vol. 11, Summer 2001.

ISBN 92-64-01530-2
New Forms of Governance for Economic Development
© OECD 2004

Chapter 3

Norway: the Challenge of Creating Regional Partnerships

by

Mike Geddes, Local Government Centre, Warwick Business School

Norway can be seen as a pioneer of the regional strategic platforms. Innovative models to foster regional competitiveness and tackle socio-economic problems have emerged in two counties, Hedmark and Oppland, which present specific economic and geographical challenges. These experiments have inspired a government reform to promote similar forms of governance throughout the country to co-ordinate policies more systematically at regional level, adapt policies to local conditions, and involve business and civil society in the orientation of measures.

In Norway, the county (regional) level of administration has an important role in co-ordinating policies and adapting them to local conditions.* Partnership relationships between public services, the social partners and even users are increasingly seen to be important to an effective regional role. The Ministry of Local Government and Regional Development has since 1995 been implementing annual Regional Development Programmes (RUPs) based on four-year strategic county plans which co-ordinate long-term policy objectives with the investments from different sectoral policies operating at the territorial level. Within a context of greater decentralisation, and the likely emergence of bigger "regions", there are important questions about how to organise strategic decision making effectively.

One possibility is that the partnership relationships which have developed around labour market councils may provide the basis for the development of regional strategies. A primary focus of the chapter is therefore on the role of labour market councils (LMCs). Some previous national studies in the OECD research programme on partnerships, in Denmark and Flanders for example, suggest that such tripartite structures, involving public authorities and the social partners, can have an influential and positive role at the regional level, expanding from labour market issues to economic development and social inclusion (OECD, 2001). However, there may also be other mechanisms for co-ordination, and therefore this study does not focus exclusively on the LMCs, but on the wider framework for partnership and co-ordination at the regional level. In turn, effective regional co-ordination implies a concern with the national policy framework and the extent to which this framework ensures that ministries and services operating at regional level pursue consistent and coherent objectives. At the same time, regional arrangements must be able to respond effectively to local actors and pressures, from local municipalities, from service users and from civil society itself.

The chapter therefore addresses questions such as: who are the important partners at regional level and what kind of structures can bring them together effectively? How can partnership at regional level both implement and co-ordinate national policies, explore new solutions to

* The author wishes to thank Micheál Ó Cinnéide for his contribution.

regionally-specific challenges, and respond to local issues? The work is based on the experience of two counties in particular: Oppland and Hedmark. Both have been at the forefront of the development of regional partnership and represent sources of innovations in regional governance in Norway.

The national and regional context

The regional level of government and administration

Norway (population about 4.4 million) is a unitary state, in which government and administration is divided among three levels: central government and administration, counties and municipalities. Norway, it is suggested, is both centralised and decentralised (Monnesland and Nautsdalslid, 2000). Central government formulates policy objectives and influences public development programmes through central government budgets. However in many policy areas responsibility for service delivery and administration is shared between central and regional and local levels of government. There are currently 19 counties, with an average population of about 230 000 and wide-ranging responsibilities in the spheres of health care, transport, secondary education, economic development and regional planning. While the counties are comparable in population terms to larger local government units in a number of other European countries, they are large in geographical dimensions, and face diverse challenges in terms of territorial development. The second tier of sub-national government comprises 435 municipal councils, with an average population of 9 000, although there are wide variations around this figure. Municipalities are responsible for local physical planning, primary education, primary health care, child care and support for the elderly.

Alongside the directly elected county authorities is a structure of state administration, with a county governor in each region with responsibility for agriculture, fisheries and environment, and decentralised regional state agencies for labour market policy (the Employment Service), national roads, business support (the Industrial and Regional Development Fund – SND) and control of education and health (see Figure 3.1). In one sense, these two parts of the regional administration are complementary – the county council focuses on the region's own needs, while the county governor and the regional state agencies focus on the implementation of national policies. In practice, it is not surprising to find that this system is characterised by considerable overlaps, tensions and conflicts, and that there has been some concern for some time about inefficient and sub-optimal policy making at this intermediate level. Recent debate about how the public sector and administration should be modernised to conform more closely to ideals of efficiency, equality and democracy has focussed to a considerable extent on

Figure 3.1. **National, regional and local government in Norway**

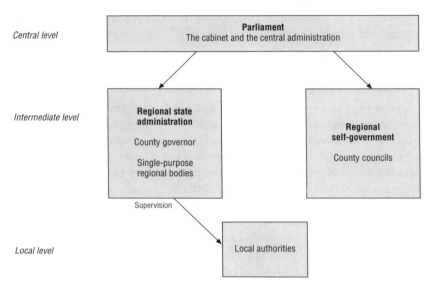

Source: Langset, 1998.

the role and legitimacy of the counties (Langset, 1998), raising questions about the possible "surplus of the regional level".

A committee appointed by government in 1998 has been looking at the distribution of responsibilities between the regional state administration, and the government has already given signals that the current counties may be replaced by 10-15 new regions, with outstanding issues about the extent of decentralisation to the regional level and whether this will remain an elected level of government, and about the impact of such changes on the municipalities.

Labour market and economic development issues

Over the last century Norway has developed from one of the poorest countries in Europe into one of the richest. Norway now has a diversified industrial structure, with about three quarters of the economy consisting of service sector industries. The manufacturing sector has traditionally been based on natural resource exploitation, including hydro-electric power, forestry and fisheries and petroleum. Norway is a small, open economy dependent on trade and thence on its international competitiveness. A trend in recent years has been the deregulation or liberalisation of the economy, leading to substantial restructuring of economic sectors. However, like other Scandinavian countries, Norway has developed and maintains a strong welfare state, and poverty and inequality are less marked than in some other OECD countries.

In the late 1980s and early 1990s the economy went through a period of sluggish growth and deteriorating competitiveness, with a rapid rise in unemployment. During this period, an Employment Commission established by the government with the social partners to establish a consensus on economic and employment policy led to the so-called Solidarity Alternative Framework, instituting fiscal, monetary and income policies to promote stability and competitiveness, and active labour market policies to facilitate structural adjustment while assisting those disadvantaged in the labour market. For much of the 1990s however there has been strong job creation with a significant increase in the employment rate and falling unemployment (Norwegian Ministry of Labour and Government Administration, 2000). As a consequence, for most occupational groups and in most sectors the labour market is tight and is expected to remain so in coming years. Labour market policy is aimed at improving the efficiency of the labour market, including measures for the unemployed and disadvantaged groups. Industrial and structural policies are aimed at achieving an optimal use of national resources, and maintaining the growth potential of the economy which in turn provides the basis for the welfare system. A particular concern is with raising the quality of human capital, including the so-called Competence Reform aimed at adults and addressing the need for competence in the workplace, in society and on the part of the individual. At the same time, such policies are subject to distributional and regional considerations. Regional development policies are based on an appreciation of the different needs of different regions. They aim to secure the development of employment and production in all parts of the country, and to support the settlement pattern in marginal areas. Regional policy measures promote the competitiveness of both "core" and lagging regions by strengthening the existing industrial base and promoting new technology, skills and jobs.

Regional partnerships in Norway

In Norway, employment, labour market and industrial policies are operated at national level through tripartite co-operation between the state and the social partners. However, it may be suggested that the powerful role of the state and the public sector in Norway (as in other Scandinavian countries) has tended to inhibit the development of the kind of partnerships at sub-national level between public, private and voluntary/community sector partners which have become a feature of local and regional governance processes in a number of other European countries. A contributing factor is that Norway is not a member of the EU and therefore the linkage between funding programmes and partnership characteristic of the EU has only impacted on Norway in a marginal way. However, recent years have begun to see the development of forms of partnership between the public sector, the social partners, and other interests, especially at regional level. While the extent and prominence of such developments varies between different parts of the country, in some places, such as Hedmark and Oppland counties, partnership relationships have a substantial history dating back to the late 1980s, and these are now the basis for further experiments in a partnership-based approach to regional economic development and co-ordination.

The Labour Market Councils in Hedmark and Oppland

Hedmark and Oppland are two adjoining counties lying to the north of Oslo. They are the only two counties in Norway without a coastline, and Hedmark lies along the border with Sweden.

Both Oppland and Hedmark have for many years been heavily dependent on natural resource-based economic activity – forestry, forest-based industries and manufacturing, and agriculture – and the need to restructure the existing industrial base and promote new and knowledge-based forms of economic activity has become pressing in recent years. As an indicator of levels of competence in the labour force, Hedmark and Oppland counties have the lowest proportions of the population with university and higher education qualifications in the country as a whole.

Oslo and its metropolitan region influence both counties to a significant degree. While the location of the new international airport to the north of Oslo is creating new development opportunities in the south of the two counties, long-term migration from the more northerly and rural areas of both counties continues, as do centralisation trends at a more local scale. While larger regional centres, areas within commuting distance of Oslo, and smaller centres at some distance from the major centres are growing or stable in the two counties, smaller municipalities and peripheral areas are declining in population.

Hedmark and Oppland thus present a combination of structural economic and geographical challenges in terms of regional economic development. Both counties have also played leading roles in the development of a partnership framework to respond to these challenges.

In Oppland, building on tentative steps in the late 1980s, the county established an Employment Committee in 1991, in the context of increasing unemployment (the same year as the setting up of the national Employment Commission). The Committee made proposals to increase employment by bringing forward municipal construction programmes, but also invited other regional and state bodies and labour market organisations to collaborate in the development of employment policy. The result was a Co-operation Committee with members from the county (the two main political parties), the county governor, the county employment office, the association

Map of Norway

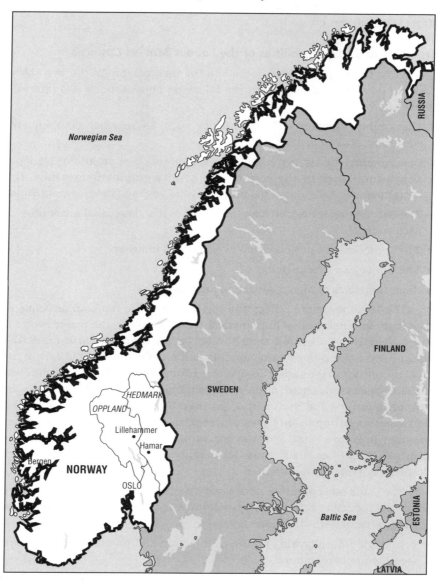

representing the municipalities, and the social partners' organisations. In 1993, as unemployment continued to rise, a national committee, the Orskaug Committee, drawing on experience in Oppland, recommended that all counties should establish Labour Market Councils.

In Hedmark, a Labour Market Council was established in 1993. In Oppland, the Co-operation Committee continued until 1995, when the Labour Market Council was created.

Structure and responsibilities of the Labour Market Councils

While there are minor variations in the membership of the two LMCs, they are essentially similar, with the following organisations and interests represented:

- The county directors of departments such as regional development, education, economic development.
- Departmental heads (or other very senior officials) from the National Education Office in the county, the county employment office, the Department of Agriculture, the Industrial and Regional Development Fund.
- The head of the Norwegian Association of Local and Regional Authorities in each county.
- The Confederation of Norwegian Business and Industry.
- The Norwegian Labour Union.
- Representatives of higher education institutions.

The LMCs therefore reflect at a regional level the national principle of tripartism in public policy. In numerical terms, however, the public sector is more heavily represented than the social partners. In both cases the chairperson is from the county administration, reflecting its lead role in the LMC. In contrast to the earlier Co-operation Committee in Oppland, politicians are either not represented, or only with observer status. While the LMCs are primarily forums for "horizontal" partnership at the regional level, the participation of representatives of decentralised national state agencies provides links to central government, while the Association of Local and Regional Authorities is a channel for the interests of municipalities, though these are not directly represented.

The LMCs meet monthly, with a small secretariat provided by the county. While the particular activities they undertake and issues they consider varies, in more general terms they have several roles:

- a strategic role: following up the county plan and producing the Regional Development Programme;
- a financial role: making a budget for the Regional Development Programme and for specific projects; and
- a co-ordination and monitoring role: ensuring that projects are carried out by one or more partners.

This range of roles faces the LMCs with both problems and possibilities.

The main formal responsibility of the LMC is to follow up and implement the strategy and activities in the four year county plans, as ratified by the county councils and national government, in the area of economic development and labour market policies. The plan is an instrument for the co-ordination of public activity in the region, providing the basis for the county's own activity and strategic guidelines for state agencies and the municipalities. The LMC thus provides an arena where decision processes and spending programmes can be co-ordinated, especially through the Annual Regional Development Programmes (RUP – *Regionalt Utuiklingsprogram*) which are the framework for the allocation of regional resources from various bodies, especially the county, the Industrial and Regional Development Fund and the Rural Development Fund. In 2000, as Table 3.1 shows, these resources amounted to NOK 141.5 million[1] in Hedmark, NOK 127.3 million Oppland. While the county plan system has been in operation since the 1970s, the RUPs were introduced in 1995 as ways of bridging between longer term planning and the annual budgeting of sectoral policies.

In addition to the role of co-ordination of spending programmes of partner agencies, the Oppland LMC also has a small budget of its own (from the county) which enables it to provide financial support of a number of specific projects in fields such as vocational and business education and training.

Table 3.1. **Funding allocated through the RDP in Hedmark and Oppland Counties (NOK)**

Funds	Hedmark 2000	Oppland 2000
Kap. 551-51 Economic development funds	9 730 000	11 000 000
Kap. 551-55 Support given to entrepreneurs	5 519 000	6 090 000
Kap. 552-56 Funds promoting economic restructure	8 000 000	3 000 000
Kap. 551-57 Interreg	1 900 000	
Kap. 551-58 Funds promoting regional co-operation	3 000 000	3 000 000
Kap. 550-60 Funds for marginalised communes	950 000	700 000
Kap. 550-61 Local development funds	7 600 000	5 800 000
Kap. 2425-51 Support for small/medium businesses	27 152 000	21 160 000
Kap. 2425-53 Loans for small/medium businesses	17 882 000	14 230 000
Local development funds related to agricultural dev.	14 500 000	16 000 000
Local investment funds related to traditional agriculture and gardening	18 400 000	20 500 000
Local planning funds etc. related to agriculture	5 200 000	5 700 000
Local funds, agricultural sector (trenching)	3 800 000	3 500 000
Olympic development funds	3 300 000	3 300 000
County municipality funds	14 600 000	13 300 000
TOTAL	141 500 000	127 300 000

The Hedmark and Oppland LMCs are now also participating in a pilot programme of the Ministry of Local Government and Regional Development, the Further Development of the Regional Development Programme, which is testing out possibilities for greater regional autonomy over the area of the two counties combined. For this purpose, the two LMCs meet together every three months. This programme supports a range of projects, including:

- The Inland College project, exploring collaboration among higher education institutions in the two counties and with a Swedish partner.
- Development of a co-ordinated business survey questionnaire, involving adding questions to the surveys undertaken by the county employment offices.
- A project to market the Lake Mjosa region to business on the basis of the high quality of life in the area.
- Co-ordination of public employment and education policy for the long term unemployed.
- Regional development contracts between the regional level and municipalities.
- Co-operation between the two counties and other partners on the implementation of the Competence Reform for adult and further education.
- Proposals to promote closer co-operation in offering public services between municipalities, employment offices, public tax offices and other possible partners.

A further objective of the Further Development of Regional Development Programme is to develop more effective indicators and evaluation mechanisms for the LMCs' activities. Evaluation needs to provide an annual appraisal of resources applied, and of the added value of the joint planning and management of resources, with a fuller four year evaluation of each county plan period.

Regional partnership in practice

The way in which regional partnership works in practice can be explored by examining a number of the activities of the Labour Market Councils:

- Implementing the county plans and Regional Development Programmes.
- Promoting the knowledge economy and economic competitiveness.
- The Competence Reform.
- The Inland College proposal.

NEW FORMS OF GOVERNANCE FOR ECONOMIC DEVELOPMENT – ISBN 92-64-01530-2 – © OECD 2004

Implementing the county plans and Regional Development Programmes

Implementing the county plans and the Regional Development Programmes are the main formal responsibilities of the LMCs.

Not surprisingly, those partners in the LMCs with most direct responsibility for the county plans – such as the county's head of planning – tend to see this as the primary focus of the LMCs' work. The development and implementation of the county plan is led by the county. Development of the plan includes a subregional consultative process via working groups including the local municipalities (thus bringing together the county's regional planning, economic development and strategic service roles with the municipalities' responsibilities for physical planning and important social services), and with some involvement of local citizens' groups. In Oppland there were six such groups (covering issues such as economic and employment development, education and competencies, environment, young people and welfare). The county planning process is therefore one of the main ways in which local issues and needs can influence the programmes of regional agencies. In addition to the municipalities themselves, some local social interests and informal organisations are represented on the subregional working groups and so are able to influence and comment on the plan during its development.

At regional level, the LMC provides an arena in which the county can develop the plan in consultation with regionalised state agencies, and with the social partners, and through which the plan, once approved, can influence their plans and programmes. However, while the LMC clearly functions well as a consultative framework in this respect, it is less clear how far there is a wider "ownership" of the county plan on the part of other agencies and the social partners. The plan is legally binding only for the county. While it provides directions for decisions for other state agencies, these tend to be driven primarily by national policy priorities and their own mandates, as will be discussed below in relation to the Regional Development Programmes. The organisations of the social partners – the regional officials of the Confederation of Norwegian Business and Industry and the Norwegian Labour Union – have relatively limited resources to participate in the LMC, and tend to focus their involvement on specific projects of interest and benefit to their members, rather than on broader policy and planning issues. Indeed, a criticism of the LMCs by the social partners' organisations is that they spend too much time on plans and not enough on concrete projects.

The annual Regional Development Programmes (RUPs) bring together resources for business support and economic development from the counties (with their regional planning and economic development responsibilities), the

SND (with responsibility for the promotion of profitable and efficient business) and the Department of Agriculture (although the rural development funding is now to be administered by the SND). The RUP is thus a significant and concrete example of collaboration between the two parts of Norwegian regional government with closely related/overlapping functions – the elected county and decentralised state agencies. While the RUP is largely funded from three (now two) sources, the county and the SND, the use made of these resources has important implications for other agencies, such as the county employment office and the National Education Office, as well as for the social partners. However, while it is clear that participants welcome the existence of the LMC as a forum in which investments under the RUP can be discussed, it is also the case that the LMC both has limited control over such decisions, and that it is one of a number of forums in which the relevant decisions are made. There are a number of issues in this respect.

In the first place, the resources allocated via the RUP remain subject to the guidelines of the respective agencies: they do not constitute a "free pot" of resources to implement the county plan. Second, only funding from certain organisations, principally the county and the SND, comes within the RUP. The activity and investments of other agencies, such as the county employment office, the Department of Agriculture and the National Education Office are not within the scope of the RUP. The specific composition of the RUP thus tends to create a distinction within the LMC between core partners (those contributing resources) and others (with interests but not committing resources). Some agencies with important responsibilities for regional development, such as transportation, have remained external or marginal to the LMCs. Third, the RUP includes only that proportion of the investment resources of the SND for which budgeting is undertaken on a regional basis, while other funds are centrally allocated. Fourth, the policies of decentralised state agencies such a the SND and the county employment offices are determined primarily at national level, so that, in general terms, such agencies contribute to regional initiatives and directions favoured by bodies such as the LMCs only as far as is consistent with national policies. Specified national targets appear to mean that while such agencies recognise that regional and subregional differences and needs exist, they may not have much flexibility to react to them. Indeed, an agency like the SND may argue that it is not efficient or realistic to think in terms of an economic development policy for a region with a population of less than 200 000. Even within the region, these agencies have other forums for consultation as well as the LMC. Thus the SND and the Department of Agriculture may work together at regional level more outside the LMC than within it. The SND works through local boards at district level including local politicians and representatives of business, agriculture and municipalities which make decisions on agricultural funds and advise on industrial ones. The SND regards its priorities as, first, businesses themselves, national government second, and then regional and local authorities and other agencies.

In summary, the LMC is the only formal body at regional level which brings together the elected regional tier of government (although the participation of elected representatives themselves is very limited) with regionalised state agencies and the social partners. As such, its existence is welcomed by most if not all of the participant organisations. But its ability to co-ordinate policy and investment across the public sector is limited by its restricted mandate and by the strength of the hierarchical principle within the regionalised state agencies, which means that much decision making still takes place within sectoral "silos".

Promoting the knowledge economy and economic competitiveness

The LMCs in both Hedmark and Oppland recognise the importance of promoting advanced technology and knowledge-based industries and businesses in order to enable their regional economies to compete more effectively in the globalised economy. In Oppland, the publicity and confidence resulting from the 1994 Winter Olympic Games held in Lillehammer provided a crucial impetus to collaborative initiatives to promote economic development and especially new knowledge-based industry. The LMC has been one of the forums which have initiated or supported initiatives such as the Lillehammer Knowledge Park which provides incubator space for business start-ups and training, including projects such as the Entrepreneurnet, an internet-based information source for people planning to start ICT businesses. While the Lillehammer Knowledge Park itself is located in the main urban growth centre of Oppland, the Entrepreneurnet has the advantage of being widely accessible throughout the region.

In Hedmark, current developments such as the Hedmark Business Park and Innovation Centre in Hamar also reflect the "trigger" of the nearby Olympics, and now also the economic opportunities for the southern part of Hedmark which is relatively close to Oslo and to the new international airport north of Oslo, while offering cheaper labour and a better quality of life. The Business Park is aimed at attracting a greater share of new development to Hedmark, while the Innovation Centre is one response to the need to restructure the traditional, forest and agriculture-based nature of the region's economy.

While these developments in both Oppland and Hedmark are the result of specific partnership arrangements (the Hedmark Business Park, for example, is the result of collaboration between the county, the SND, and private sector developers) the LMCs provide a wider framework of contact between key players at regional level which can create the context for such specific partnership arrangements.

Business interests also consider that the LMCs can create a common understanding of realities, policy challenges and opportunities among the major players in the counties. The representative of the Confederation of Norwegian Business and Industry has played a leading role in a number of initiatives and projects, especially promoting co-operation between education and industry. These include a survey of the educational levels of employees in businesses, leading to a project on vocational education for employees in the private sector, improving the take-up of opportunities. Further projects have been concerned with developing awareness of and attitudes towards entrepreneurship in schools. The small funds available to the Oppland LMC appear to have been helpful in supporting or pump-priming such initiatives.

The Norwegian Labour Union also regards the LMCs as useful means of achieving some of its objectives. These tend to be related to employment – an important part of the initial rationale for the establishment of the LMCs at a time of higher unemployment, but a focus which has become less central in changed labour market conditions. The Labour Union has limited resources (in terms of both people and money) which constrain the extent of its participation, but sees the LMC as a forum in which to influence the policies of regional agencies. In Hedmark, for example, the Labour Union participates in a committee established by the LMC assisting immigrants and the long-term unemployed who have reading and writing problems.

However, there are also instances where the LMCs have had more difficulty in fostering collaboration. One illuminating example concerns attempts to develop a joint survey of employment trends and needs among a group of agencies participating in the LMC. The main such survey has been undertaken by the county employment offices, but other organisations, especially the counties, also need information on labour market trends and needs. An experiment has therefore been undertaken to include a number of questions of interest to the counties in the employment office survey. While the LMCs have provided a forum to discuss this issue, it has proved difficult to make progress because of the vertical loyalties and differing interests of the organisations involved.

In summary, the LMCs provide a forum of contact among key regional players, which can initiate and support concrete initiatives to assist the regional economy in responding to the challenge of the knowledge economy and global competitiveness. However, the major public sector capacities for regional and local economic development remain segmented among specific agencies – the SND, the employment office, the county and others. The "unwritten regulations" and culture of the hierarchical state mean that the LMCs have only a limited ability to create synergy between them.

The Competence Reform

Focusing on continuing education and training, the Competence Reform is intended to help provide all adults with better opportunities for competence building and lifelong learning, so equipping the Norwegian labour market with the necessary injection of competence in order to secure the basis for value creation and the provision of services, in both the private and public sectors. Its objectives are to adapt educational provision to the needs of adults through innovation in education and training provision, to raise adult skill levels both to meet the needs of employers and of democratic participation in a "learning society" (Ministry of Education, Research and Church Affairs, 2000).

The implementation of the Competence Reform is an issue which highlights issues of collaboration between agencies responsible for education and the labour market, including the National Education and employment offices, the county departments of education and economic development, educational institutions at all levels, the social partners, and also voluntary organisations such as the Norwegian Association for Adult Education (a member of the LMC in Hedmark). In Oppland and Hedmark, the implementation of the reform is being handled jointly across the two counties, with the LMC representing the broad partnership framework for all institutions with an interest in the Reform. A project group has recently been established (June 2000), with a mandate to organise a permanent structure between the two counties to implement the Reform. It is recognised that this will need to overcome very different organisational cultures in the organisations concerned – for example, the need for much more flexibility in the delivery of education in schools, and for arenas for schools to meet with both business and public sector "customers", and involving voluntary adult education associations. There is a challenge to inform and motivate both businesses and workers, and in particular to engage small enterprises which are sceptical about the costs. Extensive use of ICT will be needed to reach geographically remote areas.

The Inland College

The Inland College initiative is also a project which involves collaboration between the two counties of Hedmark and Oppland. The initiative is exploring the potential for greater collaboration between the three small colleges in the two counties, in Lillehammer and Gjøvik in Oppland and Hamar in Hedmark, to enable them to offer an improved service to the population and the regional economy. Through the LMCs, funding for the project has been obtained from the RUP, and a feasibility study has been carried out. There has been support for stronger collaboration from stakeholders including the counties and the social partners, and there has also been support within the colleges themselves, although the proposals raise some difficult issues for them. A further dimension to the initiative is for collaboration with Karlstad University in Sweden, which has been facilitated in the framework of an EU INTERREG project for cross-border co-operation between Hedmark and the bordering part of Sweden.

The implementation of the Competence Reform and the Inland College initiative are current developments which challenge the regional partnership framework in Oppland and Hedmark to progress beyond its current limits, as both will require substantial advances in collaboration in which partner organisations increasingly transcend their individual remits, cultures and objectives in the interests of more joined up responses to public policy problems.

The current regional partnership framework in Norway: overview and issues

Partnerships as networked governance

Governments across the advanced world have given area-based partnerships increasing responsibilities in recent years: to stimulate economic development and address labour market challenges; to improve policy co-ordination and the adaptation of policies to local conditions; and to identify specific sub-national issues and needs which existing policies are not addressing (OECD, 2001). Partnership, as a form of "networked governance", may be able to respond to the limitations of other forms of governance – based on hierarchies, or reliant on market mechanisms. The development of new information and communication technologies pose new challenges for economic and social development, but also potentially provide new tools for a networked society and governance system (Castells, 1996). By creating new networks among actors from the three spheres of the state, the market and civil society, and from different "tiers" of the governance system (local, regional, national, supra-national) partnerships may be able to add greater legitimacy, innovative and learning capacity and ability to address the so-called "wicked", cross-cutting issues, to traditional governance mechanisms (Benington, 2001).

Experience is showing that partnership relationships can have a number of positive benefits as part of regional and local governance structures (Geddes, 1998). These benefits include:

- The development of networks of trust and common understanding among partners, including between the public and private sectors.
- More effective co-ordination and integration of policies and programmes.
- The development of innovative approaches to policy problems.
- Making better use of resources and "levering in" new resources.

At the same time, partnership as a mode of governance raises issues of inclusiveness and coherence, and of transparency and accountability. While experience in other countries shows that benefits have been reached through partnership, co-ordination and joint working has often remained localised around specific issues. Separate policy frameworks and structures have co-existed with a partnership approach, limiting the potential for collaboration. Conflicting objectives pursued at national level by partner organisations, most notably the public services but also the social partners, have limited the degree of commitment to local or regional partnerships. Mechanisms for accountability and transparency, and for monitoring and evaluation, have not always been well developed (OECD, 2001).

These are relevant considerations in addressing the questions raised at the beginning of this chapter: to what extent do the current partnership arrangements at regional level in Norway involve the important partners and bring them together effectively? How effective is partnership at regional level in both implementing and co-ordinating national policies, exploring new solutions to regionally-specific challenges, and responding to local issues and needs?

Shared knowledge and trust

Most partners in the LMCs in Hedmark and Oppland consider that the LMCs play a useful role in creating greater understanding and trust among key players at the regional level. Participants treat the meetings seriously, and there are high levels of discussion and debate. Meetings provide an important source of information on policies and developments in the region. In particular, the LMCs serve as a meeting place for senior officials from the state sector. However the social partners are less strongly represented, and elected politicians are mostly absent, indicating significant limitations to the inclusiveness of current partnership arrangements. Moreover, while most participants acknowledge the useful role of the LMCs, they do not generally regard them as particularly privileged forums – "one meeting place among many" is a common view. For most partners, equally, other channels and relationships are likely to rank above the LMC – for decentralised state agencies, national policy remits and guidance are of primary importance, while the organisations of the social partners look primarily to their memberships and to their influence at national level.

Policy co-ordination and integration

This somewhat ambiguous status of the LMCs as a regional forum is reflected in the mixture of well-developed forms of policy co-ordination and integration in some areas with others where policy still continues to be developed and implemented primarily through vertical channels. Thus the emergence of the LMCs as the forum in which investment plans are decided within the annual Regional Development Programmes, is leading to quite high levels of co-ordination and policy integration between "core" partners – including the counties, the SND and, to an extent, the social partners' representatives – within the specific policy area of business support and local economic development. There currently appears to be a potential for similarly close collaboration to develop, with a different set of core partners, around the regional implementation of the Competence Reform. At the other extreme, the nationally-driven remit of the county employment offices means that there is a relatively low level of co-operation in the area of policy for the unemployed. While rising unemployment was the issue which led to the LMCs being established in the early 1990s, with the changing economic context of a tighter labour market the main focus of regional partnership has shifted away from this original focus, and moved towards economic development issues. Nonetheless, even if unemployment is now rather low, labour market policy is still an important local development issue requiring co-ordination. For example, policies promoting geographical mobility may conflict with those of local and regional authorities promoting entrepreneurship and self-employment to keep the young people in the area.

In principle, the four-year county plans should provide the over-arching framework within which different sectoral policies are co-ordinated within the regional partnership framework of the LMC. But the fact that the county plans, while formally binding for the counties themselves, have only the status of guidelines for the regional state agencies (and have even less influence over the social partners) means that they do not play this role as effectively as they might. This suggests that there may be a need for a clearer and more concrete mandate for regional partnerships, specifying the remit and competence of the partnership, the processes by which it will operate, and what is expected of partners (as is the case in some other countries, such as Ireland and the UK for example). This issue is elaborated in the final section of the chapter.

At this point in time, though, it seems correct to say that, overall, regional partnership relationships remain subordinate to hierarchical and sectoral principles within the Norwegian governance system. The current review of the roles and responsibilities of different levels of government now being undertaken by government is clearly of relevance to this issue. If the strengthening of partnership and greater policy co-ordination at regional level are seen to be desirable, this is likely to require some revision to the guidance to regionalised state agencies from national government to alter the current balance between nationally and regionally-determined policy objectives. It would be likely to require strengthened arrangements for co-ordination between government ministries at national level, to ensure greater consistency and co-ordination in policy and funding regimes. As the OECD recommends in its "strategy to improve governance through partnerships", effective partnership requires that organisations at national level must pursue common or compatible objectives, which can then be pursued in partnerships at regional level. In practice, this means that the mission of the relevant partner organisations, such as public services, should take account of the main regional development concerns (OECD, 2001). This could suggest, for example, greater emphasis on local and regional development in the mission statement of the Labour Ministry, with an implication of more flexibility in programme management, and some funds available for determination by regional level partnerships, with such partnerships also involved in setting programme objectives and targets.

Innovation and resource enhancement

The activities of the LMCs in a number of areas, from the promotion of new, knowledge-based forms of economic development, to the Competence Reform and the Inland College initiative, indicate the potential of regional partnership to contribute to innovation in public policy, leading to outcomes which are responsive to local needs, build on regional comparative advantages, and achieve better use of resources. In particular, the Further Development of Regional Development initiative is now allowing the two counties to begin to work together to obtain synergies and economies over a wider regional area, such as in the promotion of the Lake Mjosa region. The concept of "learning regions", which has emerged from analysis of the experience of a number of successful European regions, implies effective partnership between all regional interests in creating learning networks which stimulate cultures of innovation. The promotion of regional industrial clusters and sectoral networks is seen as a route to dynamising local businesses and promoting a knowledge-based, high technology industrial future (Porter, 1990; OECD, 1996). At present the LMCs have only limited capacity and resources available to them, and consequently are not always able to play a leading role in economic innovation or in attracting resources. While realism is necessary about the extent to which economic networks and learning processes take place within regions (Lovering, 1999) it seems possible that strengthened regional partnership arrangements in Norway could have a significant role to play at sub-national level as the institutional focus for a range of "learning networks". This would, however, imply a considerable deepening of current partnership relationships (for example, greater involvement of a wider range of business interests, and at a more strategic level) as well as, probably, more substantial resources available to the partnership body to pump-prime and evaluate initiatives and disseminate learning about "what works". However, even larger regions such as given by the collaboration between Hedmark and Oppland are small in size in comparison with many comparators in Europe and elsewhere, and an important question is the extent to which such learning region functions should rest at regional or national level in the case of a country of the size of Norway. A further issue concerns the extent to which the promotion of economic innovation can benefit disadvantaged as well as advantaged parts of regions such as Oppland and Hedmark, where comparative advantage clearly favours those locations closer to the Oslo area. Bending development outcomes towards disadvantaged areas and groups is likely to require strong policy and political commitment.

Accountability and legitimacy

Evidence from partnerships in other OECD countries confirms there can be a danger that the gains from collaboration among partners may sometimes be compromised by limitations to the accountability, legitimacy and wider inclusiveness of partnerships. Partnership can contribute to the legitimacy of governance by involving a range of organisations and interests in the governance process, but it is important that this source of legitimacy complements and confirms, rather than cutting across, more traditional democratic principles and practices of accountability and legitimacy. In the case of the LMCs, the leading role of the county authorities means that there are lines of formal democratic accountability through the electoral process. However, in practice the involvement of politicians in the LMCs is very limited (and in addition the relatively low levels of electoral participation at the county level in Norway are an indication of the current limited legitimacy of the regional tier of government). It is also the case that the vertical lines of accountability of the LMCs are stronger in the upward direction towards national government than they are downward to the local municipalities and local communities, which are formally represented only through the Norwegian Association of Local and Regional Authorities. In comparison, partnership arrangements elsewhere frequently include provision for the representation of a range of local interests. Some rebalancing of representational arrangements to give greater weight to democratic and local interests would thus enhance the legitimacy and inclusiveness of partnership at regional level. This could be done partly by identifying some common objectives by municipalities and using them as a basis for the county and regional development plans. In addition to ensuring consistency in planning and vertical co-ordination, this would provide the plans with some of the legitimacy associated with municipal representation. Moreover, giving more weight to common local objectives could increase the prospects for the latter to be taken into account by nationally-designed policies in a "bottom-up" fashion (OECD, 2001). Good vertical co-operation can foster trust in the partnership framework and lead to a greater engagement by public service officers and local officials. In general the partnership framework must be responsive to the needs of both officials and politicians if they are to feel an incentive to use the partnership as a means of improving the effectiveness of their action in terms of local needs and conditions.

At the same time, issues of accountability also arise in relation to partner organisations. In the LMCs, lines of accountability and reporting between the partnership and partner organisations, and between individual representatives and their organisations, vary considerably. In the case of the county and some other public bodies, there are formal procedures (such as committee proceedings) for reporting. In the case of other partners, such as the trade unions or employers, reporting may take place at regional meetings of the respective memberships, but there is recognition on the part of those representing such interests that more formal and structured processes might be desirable, although this would have resource implications. Evidence from elsewhere has shown that a prerequisite for active involvement of trade unions and business in partnership, and for reporting, is that these organisations identify and promote a clear policy on the issues dealt with by the partnership, such as local development (Geddes, 1998; OECD, 2001). Social partner representatives on partnerships can take the initiative within their organisations to introduce and implement such policies. The relatively informal nature of accountability and reporting in and around partnerships can enable them to act quickly and innovatively. However, factors such as the increasing use of new communication technology may open up new possibilities for accountability and transparency. It seems likely that if the current role of the LMCs were to be extended there would be a case for strengthening arrangements for accountability and transparency, both in terms of the democratic process and in relation to the reporting arrangements between the partnership body and participating organisations.

Monitoring and evaluation

One important procedure which underpins accountability is effective monitoring and evaluation. The LMCs currently have formulated proposals for instituting a system of monitoring and evaluation, and it might be that these should be piloted as part of the Further Development of Regional Development initiative now provides a framework within which these can be piloted and developed.

It is widely recognised that there are difficult methodological issues in evaluating the impact of partnership working (for example, see Monnier, 1997). Evaluation of the outcomes of partnership working requires forms of evaluation, which are appropriate to the pluralistic nature of partnership. Evaluation of partnership needs to acknowledge and reflect differences in objectives and expectations among partners, as well as jointly agreed goals.

Because the nature of partnership is often a matter of negotiation and compromise, evaluation procedures developed in less complex situations may not be sufficient. Where the gains of partnership are seen as much in terms of process as of product, what are relevant measures of success? To what extent can the achievements of local partnerships be attributed specifically to the partnership framework, not merely to the programme resources which they control? (Geddes, 1998). Nevertheless, detailed analysis of impacts and outcomes is essential to guide and consolidate the partnership process and to ensure the achievement of goals and the effective use of financial and other resources. Experience elsewhere suggests that effective performance management and monitoring and evaluation may need to draw together a number of elements: quantitative accounting of inputs, activities undertaken and outputs alongside more qualitative assessment of the views of partners and stakeholders; both formative and summative dimensions; internal monitoring systems and external audit and validation. Monitoring and evaluation should attempt to identify what the partnership has done to improve governance and the implementation of partners' policies. Performance targets and indicators should be validated by each partner organisation, and evaluation should be seen as a way to stimulate discussion of the relevance of the work of the partnership, to optimise institutional involvement and to avoid duplication (OECD, 2001).

The detailed arrangements for monitoring and evaluation of regional partnerships in Norway will depend upon the way in which the partnerships develop in the future. Nonetheless, some elements of a robust system which can underpin both accountability and performance management might include:

- Quantitative monitoring on a regular basis of data concerning both partnership processes and activity. "Process" indicators to be monitored might include information on involvement by individuals and organisations in the partnership at various levels (Board level, involvement in specific projects and initiatives, etc.). Such information would indicate the degree of inclusiveness of the partnership and the commitment of partners. Similarly, monitoring of mechanisms for accountability and reporting to and from partner organisations, and communication with other stakeholders, would give an initial measure of accountability.

- "Activity" monitoring would include data on the projects and initiatives undertaken by the partnership, including information on financial and other resources committed; activities undertaken; and outputs achieved to enable monitoring against performance targets. Wherever possible, data should be collected which provides information on the specific results from working in partnership, and which relates to the strategy and objectives of the partnership, including in particular information concerning the benefits (and costs) of joint development, funding and implementation of projects and initiatives within the partnership framework. A requirement to provide monitoring data of this nature should be established at the inception of programmes or projects.

However, quantitative data such as the above will need to be supplemented by more qualitative and evaluative information. This may relate to issues such as:

- The extent of development within the partnership of trust and shared understanding of problems and possible solutions among partners; and the extent to which such trust and shared understanding contributes to the wider development of "social capital" in the locality.

- The contribution of different partners to the partnerships' strategies and action plans; the extent to which different partners and stakeholders – including local community interests and target groups – claim ownership of the strategy and specific actions; and the extent to which the partnership strategy reflects the interests and objectives of different partners and interest groups.

- The effectiveness of working processes within partnerships; including the degree and depth of involvement of different partners (and how this changes over time), and whether partnership processes encourage or discourage equality of involvement of partners; questions of accountability; methods of dealing with problems and disagreements; mechanisms for communication and reporting between the partnership and partner organisations and stakeholders.

- The performance of partnerships as learning networks; including training and capacity building issues and resources.

- The outcomes of partnership working: the extent to which shared understanding, trust and common objectives among partners can be shown to lead to more effective and innovative approaches to issues; and to the more effective utilisation of resources and the acquisition of additional resources; and the extent to which the partnership succeeds in influencing the policies, actions and expenditures of partner organisations in line with the partnership strategy.

The collection of qualitative information of this kind will require that procedures are established and adequately resourced within the partnership to enable information collection, analysis and learning to take place as part of the "core business" of the partnership. External evaluation should then be used to review and validate internal monitoring and evaluation results and processes.

Conclusion: scenarios and options for the future

This chapter suggests that the future for regional partnership in Norway is quite open. In general, the partnerships surveyed have shown a greater ability to stimulate local initiatives and promote inter-regional co-operation than to co-ordinate national policy and adapt them to local conditions. There may be a number of future possibilities for partnership arrangements as part of the regional level of governance in Norway.

One possible future is that regional partnership arrangements will have a restricted (but nonetheless valuable) function as a forum for the exchange of information between key regional actors, especially service providers, and for co-ordination between services which remain essentially vertically-organised. This is a function which is valued by participants in the LMCs as they currently exist. It would imply, however, that some of the important challenges for public policy, including those requiring more integrated, joined up responses across the public sector and beyond it, would be the responsibility of other levels of governance – national and local.

A second set of possibilities are for more strongly developed partnership-based arrangements at regional level. Movement in this direction would mean a strengthening of partnership beyond – maybe quite considerably beyond – the current role of the LMCs. There are at least two distinct possibilities for strengthened regional partnership arrangements. One is associated with a primary focus on the developmental economic role of governance at the regional level. In a number of countries, executive regional development agencies (directed by a board composed of influential regional economic actors from the business community the public sector and some other interests) have a powerful role in regional economic development and urban and rural regeneration. These agencies often have substantial investment resources and autonomy over the application of these resources, and act as a hub of regional economic innovation and learning networks. They operate frequently – though not invariably – at arms length from the democratic process. In Norway, movement in this direction would imply an enhancement of the kind of partnership now developing around the RUPs. In particular, perhaps, evidence suggests that effective regional learning networks require extensive and active business participation, not merely that of organisations representing business interests.

The second variant of strengthened regional partnership is one in which strategic partnership arrangements are developed in close alignment with representative democratic government institutions at regional level. In this model, a strategic partnership is the forum in which elected local/regional government negotiates a collective vision and values for the area with other key actors from the public and private sectors and with community interests, enabling democratically elected local government to exercise a "community leadership" role alongside its service delivery functions (Larsen and Offerdal, 2000). In Norway, this would involve finding ways to overcome the limited degree of "ownership" of mechanisms such as the county plan which are intended to provide strategic policy direction. It would imply a wider and deeper scope of partnership arrangements than those currently represented by the LMCs, including fuller representation of local communities and other interests, greater engagement on the part of elected politicians, and greater freedom for public service agencies to balance national policy priorities with regional ones.

In principle, the greatest benefit is likely to be gained from a combination of the advantages of these two variants, in which partnership arrangements enable a wide range of interests to contribute to democratic and inclusive governance, aligning objectives of economic growth and competitiveness with social, regional and distributional goals. The extent to which partnership at the regional level can contribute to such outcomes in the Norwegian context will, of course, depend on the wider future of the regional tier of government in terms of service provision, as a developmental economic agent, and as a democratic arena. There is of course a danger that strengthening the role of partnerships will lead only to more overlap, more complex accounting mechanisms, more time required for accountability and agreeing roles and responsibilities. To avoid such a danger, it needs to be clear that regional partnerships are able to play a significant role which complements the contribution of other organisations. As a step in this direction, it is possible to sketch out some of the changes which might be necessary to enable partnerships to contribute real "added value" to regional governance. These points draw on the issues discussed in the previous section of the chapter, and relate to the composition; remit and powers; resources and capacity; accountability; and, last but not least, to the culture of regional partnership bodies.

Composition

If partnerships are to contribute to democratic (rather than elite) governance, it is essential that elected democratic representatives play an active role within them. At the same time, partnership arrangements should not supplant democratic local governance: in this respect their role should be as a "friend", not a competitor to representative democratic processes. But a friend sometimes needs to be critical: if partnerships are to be critical friends to the democratic process, their composition also needs to provide scope for the representation of interests which may not be fully reflected by representative democracy, especially less powerful, marginalised social groups. In the Norwegian context, this would suggest that the composition of regional partnerships might be widened in two main ways: by the more effective representation and participation of elected regional politicians; but also by the representation of other social interests, either by the involvement of elected councillors from the municipal level, and by local voluntary and community interests and organisations. This would help to ensure that local needs and objectives are taken more fully into account in a bottom-up fashion in regional and national policies.

At the same time, attention should also be given to the fuller representation of other interests, such as those of the social partners, including different sectors of the business community. The experience of other countries offers a number of models of interest representation which could be drawn on in this respect, in order to both widen and deepen involvement in regional partnerships.

Remit and powers

There are at least two areas in which the remit and powers of regional partnerships might be strengthened. First, a stronger role for regional partnerships in developing (as well as, as now, implementing) the county plans would help to ensure that the plans are more representative of the full range of regional interests, and as a result that ownership of the plan is more widely shared. While the democratically-elected county municipality should remain ultimately responsible for the plan, it would develop the plan in close collaboration with the partnership.

Second, an extension of the remit of regional partnerships in relation to those of the regional state administration might be achieved through regional-level "public service agreements" negotiated within the partnership framework. Such agreements would be negotiated through a structured dialogue between the central administration, the decentralised regional state agencies, and with the involvement of the partnership. They would provide a framework in various policy areas, such as labour market policy and economic development, and potentially others, such as education, or transport, within which a new balance could be achieved between national and regional priorities, alongside better synergy at regional level between the expenditures and programmes of state agencies. Such regional public service agreements would be required to demonstrate the "added value" or leverage which they would bring to public policy and expenditure. As the OECD suggests (2001), proposals such as these to promote more effective partnership at regional level would also require strengthened arrangements for co-ordination between government ministries at national level.

Together, these proposals would offer partnerships a pivotal – and challenging – role in guiding the development and implementation of regional strategies which reflect the needs of local communities and different regional interests, as well as national policy directions and the challenges of regional development in the context of an open and competitive economy.

Resources and capacity

An enhancement of the composition and remit of regional partnerships would require a strengthening of their capacity. Partnerships would require an independent staff to undertake a wider role. This would need to include a capacity and competency for policy development; performance management; effective consultation and liaison with regional and other interests; and for monitoring and evaluation. If partnerships begin to play active roles in fields such as regional economic innovation, this would require the appropriate technical capacity, including the skills to develop and evaluate initiatives and disseminate learning. The resources available to the partnership to enable it to build such new capacities should be independent of any particular partner interest. One possibility is that for some specific competencies (e.g. in relation to economic innovation) partnerships might be able to draw on a national resource base available to all regional partnerships.

Accountability

These proposals would require stronger and more transparent procedures to ensure accountability. These would include:

- First, clearer guidelines on the composition of partnerships and the representation of interests.

- Second, procedures within the partnership to ensure that all interests are able to contribute on as equal a footing as possible, and that the internal working and decision-making of the partnership is transparent.

- Third, mechanisms to promote accountability between the partnership and partner organisations. The OECD suggests important principles in this respect, such as a clear distribution of responsibilities between partners and partnerships, and agreed mechanisms for "reporting back" by representatives on the partnership to their constituencies (business and trade unions, for example).

- Fourth, for two-way accountability between the partnership and the national administration. This would require the drafting and agreement of guidelines and protocols between the relevant parties.

The availability of monitoring and evaluation information on a regular basis and in a form which promotes a developmental rather than a judgmental approach is an essential basis for accountability. As discussed in the previous section of the chapter, effective monitoring and evaluation of partnerships is likely to include a number of elements, ranging from quantitative monitoring against targets and performance indicators to more qualitative evaluation of the effectiveness of processes and the views of partners and stakeholders.

Partnership culture

The notion of "partnership culture" is elusive yet of critical importance. It implies a break with closed, institutional or sectional cultures, not just in the state but among all partners and interests. It implies dialogue, between a regional partnership and the central administration and between regional interests and local actors. Such a dialogue does not imply the collapse or abandonment of the strategies and goals of specific organisations and social interests – quite the reverse. It should mean a clearer and more transparent enunciation of interests, aims and interests, and a more deliberative, less oppositional public process in which differences and diversities are clarified and contested, so that wider alliances of interests and actors can develop around specific themes, programmes and initiatives. The evidence from countries where partnerships have been in operation for some time is that the achievement of such a partnership culture requires a programme of cultural change to which all partners and key actors are committed, from national government to local grassroots organisations.

Some steps forward

There has been continuing debate, and further developments, in the last few years about the responsibilities for developmental and sectoral policy at the regional level. Two different national governments have presented White Papers to the Parliament on the issues involved, and the current centre-conservative government got Parliamentary support for its new position in June 2002. The outcome of these political processes can be summed up as follows:

● The politically-elected county councils will have the role of leading developmental actor at regional level, and will conduct their policies through a partnership including state agencies, municipalities and private sector.

● The municipalities will be the prime providers of social services to their inhabitants.

● The state agencies at regional level will be implementers of national sector policies, among them labour market policy, in collaboration with the other members of the partnerships.

The reform is accompanied by a significant change in how the specific funds for regional development are to be transferred to the county councils. From 2003, on the funds will be provided as *a lump sum* with a large *flexibility in usage*, instead of through eight different streams of funds with different rules and formal frameworks. The funds for regional development are now completely *decentralised*, compared to a regime of *delegation* up to this year (Knutzen, 2003).

These changes potentially offer more scope – or more challenge – to the regional politicians to make good use of the greater flexibility in the deployment of the regional development funds, and to work with the partnerships accordingly. At the same time, there may be a danger that the participation of the partnerships in this process could blur accountability issues. However, the reform has not transferred any new tasks to the county councils from the state agencies, which was strongly advocated by the politicians at regional level. Neither has it so far provided the state agencies at regional level with more leeway for regional adjustments within the national sector based policies. The White Paper simply stated that this latter issue will be under continuous consideration. The challenge to central government to commit itself more wholeheartedly to the principles and practice of regional partnership thus remains "on the table". These recent reforms thus represent some steps forward towards more effective joined-up, cross-sectoral regional policy making, but at the same time they indicate the difficulties which continue to confront this objective.

Note

1. NOK = 0.123 EUR (1 EUR = 8.12 NOK).

Bibliography

Benington, J. (2001), "Partnerships as Networked Governance: Legitimation, Innovation, Problem Solving and Co-ordination", in Geddes, M. and Benington, J. (eds), *Local partnerships and social exclusion in the European Union: New modes of local social governance*, London: Routledge.

Castells, M. (1996), "The Information Age: Economy, Society and Culture", Vol. 1: "The rise of the Network Society", Oxford: Blackwell.

Geddes, M. (1998), *Local Partnerships: A Successful Strategy for Social Cohesion?*, Dublin: European Foundation for the Improvement of Living and Working Conditions.

Knutzen, P. (2003), "Norway: Developing an Integrated Approach in the Regions", in OECD (2003), *Managing Decentralisation: A New Role for Labour Market Policy*. OECD, Paris.

Langset, M. (1998), "Intermediate Level of Public Administration and Government in Norway: Structure, History and Recent Developments", in Larsson, T., Nomden, K. and Petiteville, F. (Eds), *The surplus of the intermediate level in Europe?*, Maastricht: European Institute of Public Administration.

Larsen, H.O. and Offerdal, A. (2000), "Political Implications of the New Norwegian Local Government Act of 1992", in Amna, E. and Montin, S., *Towards a New Concept of Local Self-government?* Bergen: Fagbokforlaget.

Lovering, J. (1999), "Theory Led by Policy: The Inadequacies of the New Regionalism", *International Journal of Urban and Regional Research*, Vol. 2, No. 23.

Ministry of Education, Research and Church Affairs (2000), "The Competence Reform: Plan of Action 2000-2003", Oslo.

Monnesland, J. and Nautsdalslid, J. (2000), "Planning and Regional Development in Norway", *Built Environment* Vol. 1, No. 26.

Monnier, E. (1997), "Vertical Partnerships: The Opportunities and Constraints They Pose for High Quality Evaluation", *Evaluation,* Vol. 1, No. 3.

Norwegian Ministry of Labour and Government Administration (2000), "The Norwegian Labour Market 2000", Oslo.

OECD (2001), *Local Partnerships for Better Governance*, OECD, Paris.

OECD (2000), *OECD Economic Survey: Norway*, OECD, Paris.

OECD (1996), *Networks of Enterprises and Local Development: Competing and Co-operating in Local Productive Systems,* OECD, Paris.

Porter, M. (1990), *The Competitive Advantage of Nations*, Macmillan, London.

ISBN 92-64-01530-2
New Forms of Governance for Economic Development
© OECD 2004

Chapter 4

Mexico: Regenerating Participatory Planning and Development Processes

by

Micheál Ó Cinnéide,

Department of Geography,

and

Michael Keane,

Department of Economics, National University of Ireland, Galway

Mexico has experienced in recent years an approach to development that is more inclusive in design, more flexible and more focused on priorities as perceived and identified by local stakeholders. Through participatory processes in the preparation of strategic plans at national and various sub-national levels, and through the decentralisation of functions and financial resources, the government is attempting to create an enabling institutional environment in the regions and at local level that has the capacity to be responsive to a wide variety of conditions. Finding the most appropriate ways to reconcile participatory and representative democracy is a challenge that remains to be tackled.

The socio-economic context

Mexico is the 14th largest country in the world with a land area of approximately two million square km. Situated between latitudes 14 and 33 degrees north of the equator and characterised by geographically diverse terrain, including large mountain ranges, elevated plateaus, extensive plains and fertile valleys, it has highly varied sub-climates, ranging from warm and temperate sub-humid climates to dry and even arid conditions. There are lush rainforests where the vegetation reaches heights of over 40 metres in areas of over 400 cm of annual rainfall. Other parts of the country are deserts with extremely sparse vegetation. Some mountainous areas are snow-covered throughout the whole year. There are many other ecological sub-types, including bushland, grassland, conifer and broadleaf forests, palm groves and jungle, highly developed mangroves, and pioneer plant communities in coastal dune areas. This variety of landforms, climate and natural vegetation represents a diverse range of natural conditions as a backdrop to the development of Mexican society.

Government structure

Mexico is a federal republic with an elected representative and democratic system of government. It has three tiers of government, namely, the central or federal level, the state level, and the local level. The federation is divided into 32 entities, consisting of 31 states and one federal district. The states, in turn, are subdivided into municipalities, totalling almost 2 500 and the single federal district is subdivided into *delegaciones*.

Federal government is organised into three functional branches, consisting of the executive branch, the legislative branch, and the judiciary, with checks and balances defined in the constitution. Although the branches are officially autonomous, federal power was concentrated, until recently, in the executive branch, and especially in the president, who constitutionally is Head of State and Chief of government, and is elected by popular vote for six-year terms. The legislature is comprised of an upper house, *Cámara de Senadores*, and a lower house, *Cámara de Diputados*. The upper house is geographically representative, with three senators being elected for every state, although additional senators are elected in accordance with a proportional representation system, giving a total of 128.

The 31 states are organised in a similar fashion to the federal level. They too have the same three branches of government, with a governor elected every six years as head of the executive branch. Each state has a legislature that is elected every three years, with the number of deputies varying from one state to another, depending on population size. The states are subdivided into municipalities which are governed by an *ayuntamiento,* or council, led by the municipal president, or mayor, and comprised of a variable number of trustees and councillors (*regidores y síndicos*), all of whom have the same hierarchical status and are elected every three years. It should be mentioned that none of the above mentioned positions are open to immediate re-election. The excessive centralism that characterised the federal government was replicated at state level (OECD, 2002). Power was concentrated in the hands of governors, that ruled largely at the behest of the president, and through which the presidency had a direct line of influence over the municipalities, among others, by exercising a great deal of influence over the allocation of federal resources and over the appointment of the mayors.

The main functions of central government relate to national security and defence, the preparation of national laws and programmes, resolving judicial conflicts, and managing the economy. The competencies of the states are often not clearly outlined in the legal framework and vary from one to another. In general, however, they provide public services such as basic education and public health, among others. The national constitution establishes that states are free and sovereign and that they have general competence to perform all those functions not reserved for federal level (OECD, 2002).

Population

According to the results of the 12th Population and Housing Census, a total population of 97 483 412 was residing in the country as of February 2000. This ranks Mexico as the 11th most populous country in the world. Average annual population growth rate for the period 1990-2000 was just less than 1.9%. However, it is important to distinguish two periods, namely, 1990-1995, when the annual population growth rate averaged 2.1%, and 1995-2000, with an average annual growth rate of 1.6%. These figures confirm a gradual decrease in demographic growth, associated with declining fertility rates and international migration, mainly to the United States. Selective out-migration, comprised mainly of young adult males, has left a structurally unbalanced residual population of 47.6 million males and 49.9 million females, or approximately 95 males per 100 females. Taking recent growth rates into consideration, the current population is estimated at over 101 million people, of which an indigenous population, variously estimated between eight and 12 million people, represents a significant ethnic minority grouping.

Population density averages approximately 50 per square km but this varies enormously, with, for example, an average of 6 inhabitants per square km in Baja California Sur, while entities such as Distrito Federal, Estado de México and Morelos have 5 643 611, and 313 persons per square km, respectively. Settlement sizes in Mexico are highly polarised. At the one extreme there are 201 138 predominantly rural settlements with 2 500 or less inhabitants. These account for 25% of the total population. This population dispersion represents a huge development challenge because of the high costs of delivering basic services required to alleviate deprivation and to facilitate human investments required to escape poverty (OECD, 2002). At the other extreme, over 30% of the population are living in cities with more than one million inhabitants, the largest of which is Mexico City, one of the most populous cities in the world. The balance of the population is in settlements ranging from 2 500 to 500 000 with intermediate cities of 100 000 to 500 000 showing strong growth in recent years.

Internal and international migration is a common response to a deficit of economic opportunities in many parts of Mexico. Pressure on rural labour markets, because of traditionally high birth rates and agricultural adjustments leading to reduced demand for farm labour, has given rise to strong rural-to-urban migration flows, and rapid growth in urban population, creating huge housing and related social challenges in many cities. Attracted by higher wages in the United States, large numbers of Mexicans migrate to that country. As well as relieving local labour markets within Mexico, these emigrants contribute significantly to the country's economy, principally through remittances sent to family members left at home.

Economy

For over three decades following the Second World War, the Mexican economy underwent impressive growth. Import substitution represented the main plank of industrial development policy. Throughout this period the state was the dominant economic player and the nation's largest employer, investor and entrepreneur (Canak and Swanson, 1998). It pursued a policy of low taxation to help create an environment that was attractive to both foreign and domestic investors. Successive governments resorted to heavy borrowing from foreign banks and international development agencies to finance large-scale infrastructural investments. Mexican dependency on oil revenues was greatly exposed with the collapse of oil prices in the early 1980s. This together with a steep rise in international interest rates led to a severe balance of payments crisis in the country by 1982.

A major shift in economic development policy ensued. The balance of payments crisis highlighted the unsustainable nature of the Mexican import-substitution development policy (OECD, 2002). A process of fully integrating the Mexican economy with the global economy was signalled with entry to GATT in 1986 and the privatisation of many state-owned industries. The transition from the highly protectionist policies of the past to an open market economy was nevertheless to prove highly problematic. A further debt crisis in 1994 and the associated need to implement severe austerity measures, resulted in the bankrupting of many businesses, large scale redundancies, severe social problems, and led the economy to contract by 6.2% in 1995 (Ros, 2000). However, the neo-liberal economic model was copper-fastened through the signing of several other trade agreements, principally the North American Free Trade Agreement (NAFTA), which took effect from January 1st 1994. Mexico now trades at reduced or zero tariff with over 60% of the world (Lichfield, 2000). Foreign trade has become the engine of its economy. Between 1990 and 2000 its exports grew at *circa* 15% per annum, so that they constitute about one-third of GDP, and their composition has changed dramatically, to the point where manufactured goods now represent almost 90% of the total, a doubling over 10 years (Hakim, 2002).

These policies have succeeded in stabilising the Mexican economy, and resulted in impressive growth rates of over 5% per annum in the latter years of the 1990s. It currently ranks as the 12th largest economy in the world (Hakim, 2002). By providing a huge market that accounts for approximately 90% of Mexican exports, by being the primary source of foreign investment in the country and the origin of most its tourists, and by being the destination for up to 300 000 Mexican emigrants per annum, the United States exerts an enormous influence on the Mexican economy. Its buoyancy throughout the 1990s and the signing of NAFTA lifted Mexico out of its 1994-1995 crisis and maintained steady growth in the country until the downturn in the United States in 2001, with a slight recovery being shown in 2002.

Social problems

Although overall Mexico has successfully embarked on a transition to an open market economy, it is still faced with many intractable socio-economic problems. In particular, the new economic policy has not equally benefited all segments of society. It appears the benefits of economic growth have accrued relatively more to advantaged citizens rather than the disadvantaged (OECD, 2002). Southern regions of the country have been hit hard as much of the economic activity in these areas is not geared to avail of opportunities afforded by trade liberalisation (Fernandez de Villegas, 2000). Traditional agriculture is not in a position to compete with relatively cheap mass produced imported foodstuffs. Most of Mexico's rural population lives on subsistence agriculture and is confronted with problems relating to security of land tenure, small size of holdings, low levels of education, limited access to credit facilities, and pervasive poverty. They remain largely outside the influence of government policy, which is more focused on the development needs of agri-business, especially the export oriented sector (Canak and Swanson, 1998). Modern agricultural activity has developed mainly in the north of the country where there are strong locational advantages associated with proximity to the North American market.

Modern industrial development strategy has been concentrated on attracting foreign investment. An impressive number of jobs have been provided by the *maquiladoras,* with total employment in these plants growing from 0.5 million when NAFTA was introduced in 1994 to 1.3 million in 2000 (Lichfield, 2000). They now account for 52% of Mexico's manufacturing exports (OECD, 2002). However, they have failed to develop any significant local linkages as evidenced by the fact that in 1996, only 2% of total value of intermediate inputs were sourced in Mexico (Tamayo-Flores, 2001). Consequently, the multiplier effects in the domestic economy are rather limited and the strong growth in manufacturing exports is not reflected in an equally strong growth of employment. Based on a detailed analysis of the employment impacts associated with structural adjustments by Ros (2000), it appears that in order to compete effectively at home and abroad, manufacturing industries in Mexico have been forced to rationalise production by adopting new technologies to reduce labour requirements, thus limiting their contribution to job creation.

Official unemployment rates in Mexico are generally very low and do not reflect the reality on the ground. With only an extremely limited welfare system, much of the working population of Mexico derives a living in the informal economy. Estimates of the size of that economy vary considerably. One recent government estimate claims that 9.3 million of an economically active population of 32.6 million worked informally (Lichfield, 2000). Other estimates are much higher. In any case it is clear that a large proportion of the total labour force is engaged fully or part-time in the "shadow" economy. For the vast majority of people consigned to this sector the end result is a meagre and insecure living on the margins of society. Another undesirable side effect is that it denies the state much needed revenue to effect social and economic development programmes.

Estimates of the number of people living in poverty in Mexico also vary considerably, depending on how it is defined and the manner in which data are compiled, but it is generally agreed that it is a widespread and pervasive problem. Although there is minimum wage legislation on the statutes, it is largely meaningless as a measure of well-being or poverty, as it is widely accepted that a large proportion of those who are economically active, work for wages below the legal minimum. Inequality is a major problem. Up to 25% of Mexicans do not have enough money for food and clothing. Extreme poverty rates vary from less than 10% in northern regions to over 40% in the south (OECD, 2002). Poverty and associated social problems are particularly acute among the indigenous population. The poor live in *barrios* (neighbourhoods), many of which do not have planned streets, potable water, sewage or other services (Canak and Swanson, 1998). Mexico's economic elite has a lifestyle similar to wealthy citizens in other developed countries and tends to live in large houses in select residential neighbourhoods. Of the 21.9 million houses registered in the 12th Population and Housing Census, 2000, 78% had drainage, 89% had piped water available inside the dwelling and 95% had access to electricity.

The education system reinforces the social divide as the better-off sectors avail of it to a much greater extent than the poor, many of whom tend to drop out of school before completing the full primary cycle. Access to the relatively well-funded tertiary education is very much the domain of the upper social strata. An illiteracy rate of 9.5% was recorded among the population of 15 years or over in 2000. In recent years, government has sought to grapple with these problems through the introduction of targeted poverty programmes such as OPORTUNIDADES. This programme is targeted at areas with high levels of deprivation and is designed to integrate actions in the three complementary fields of basic education, health care and nutrition. Basically it provides food and clothing to poor families on condition that the children attend school and mothers address health issues through attendance at clinics.

The National Development Plan, 2001-2006, includes a national programme for social development (CONTIGO), that is aimed specifically at overcoming poverty. It acknowledges that the complex array of problems associated with poverty requires prioritisation of public actions on a long-term basis to provide coherence to initiatives adopted in the short term. Special emphasis is placed on pursuing an inclusive strategy that captures society's views on how best to overcome poverty and that enlists their support with its implementation. Actively involving people living in poverty in all aspects of the programme is a priority. It seeks to establish a co-responsibility pact with society to tackle poverty in a manner that stresses the development of the human capacity to create social and economic opportunities that will lead to the eradication of poverty in an equitable and sustainable fashion.

Regional disparities

Regional disparities in the levels of economic and social development are particularly stark in Mexico (OECD, 2002). The north of the country including Mexico City is characterised by generally higher levels of development than the generally lagging southern regions. Regional development problems are particularly acute in the southeastern states of Guerrero, Oaxaca, Chiapas, Campeche, Tabasco, Veracruz and Quintana Roo. The level of *per capita* income in the Southeast Region is less than one half of the income in the Northeast Region (Lichfield, 2000). However, the south also has considerable resources and development potential. It has a warm climate with considerable precipitation that provides good growing conditions and an abundant water supply. Large reserves of oil, gas and other mineral resources are located there. Problems of environmental degradation do not correspond fully to a north-south divide, but the southern regions have escaped the worst excesses of this blight. Yet, the south has greater poverty, higher illiteracy rates, faster population growth, a larger and more dispersed rural population, more traditional and mainly subsistence farming systems, less industrialisation, and generally much lower levels of productivity than the north.

The north of the country displays a great deal of internal heterogeneity, ranging from the vast urban metropolis of Mexico City to small and sparse rural settlements in states such as Baja California, but it is generally at a much more advanced stage of development than the south. Recent developments have tended to exacerbate the north-south divide, leading to the assertion of the existence of "two Mexicos", with the more prosperous north racing ahead and the impoverished south struggling along and still largely neglected by government, notwithstanding the increase in public expenditure in the area and the establishment of region specific programmes such as the Plan Puebla-Panamá. The development of the primary road network and other transport systems are centred on Mexico City and strongly favour the north. NAFTA and the export led economic development strategy of recent years has reinforced regional disparities by providing further advantages to areas adjacent to the United States, resulting in the explosive growth of *maquiladoras* and related employment opportunities (OECD, 2002). The poor transport infrastructure renders it extremely difficult for firms located in the south to compete successfully in national and international markets.

The present government acknowledges the existence of huge regional disparities and is committed to overcoming them. It is pursuing a regional development strategy that is designed to be economically competitive, socially inclusive, environmentally sustainable, territorially orderly, and financially feasible. The ultimate aim is to reduce the development gap between the regions and to promote social inclusion (OECD, 2002).

Participatory planning and development practices

Like many other countries in the industrial world Mexico, in recent years, has acknowledged the value of decentralisation as a major institutional framework. A new governance context has emerged which points the way towards reducing the role of the federal state in general by delegating central authority and introducing more interregional competition with suitable checks and balances. The Mexican government has also acknowledged the regional and local level as important elements in this evolving governance framework and it has worked to develop supports for many regionally based initiatives in economic development and promotion. Important elements of this emerging framework include:

- a growing commitment at the federal level to create a joint system of government with other levels of government;
- the revitalisation of old tools of participatory planning;
- a new commitment to working with public bodies by the private sector;
- new political and administrative agencies, very often involving the business community; and
- a strong commitment to using development planning and project management at all levels of government.

Taken together these tendencies amount to a significant shift from a highly centralised government, in which the President had unparalleled ascendancy (*presidencialismo*) to one that reduces the role of the centre in general by sharing responsibilities, through the introduction of more intergovernmental competition with systems of checks and balances across the different levels of government. These developments have important consequences for the distribution of the institutional capacity to make and influence decisions regarding the long-term future development of different areas in Mexico. Their focus is very much on designing mechanisms to link the federal with the state and the state with the municipal, strengthening the governance capacity of the lower tiers of government and facilitating greater local participation in decision-making.

Government relationships and reforms

Municipal government in Mexico is severely limited and represents the weakest tier of Mexican government (OECD, 2002). Although the constitution provides for a federal structure with an autonomous local government system in the form of *municipio libre*, municipalities, in practice, have only a limited range of responsibilities, relating mainly to the provision of public services, such as water and sewage, public lighting, cemeteries, roads, parks and public security. They do not have any legislative function and can only make regulations within the framework of state and federal law. Municipalities are empowered to levy some tax revenues and raise loans, but tax rates and those loans going beyond any particular administration's term of office, have to be approved by the state legislature. The reality is that municipalities are heavily dependent for their revenue on federal and state transfers, and this has the effect of considerably limiting their autonomy. As was the case of the state level, the independence of the municipal level of government traditionally has been greatly diminished through mayors being chosen by the former ruling party. Furthermore, although Mexico undertook some significant decentralisation of spending in the 1990s, the federal government still retains the lion's share, so that municipalities, in particular, have very limited budgets (Cabrero Mendoza and Martínez-Vázquez, 2000). The current reality is that municipal government in Mexico is severely limited and represents the weakest tier of Mexican government (OECD, 2002).

Throughout the 71 years up to 2000 during which the *Partido Revolucionario Institucional* (PRI) ruled Mexico, the country was run in a highly centralised and authoritarian fashion. The PRI controlled the legislative and executive branches of government. They also controlled labour unions, rural associations, the business community and the press (Hakim, 2002). Despite a constitution that envisaged strong local government and legal provisions that sought to invest significant authority at each of the three levels of government, the federal presidency retained a firm grip on power. Centralised presidential control over resource allocation, combined with party political patronage, meant that the whole system of government, and especially the local level, was largely stifled and unable to respond to locally identified priority needs.

Government modernisation and decentralisation in Mexico have progressed slowly and somewhat erratically over the past two decades. With the recent emergence of a multi-party democracy, Congress is playing a more active role and a system of checks and balances between the various arms of government is evolving. An important series of reforms and decentralising initiatives in the 1980s sought to strengthen state and local government. Committees for development planning at the state level (COPLADE) and at the municipal level (COPLADEMUN) were created by the National Law of Planning, with powers to decide the priorities and aims of public investment.[1] Municipal reforms, established by amendments to Article 115 of the Mexican Constitution, gave local government the task of administering property taxes as well as a wider array of public services. These reforms are regarded as being largely ineffective (Cabrero-Mendoza, 2000). The committees for development planning did not result in more decentralised or open policy making.

"Instead, when they functioned at all, they turned out to be largely ceremonial forums to legitimise decisions already taken by the governor and a small group of federal officials, exactly as was done before. Because of the lack of administrative capacity of municipal governments, in most cases, the state governments continued administering the property tax at the request of the municipalities. Curiously, the decentralisation measures never contemplated specific actions to strengthen the administrative capacity of municipal governments. This situation still prevails, with the exception of the urban municipalities that tend to have a higher degree of administrative capacity" (Cabrero-Mendoza, 2000).

Significant electoral reforms have been introduced in Mexico in recent years. Mexican elections have been made fair through measures such the establishment of impartial electoral authorities, strict penalties for electoral crimes, the compilation of a reasonably accurate register of voters, and state funding for the publicity campaigns of the various parties. Such basic democratic liberties, together with freedom of expression through independent media, enable society to hold governments accountable for their actions, thus putting pressure on them to improve performance. The election of the centre right National Action Party (PAN) candidate as president in 2000, at the expense of the PRI, which held power for 71 years, represents a milestone in the development of a full democracy in the country. The current presidency is strongly committed to a continuation of the reform process and a real system of co-governance is starting to appear in several areas of policy making (OECD, 2002).

Growing electoral pluralism and improved electoral transparency, combined with a willingness of central government to devolve power, are leading to a stronger system of government at state level. A recent study of six states in Mexico found that government bureaucracy was being modernised and governors were seeking to share power with legislatures, while local congresses were exercising greater checks and balances *vis-à-vis* the executive branch. Furthermore, the judiciary, particularly at national level, was reported to be developing jurisprudence relating to inter- and intra-governmental relations (Ward and Rodríguez, 1999).

Progress towards accountable local government has varied significantly within Mexico. Less accountable and authoritarian power structures are reported in many rural areas, especially in the south, but modern and democratic administrations are in place in many northern cities (Fox, 1995). In these latter cases innovations involving leadership style, citizen participation, improved intergovernmental relationships, and better public management systems are being gradually introduced. Vertical and horizontal intergovernmental partnerships, local mechanisms to enhance participatory democracy, and the recruitment of professional staff, are all indicative of sustained progress in the development of the local government system.

However, many weaknesses are still associated with the transition to better local government in Mexico. Structural obstacles are found to be the most critical. The fact that mayors, for example, can only be elected for a single three year term means that they have little or no incentive to perpetuate the success of their programs beyond their own term in office. As municipal governments cannot mandate legislation and carry little influence at state congress level, it is difficult for them to institutionalise new programmes or decision mechanisms. The implementation of innovations relating, for example, to new management systems, often have negative outcomes, because they are not sufficiently explained and transparent to the people whose lives they are intended to improve (Cabrero-Mendoza, 2000). These and other difficulties are retarding progress toward a fully responsive and satisfactory system of local government in Mexico.

Citizen participation in public policy making traditionally has not been encouraged or facilitated in Mexico. On assuming power in the 1930s, the PRI organised society into a corporate structure of mass party organisations that acted as a control and support apparatus for the ruling party, delivering votes for political favours in a highly clientelistic fashion. This practice retarded progress toward participation by civil society in development affairs. With the enhanced democratisation of civil society in recent years this system is gradually being eroded. However, a recently completed study of projects supported by multilateral development banks concluded government was limiting information made available to the public regarding the projects and generally frustrating or blocking societal participation in them (Fernández de Villegas, 2000). In this regard, the recent adoption of a Freedom of Information Act is a significant positive development. Another comparative study of World Bank funded rural development projects in Mexico and the Philippines found that: a) variation in the commitment to pro-social capital reforms within the Mexican state apparatus was resulting in significant differences in the enabling environment; b) projects that start off as participatory often fail to remain so as they are captured by state actors opposed to sharing power with civil society; c) social capital promotion, although frequently represented in terms of shared norms and negotiated consensus actions, is often controversial and even conflictual, as the process involves the redistribution of power, and tends to be resisted by vested interests; and d) social capital is unevenly distributed across groups, sectors and regions (Fox and Gershman, 2000). Based on this evidence it appears that, although civil society in Mexico is becoming more organised and independent, the development potential associated with actively involved citizenship has not always been fully recognised or exploited in a manner that would contribute to the effectiveness and efficiency of development initiatives and increase public accountability through meaningful participatory processes.

In conclusion, considerable reform of government, involving the decentralisation of functions, competencies and resources to state and municipal levels, has been introduced over the past 20 years. The main goal of these reforms is to enhance the capacity of the lower levels of government to promote economic and social development in the different regions of the country in a manner that is sensitive to local needs, opportunities and priorities. State and municipal governments are being gradually included in the decision making process regarding federal expenditure in areas such as social assistance programmes, regional development strategies, and integrated policies for the promotion of intermediate sized cities. This process is driven by the recent democratic reforms and the development of political pluralism, that have broken the traditional stranglehold of the presidency over governors and mayors and generally made the political system more accountable and responsive to local constituents. Although significant obstacles remain, this is leading to innovations aimed at increasing the efficiency and effectiveness of state and local government and to a system of decision making that is more orderly and systematic.

Federal initiatives

The July 2000 presidential election was an important event that has helped to accelerate the political changes whose origins have a long history but that can be more clearly located starting in the mid-1980s. The growing commitment to inclusive government at the federal level is reflected in President Fox's numerous calls for the involvement of civil society and the private sector in decision-making, for better co-ordination across federal, state and municipal levels of government and for the definition of a long-term vision of the sustainable development of Mexico.

The President's economic strategy has three clearly enunciated objectives: a) achieving high and sustainable rates of economic growth, b) creating economically stable conditions that eradicate the recurrent cycles of inflation and devaluation, and c) improving the lot of the most economically vulnerable members of society, by ensuring they are provided with opportunities to benefit from economic growth. In support of these objectives, Fox has stressed several fundamental underlying principles of his economic policies, including: a) sustainable development policies based on the generation of small fiscal surpluses and simultaneously reducing dependence on oil revenues, b) facilitating the development of the primacy of the private sector by placing it at the very heart of economic activity and relegating government to a support and facilitator role, c) improving the functioning and performance of key economic sectors by exposing them to truly competitive markets, and d) improving the functioning of the labour market.

Underpinning the efforts of state and municipal governments to create and experiment with new mechanisms for co-operation and participation is the federal government's goal of establishing a permanent planning process where state (and municipal) levels of government, rather than only the federal authorities, define guidelines, priorities, schedules and solutions for their own problems. Towards making this a reality, a number of federal initiatives whose broad thrust has been to actively incorporate the state and municipal governments into the administration and management of public resources and into the decision-making process regarding the allocation of public funds can be identified. These include:

1. The introduction of strategic planning involving all levels of government and both public and private actors in the preparation of the 2001-2006 National Development Plan.

2. The division of the country into five meso-regions for planning purposes regarding infrastructures and key public investments.

3. The commitment towards achieving longer term policy-making, through the Mexico 2020-25 vision, and the establishment of a stronger consultation process with civil society.

4. The introduction of a programme for micro-regions in order to overcome poverty and promote their development.

5. The use of framework agreements for the allocation of resources (funds and information/technical assistance) by federal ministries to state governments.

6. The continuing refinement and elaboration of broad fiscal reforms that provide for increased resource and responsibility devolution from the federal to state and local levels.

Salient features of several of these initiatives are examined below.

Strategic development planning

Much of the initial period of the Fox administration has been spent promoting programmes of institutional improvement across the three levels of government. The government has established a regional planning system with a new scheme of intergovernmental relations and institutions around it. The Office for Strategic Planning and Regional Development (OSPRD) is located within the Executive Office of the President. One of the key objectives of the OSPRD is the development of a long-term strategy regarding public policy, that is linked with the implementation of a National Participatory Planning System (NPPS) and with measures contained in the National Development Plan 2001-2006. The NPPS promotes planning and policy making through a process of consultation and agreement with all political levels and with civil society together with evaluation of the policies of the executive branch and the activities of all the agencies and bodies of the federal public administration. A key element in this process is the creation of a long-term vision, Mexico 2020-25, that aims to make successive federal administrations accountable to the population in the long term.

The OSPRD is also seeking to foster regional development through a model that incorporates inter-state and inter-sectoral co-ordination and commitment mechanisms. This model seeks to create a space for dialogue and both horizontal and vertical co-operation between the federation and states, between states and municipalities and within state governments and the federal administration, while also allowing for the participation of the private sector and civil society in the definition of common goals (OECD, 2002). The primary role of OSPRD is one of encouraging and supporting regional level responses towards the planning, financing, implementation and evaluation of large-scale projects. For this purpose, meso-regions made up of a number of adjoining states with common interest in the projects, have been defined.

More specifically, this model provides for the creation of regional management mechanisms, in which the main regional development actors, the federal and state governments, the community and the business sector, participate. There are three levels of response: *a)* consensus building, *b)* co-ordination and structuring, and *c)* operations. The forum for consensus building is the Regional Council, with a technical secretariat in charge of both co-ordination and operations. The Technical Secretariat includes a permanent representative from each state, as well as a representative for each issue on the regional development agenda. The role of the Secretariat is to incorporate both state and sectoral considerations in the regional plans and to manage the operations of the planning process as a whole.

Decentralisation of resources and functions

Revenue collection in Mexico is highly centralised with as much as 90% of total revenue accruing to the federal government. Local taxes make up only 7% of total state and municipal revenues although there is considerable variation across states, with a tendency for some wealthier regions to generate a larger share from own resources. Generally, however, states and municipalities depend mainly on transfers from the federal government. These are comprised of a large unconditional grant (branch or *Ramo* 28) that accounts for 38% of sub-national revenues and a set of conditional grants (*Ramo* 33), comprising 47% of sub-national revenues. *Ramo* 28 is comprised mainly of *Fondo General de Participaciones,* of which states are required to transfer at least 20% to municipalities. Municipalities rely heavily on this funding. Other federal revenues account for a further 7% of sub-national revenues (OECD, 2002). Congress has recently approved a tax reform package that confers modest new taxing powers on sub-national government but there appears to be some reluctance to avail of these.

In contrast to the continuing concentration of taxation on the federal level, considerable responsibility for the administration of a number of public services and programmes has been devolved to sub-national government. States have been given responsibilities relating to basic education, health care, social infrastructure and other such programmes. Conditional transfers (*Ramo* 33) were introduced in 1997 for the purpose of funding these devolved responsibilities. *Ramo 33* consist of seven separate funds, of which those relating to basic education and health care, are the most significant. The actual devolution of responsibility and control that is associated with these transfers are very limited as they provide little scope for innovative and locally tailored responses and initiatives on the part of sub-national government.

The decentralisation process was first introduced in the education sector in 1992 after the signing of agreements to modernise education programmes, to improve employees' incomes and teachers' working conditions and to decentralise basic education services to the states. All operational aspects of the school system were decentralised to the states, but the federal government remained in charge of financing the system. Large parts of this federal expenditure are in the form of transfers to the states (Corbacho and Schwartz, 2002). In 1996 the National Agreement for Health Services decentralisation, as well as co-ordination agreements, were signed between the federal government, the 31 states and the Federal District.

The Ministry of Social Development (SEDESOL) plays a central role in the process of decentralising resources and designing programmes that give new responsibilities and opportunities to states and municipalities. Regarding poverty alleviation programmes, traditional initiatives took the form of distributive aid programmes. The most noteworthy of them was the *Programa Nacional de Solidaridad* (PRONASOL) introduced by President Carlos Salinas in 1988. The objectives were: *a)* to improve the living conditions of marginalised groups, *b)* to promote balanced regional development, and *c)* to promote and strengthen the participation of social organisations and local authorities. This programme was mostly run by the President's office. Despite initial hopes that it would herald a significant step towards decentralisation, Salinas was able to bypass in a highly discretionary way state governors and municipal mayors and allocate funds directly to local community groups and other organisations.

Essentially, PRONASOL emerged as a community participation programme that worked in a rather simple way: any organised group, be it state or municipal government, a resident's group or a local association, approached local PRONASOL officials and presented a project for any type of public work. After analysis and negotiation, and once the project was approved, PRONASOL put up most of the financial resources required for the project while the group contributed the labour and, wherever possible, local resources. PRONASOL functioned largely in parallel to state and municipal governments. Nevertheless, towards the end of 1994 an effort was made to involve the two levels of local government more closely in the programme.

The general assessment is that the programme failed to make any contribution to institutional capacity building at the local level (Cabrero, 2000).

It was, after all, a presidential creation which, by bypassing the lower levels of government, handed out resources in a highly clientelistic fashion. Later budgetary reforms began the process of depoliticising the allocation of resources to state and local levels of administration. Also, the nature of the poverty alleviation strategy began to focus more on co-responsibility and targeted programmes (e.g. PROGRESA, where in exchange for health care vouchers and food baskets, households committed to keep children at school).

In this respect, recent social programmes are focusing more specifically on capacity building with the aim of enabling the beneficiaries to pursue self-help projects through financial mediation (e.g. the provision of seed capital), business mediation (e.g. teaching basic business skills) and social mediation (e.g. developing the capacity of people to organise and network). In general, these newer programmes are not as much intended as short-term support measures, but as more long-term mechanisms to help people to improve their condition and escape poverty and its consequences in a sustainable manner. For this reason in recent years there has been a shift from pure income transfers to transfers conditional on recipients investing in human capital. In principle, many of these programmes are targeted to specific population groups (Corbacho and Schwartz, 2002). In 1990, total expenditures in these various programmes amounted to 0.7% of GDP and increased to 0.9% of GDP in 2000. Until 1995 these programmes were mostly run by the federal government, but have been gradually decentralised to the states and municipalities since then. In 2000 over 50% of all expenditures for poverty reduction were directed to programmes for human capital development, about 30% to programmes for basic social infrastructure and the remaining 20% for programmes in employment and productivity enhancement (Table 4.1). Also, the nature of the programmes began to focus more on co-responsibility and later at attempts at building individual and household economic capacity.

A good example of this new approach is OPORTUNIDADES (initially called PROGRESA). It is the flagship anti-poverty programme and operates within the framework of a multi-sectoral development strategy known as CONTIGO. It seeks to foster human development by linking income transfers to households to compliance with a schedule of preventative health check-ups and vaccinations and continued primary and secondary school enrolment of children up to the age of 16 years. Families that enter the programme remain in it for a minimum of three years. When it started in 1997, the programme operated only in one state. Since then, the programme has expanded to incorporate a total of 2.6 million families by the year 2000 (Corbacho and Schwartz, 2002). PROGRESA represented less than two per cent of total expenditure for poverty reduction in 1997 but this had been increased to almost 20% by 2000. Originally confined to rural areas, it is currently being extended to the urban poor.

Table 4.1. **Mexican expenditure for poverty reduction 1990-2000**

	Total	By level of government			By strategy		
		Federal	State	Municipal	Human	Basic social infrastructure	Employment production
	% of GDP	% of total	% of total	% of total	% of total	% of total	% of total
1990	0.7	100.0	0.0	0.0	35.9	51.0	13.1
1991	0.9	100.0	0.0	0.0	31.7	58.5	9.9
1992	1.0	100.0	0.0	0.0	36.2	52.0	11.8
1993	1.0	100.0	0.0	0.0	41.7	47.2	11.1
1994	1.0	100.0	0.0	0.0	42.9	47.1	10.1
1995	1.0	100.0	0.0	0.0	49.0	37.4	13.6
1996	0.9	99.7	0.3	0.0	51.7	34.6	13.7
1997	0.9	98.7	1.3	0.0	49.3	34.7	16.0
1998	0.9	63.9	9.7	26.4	48.9	34.5	16.7
1999	0.9	62.9	8.8	28.4	47.7	35.5	16.8
2000	0.9	64.3	8.4	27.3	48.3	35.5	16.2

Source: Corbacho and Schwartz, 2002.

A major development challenge in Mexico is how to address structural problems in the poorer rural regions, where there is very limited productive or social infrastructure, associated in large measure with the small size and dispersed nature of settlements, all of which seriously hinder development possibilities. In this regard, a strategy of co-ordinated action focussing on 263 micro-regions is being pursued. The main features of these micro-regions are that: 55% of the population has no access to running water supply, 85% of households have no drainage or sanitary service, 37% have no electricity, almost 40% of those 15 years of age or over are illiterate, 79% of households have soil floor, 78% of houses are overcrowded and 87% of the economically active population earn less than two minimum wages. The overall goal of the programme is to get the relevant government ministries (11 in total) to subscribe to a coherent strategy and also to convince the municipalities involved and the private sector to participate and co-operate in implementing agreed solutions.

A key aspect of the strategy in these micro-regions is to concentrate actions in one centre in each micro-region, the Strategic Community Centre. This location has to be easily accessible from all other locations in the micro-region, it must have over 500 inhabitants, it needs to have good communications (especially usable roads during most of the year), it must provide some education and health services and it should have basic infrastructure. Thus, locations with these advantages are designed to be poles for local and regional development in the micro-regions.

The micro-region programme avails of funds from different national programmes, which means that several ministries are involved. Co-ordination amongst the different ministries is achieved through an Inter-Sectoral Committee for Micro-Regions, which is chaired by the President of the Republic. Projects supported through the micro-regional programme are normally chosen by Municipal Development Committees and the local COPLADEMUN. In situations where the COPLADEMUN does not work well or where more social participation is warranted, then Community Assemblies are used. The various participants discuss the main local needs and agree on local development priorities. Local representatives then meet with state and federal officials to make the final choice within the framework of overall state and federal policies. The COPLADE provide the mechanisms for the vertical matching of actions and resources and ensuring that projects are technically and financially sound.

Tourism is an important sector in Mexico. Historically, tourism planning and policy at the state level was controlled by the tourism *delegaciones* of the federal ministry (SECTUR). Since 1993 most of the activity in the tourism field has been transferred to the states. Public expenditure agreements are key instruments used by the Federal Ministry of Tourism in its relationships with the states. The Ministry is responsible for tourism planning and development programmes. It collaborates closely with the states on these matters. Initiatives are proposed by various states and framework agreements are made for funding of agreed project proposals. The Ministry plays an important evaluation and monitoring role in this collaborative planning and development process. States with significant tourism sectors form consultative committees to advise on development plans. The Mexican Tourism Board was established three years ago with 15 public sector representatives (3 federal, 8 state and 4 municipal nominees) and private membership comprising 14 representatives and it, too, has an advisory role.

The National Tourism Fund (FONATUR) is an early example of a shared approach to tourism development. It was established in the 1970s and its focus has been on real estate development at a number of key tourism sites throughout Mexico. A more recent example of this shared approach to development in tourism is the Escalera Naútica programme that includes Baja California, Baja California Sur, Sonora and Sinaloa. Development plans and joint funding arrangements are agreed as part of a two way process of dialogue and consultation between the Ministry and the states. One objective in tourism development is to try and concentrate resources on the strategies that are so agreed. This helps to improve the co-ordination of the different levels of government and to enhance communications and working relationships with the private sector.

State and municipal level initiatives

Examples of how several of these initiatives work in practice, as seen from the perspective of state and local level actors, are reported here. The analysis is based primarily on a study of two states, Guanajuato and Sinaloa, both of which are advanced, relative to other Mexican states, in terms of planning and administrative reorganisation.[2] Guanajuato and Sinaloa provide interesting examples of attempts to modernise and extend their systems of governance and these different contexts offer various perspectives on how relatively recent attempts at capacity building at state and municipal levels have worked. The practices reported here, however, are not to be taken as necessarily representative of governance measures that have been effected throughout Mexico, but more as illustrative of developments in the more progressive states and municipalities.

New governance initiatives in Guanajuato

A considerable economic dynamic can be found in Guanajuato's central industrial corridor in which an FDI (foreign direct investment) driven industrial concentration is emerging. This dynamic is supported by a large network of medium-sized cities (6 with a population in excess of 1 million and 12 with 100 000 or more). In contrast, on either side of this economic corridor lie depressed rural communities and small urban centres where it is difficult to retain economic activity, services and populations. This unevenness in economic development in Guanajuato is reflected in aggregate indices which signal low levels of educational achievement and high levels of marginalisation in the state relative to the Mexican averages (OECD, 2002).

A key focus of the state's six-year development plan is to strengthen the economic dynamic of the central corridor through new transport infrastructures (e.g. a proposed high-speed train and improved highway links) and an enterprise zone area (Puerto Interior). These are large-scale projects of supra-regional significance and as a result they are being planned within the framework of the Centre-West meso-region. Guanajuato also has an automotive training centre that serves the training needs of the larger region, where significant FDI in the automotive sector has located.

The pressing need for economic promotion, international visibility and investment in infrastructure to ensure the essential economic conditions for successful integration into the global economy constitute a new and constant challenge for government at all levels in Mexico. The meso-region plays a strategic role in linking the National Development Plan with state plans. The state then seeks to carry these bigger strategic lines into its own state planning and down to cities and municipalities. The COPLADE is the mechanism for municipal involvement in state level planning in Guanajuato.

Map of Mexico

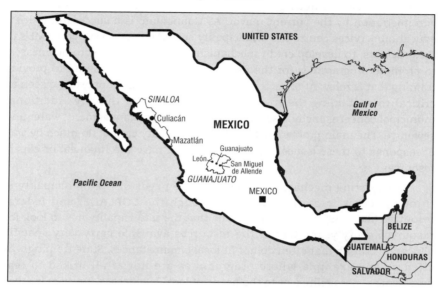

All municipalities have a representative on this body. Municipal administrations bring projects and plans to the COPLADE. The COPLADE is served by a technical committee, which advises on priorities and projects throughout the state. At the COPLADE there is competition amongst the 46 municipalities in the state for resources and some balance must be sought between local and regional benefits and needs. The COPLADE is very much a political instrument and in Guanajuato there is the view that it is difficult to adjust the mindset of the key players from traditional questions of social development to newer challenges and tasks in economic development.

A key issue in Guanajuato, referred to above, is the low level of human resource development in the state. Training, particularly training connected to the labour market, is therefore a critical issue. There is a commission working on this problem at present. A major task for this commission is to make a connection with businesses, particularly small businesses in order to identify good responses to training needs in the state. It is proving to be very difficult to make this connection and this is symptomatic of deficits that exist locally in the development capacity of civil society. These deficits are clearly evident also at the municipal level. The process of democratisation and participation was recently advanced in the municipality of Guanajuato with the creation of a COPLADEMUN. A network of 40 neighbourhood committees feeds into this advisory body. It has managed to go beyond issues of infrastructure and to try and address social and human development issues. The office of Director of Economic Development for the municipality was created within the administration by the current mayor. As Guanajuato is a successful tourist/education/services centre the municipality sees the need to support SME's in these sectors, to develop credit mechanisms for SMEs and micro businesses, to promote programmes for the improvement of businesses and to provide training that is relevant to sectoral needs. These specific supports are seen as critical to sustaining the trade and services base of the city. Additional municipal concerns include security, housing, traffic management, water and sewerage. The main problem is that the municipality cannot do much by way of response to these issues because it does not have the financial or expert resources.

The existing mechanism to advance the needs of the municipality is through access to state resources (through the COPLADE) and federal resources (*Ramo* 33). The system means that the municipality has to look for resources every year. Most of the resources available carry very specific allocation criteria that often do not fit local circumstances. State training was cited as one example where programmes are not at all linked to real employment possibilities or to the needs of local businesses. Tourism is a key local sector and the municipality has worked successfully with the state in tourism promotion and strategy. The municipal administration is currently trying to use a public-private partnership agreement to provide a water treatment facility for the city. It already has experience with partnerships in traffic management and car parks.

The municipality of San Miguel de Allende is also trying to initiate a process of planning and participation through the mechanism of a recently established COPLADEMUN. A 14 member urban council representing 78 urban colonies and a 34 member rural council representing 538 rural communities are part of a technical committee. These representatives work along side the municipal administration to identify local needs and priorities and to develop a plan for the municipality. The committee works primarily though commissions. These mechanisms are totally advisory. The signature of the COPLADEMUN is described as giving social validation to decisions that are made by the municipal administration.

Tourism is an important industry in San Miguel and the municipality has worked with the state on a development strategy, specifically in relation to tourist routes and guides. The municipality has recently completed through FONATUR a study of tourism development and the urban image of San Miguel de Allende. The preparation of this report entailed a substantial amount of public/private discussion and collaboration. One particular focus was on new rural tourism opportunities in the communities adjacent to the city. The municipal administration is co-ordinating this effort and work is being done through a tourism commission of the COPLADEMUN. Other immediate concerns for the municipality of San Miguel de Allende revolve around strengthening the arts and crafts sector and developing the requisite water resources for tourism development.

The Mayor of San Miguel is a member of the COPLADE where he can seek state funding for projects. A recent example is that of a private museum that received partial funding from the state. Direct approaches to the federal level are made informally and, as appears to be the case in other places, these approaches are often made on the basis of personal relationships. *Ramo* 33, which is a main funding line at the federal level, is perceived as being inflexible. However, it is interesting to note that, at the local level of the COPLADEMUN in San Miguel, new controls and reporting systems for each type of project are being enforced. *Pro forma* documents must be used, signed and approved at the level of the local colonies and in the case of key infrastructural projects, the relevant documentation must be validated by the appropriate secretary in the municipal administration.

Because of the importance of arts and crafts in the local economy of San Miguel de Allende training is important. The state is responsible for key training functions but the municipality has taken an initiative in the provision of training and small credit schemes to micro businesses. This programme focuses on accounting, marketing, administration and sales skills and a MXN 2 500 maximum credit facility (without guarantee) for micro businesses. It is administered through the Office for Economic Development with the assistance of local notaries and some international sponsorship. To date MXN 5 million have been allocated to over 300 entrepreneurs under this scheme. A constraint in federal training programmes is that everything is geared towards existing businesses. The city has tried to develop workspaces for young people and older women and they are looking for support from the existing commercial sector to enable these producers to market their products. However, the administration is not very familiar with this area of local economic development, and it has no technical resources to manage and monitor these activities.

León is a municipality in the state of Guanajuato largely focused on industry which became a metropolitan area (population greater than 1 million) in 1995. It is a major manufacturing city, strongly dependent on the leather industry, and its strategic location in the central industrial corridor has made the transport, storage and communications sector an important growth area (Table 4.2). Partly because of its narrow economic base, the municipality of León has had to work hard at maintaining its economic position and competitiveness. In this regard, successive municipal administrations have demonstrated a high degree of innovation in terms of facilitating the participation of citizens in decisions on investment and other public projects.

Some of the key mechanisms developed for this purpose are summarised in Figure 4.1. Of particular interest are the Municipal Planning Institute (IMPLAN) and the Directorates for Economic and Social Development and their links to civil society though a variety of instruments, for example, SAPAC, which sets and manages water charges for the municipality.

The main concerns of businesses in León are about their ability to perform and to be competitive in regional, national and global markets. These are also key concerns at the state level. Market pressures means that Mexican cities sometimes see themselves in strong competition with each other. As noted earlier, León has grown on a strong manufacturing and service base and a key issue for the Economic Council is that the municipality has a policy and a strategy that will help maintain the position of key existing sectors and develop new ones. In this respect the Council acknowledges the importance of state planning and indeed of meso-regional planning. This planning is only beginning in Guanajuato and in the meso-region to which it belongs. The main criticism is that, to date, it has not included the business sector in the planning process. There is a process under way of having better working relationships between business and government but it is a process that is still driven mostly through personal contacts and relations. The desire is that this relationship should become more formal. The business sector is somewhat tired of mechanisms (*e.g.* working commissions) that are guided by the public administration. There is the view that there is much rhetoric but little resources to develop solutions. Similarly, there is a criticism that what is being said and proposed at the federal and state levels concerning development planning is all too general and of little value in helping the Economic Council of León address local challenges.

The provision of training for the labour force is a specific priority requirement of the business community of León. Training is a state responsibility but the reality is that there are many agencies involved in its delivery and the key issue is getting co-ordination. Two important federal

Table 4.2. **GDP shares by major divisions of economic activity in León, 1990-2000**

Activity	% share 1990	% share 2000	Annual average rate of growth
Manufacturing	18.0	19.7	1.9
Construction	4.2	3.9	1.2
Commerce	2.0	2.0	1.5
Transport	8.3	10.6	2.6
Financial	13.9	14.2	1.6
Social and personal	21.1	18.3	0.08
GDP	100	100	1.5

Source: Fomento Económico Municipal León.

Figure 4.1. **Key development structures and relationships in León**

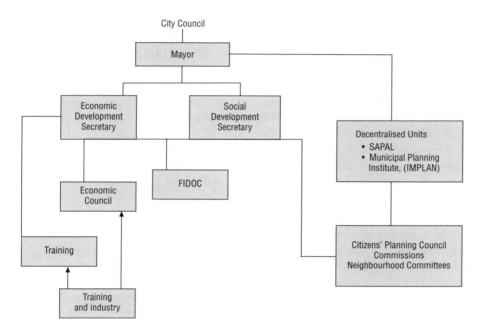

supports for company training are CRECE (*Centros Regionales para la Competitividad Empresarial*) and PAC (*Programa de Apoyo a la Capacitacion*). CRECE is a nation-wide federal support programme that provides advice, diagnosis and business planning for SMEs. The PAC federal programme provides training supports to micro-, small- and medium-sized companies. In León, the Chamber of Industry acts as the provider for PAC. Training programmes are provided at the individual enterprise level. A condition of eligibility is that the employees must be affiliated to the Mexican Institute for Social Security (IMSS), a social security system for private workers. All enterprises must affiliate their workers to the IMSS but many fail to do so. In León, where less than 50% of the workers are insured, this acts as a serious constraint and raises the question of what should come first: getting workers in companies trained and simultaneously getting businesses and all their workers registered in the formal economy, or (as is the case at present) requiring businesses to register first, and only then to provide the training.

The municipality of León is proactive in trying to fill training gaps and provide the necessary co-ordination. It administers Local Employment Exchange Centres, where companies can recruit workers. It also sponsors community training where people are assisted in job search and in looking at part-time and self-employment opportunities. It supports a Management Training Programme by co-ordinating the training efforts of educational institutions, training organisations and government resources and placing these at the disposal of companies who seek assistance. Training programmes are organised in collaboration with the Chamber of Commerce and the Chamber of Shoe Producers. Shoe manufacturing is an important sub-sector in León with as many as 1 500 small and micro enterprises seeking to innovate and in need of technical support. The municipality, in co-operation with the private sector, has begun a city training strategy, which seeks to develop critical mass in key skills. It has made a number of proposals regarding key training needs to the state and federal government but progress on these proposals has been very slow with much depending on individual personal contacts.

The Municipal Planning Institute was created in 1996 and it is a concept found in a number of large and middle-size cities in Mexico. The creation of these institutes in León and in other cities represents an attempt to put in place a more professionally driven approach to urban management and planning. Plans and projects are advanced by the institutes in consultation with entrepreneurs (Economic Council in Figure 4.1) and citizens (Citizens Planning Council in Figure 4.1). This mechanism allows the municipality to develop a stable framework for decision making that is independent of politics and changes in the political leadership.

In León, there is a direct link between the work of the Planning Institute and efforts at neighbourhood capacity building that are co-ordinated by the Social Development Directorate. Specific planning projects and other task objectives are typically facilitated by commissions with ordinary citizens as members. In addition, commissions have representatives of sectors that come within its particular remit, *e.g.* representatives from educational interests if the commission is about education. Also, there can be representation from the federal level of government on commissions but only in a supporting and informal role. In addition, people from NGO's are afforded an opportunity to participate on these commissions.

This type of approach, labelled under the heading decentralised units in Figure 4.1, has a long tradition in León. For example, it predates the Federal reforms of the 1980s that saw the introduction of the committees for development planning. While the federal and state levels sought to refine and deepen the mechanisms for citizen participation in these committees, the municipality of León developed its own mechanisms. In the middle of the 1990s, the municipality undertook a survey to evaluate its working relationships with its citizens. It showed that the level of social development contained in their processes of involvement with citizens was limited. Social development in

Mexico has a strong connotation of creating infrastructures (*e.g.* sewage facilities, paved roads and public lighting) and of providing public assistance through different compensatory policies (*e.g.* food baskets, milk, and blankets in winter). As a result of the evaluation, a new mission, which sought to promote empowerment through an improvement in the existing mechanisms for consultation and participation, was identified as a priority. A key goal was to change the perception that the social development process was the sole responsibility of government and to stress the idea of the people concerned being involved meaningfully through a bottom-up approach. This goal would be achieved through neighbourhood planning committees. The three targeted areas of work were social infrastructure, services and economic opportunities.

These committees have agreed mechanisms for the selection of a representative membership and for local community consultation on needs and investment priorities. The committees assemble the facts, identify the problems of the neighbourhoods that they represent and essentially compile lists of pressing needs. Through the citizens council, these are brought to the attention of the administration and are again prioritised by the municipal government. The process stops there and it is the task of the mayor and his administration to seek the resources that are needed to give effect to these. The municipality, however, has very limited resources at its disposal to invest in this process. Like all municipalities in Mexico, it has very limited capacity to raise revenue and depends heavily on transfers from the state and federal government. An explicit federal/state/municipal budget line is contained in *Ramo* 33 but its formula-based approach is found to be too rigid and does not reflect the needs or strategies of the municipality and its communities. An ideal solution to the funding problem, in the view of local actors, would be an unconditional global grant. The administrative experience in León suggests that it has the capacity to administer and account for this form of financial assistance. Another possible solution would be to lessen dependence on federal transfers through generating revenue from localtaxes.

One instrument with limited resources to meet some neighbourhood needs is FIDOC (*Fideicomiso de Obra Publica por Cooperación*) which was established in 1996. FIDOC is a co-operative programme between the municipality and the citizens for neighbourhood infrastructure improvements. It is based on a 50:50 or 70:30 joint funding arrangement between government and the community. It began in 1996 with resources of USD 700 000. The specific aims of FIDOC are: *a)* to carry out infrastructural work like sewerage, paving and electrification in neighbourhoods where these services are lacking; *b)* to raise the resources to do this work, and *c)* to manage the schemes of work and the general financial position of the programme. The needs and requests of the neighbourhood committees are ultimately considered by the committee of the COPLADEMUN. This committee agrees priorities and decides on the projects to be funded. Public funding is then sought through *Ramo* 33 while citizens of the neighbourhoods included contribute 50% or 30%, depending on local circumstances. Citizen contributions are organised as a monthly bank payment. The whole procedure is governed by the State Law of Guanajuato.

FIDOC is a concrete example of the type of engagement that takes place between the municipal administration and many of its citizens. A measure of the scale of activity under FIDOC is shown in Table 4.3. There is, however, no evidence yet of going beyond task objectives of developing social infrastructure and basic neighbourhood services towards process objectives of capacity-building in support of human, social and economic development.

Participatory models in Sinaloa

The economy of Sinaloa relies heavily on agriculture, horticulture, agri-food industries, textiles, fishing and aquaculture. As these economic activities are vulnerable to national and global competition, the business community argues that sustained policies and programmes of development of economic services and infrastructure are vital for competitiveness. Since the early 1990s local businessmen have been important "change agents" advocating systems for long-term planning and seeking to work on this task with the state government. A major thrust of the state administration in Sinaloa is focused on economic diversification and development. The key economic development structures in Sinaloa are described in Figure 4.2. The state acknowledges the role and views of business to the extent that important decision-making capacities in relation to economic development now reside in an economic development council (CODESIN) which is a public-private partnership. CODESIN has 12 members, eight private businessmen and four government members. It is a vehicle that reflects the vision of business people and that is sympathetic to the needs of business people. There are no other constituencies represented on CODESIN and there are no plans to add to its membership. It is fully funded by the state through 20% of the salary tax collected by the state. The Secretary for Economic Development for the state of Sinaloa has a pivotal role in managing CODESIN and in linking the

Table 4.3. **Citizen contributions and public investment under FIDOC, 1998-2001**

Million pesos

	1998	1999	2000	2001
Citizen's contribution	10	20	28	41
Public Investment	26.4	42	72.8	95

Source: FIDOC 2001.

strategies agreed at CODESIN to the administration and economic policies of the governor and the state government. CODESIN plays a pivotal role in formulating and implementing the supply-side policies and programmes that are necessary to attract inward investment and to promote endogenous development

The development of a cluster strategy for textiles and support mechanisms for food-producer groups are illustrative of this partnership/ networking relationship between the state and the business community. State funding and private credit facilities are made available to investors in the textile plants. Municipal support for the cluster strategy takes the form of providing serviced sites and local tax exemptions. One element of the strategy is to try and locate some of these textile operations in the smaller towns of central Sinaloa. The agri-food sector is a key sector in Sinaloa.

For the food product groups (each of which usually comprises 10 owners) the state funds a "growing" manager for three years. The task of the manager is to look at strategic issues for the sectors and provide support to the individual owners in the group to address significant problem areas. There is also a food industry council that acts as a forum for issues relating to the broader food sector.

The business sector in the state is generally organised through a Business Council. This council has sought to work with state and municipal governments to a) support long term economic planning, b) ensure some continuity and consistency in public administration and c) create some counterbalances to discretionality of public officials. The ECO-Region concept is one notable project created by the Business Council with support from state government, CODESIN, SAGARPA (Federal Ministry of Agriculture) and SEMARNAT (Federal Ministry of Natural Resources and Environment). It is an educational/advisory pilot project that seeks to develop principles of good practice in relation to matters that are of pertinence to the agri-food industry, such as land and water management, pest control and the sustainability of agricultural communities.

There is a spatial substructure to CODESIN in the form of northern zone, central-northern, central zone and southern zone councils. These regional councils are a conduit through which local businesses get to know about state programs and policies and through which they can get their views conveyed to the state administration. The regional structure allows for the participation of municipal presidents alongside business people and members of chambers of commerce. CATAM is the acronym for one experiment supported by the regional council of CODESIN in the central zone. It involves a partnership between business people, civil society and municipalities dealing with issues concerning long-term municipal management. As municipal presidents in

Figure 4.2. **Key economic development structures in Sinaloa**

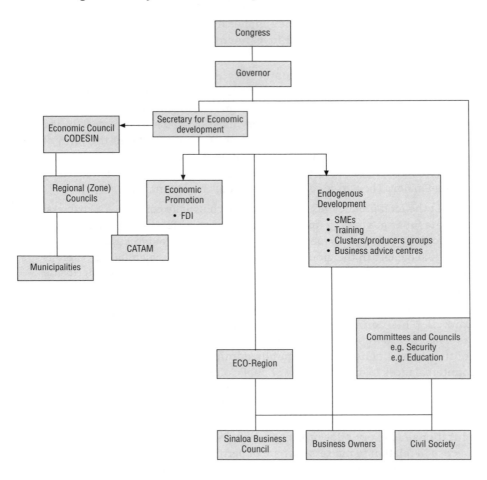

Source: OECD.

Mexico are only elected for one three-year term without the possibility of immediate re-election, continuity is greatly hindered and attention is sometimes largely focused on actions and reforms oriented towards yielding short-term results. What this means is that political leaders usually have no incentive to perpetuate the success of their programmes beyond their terms of office. Municipal management is further hindered by the lack of technical and professional staff and by an insufficient number of permanent "civil service type" employees, and a correspondingly high turnover rate of bureaucratic personnel.

The CATAM initiative is only one year old and it has received technical support through the International City Management Association (ICMA) sponsored by USAID to hold training workshops for mayors and their limited support staff and to enable them to undertake study visits relating to urban planning and city management models. Anticipated outcomes from this initiative are that improved advice and expertise will be available to the mayors of the participating municipalities and that a structure to ensure continuity in development policy from one mayoral administration to another – thereby eliminating the sudden changes that often accompanied these transitions – will be put in place.

The economic development and diversification needs of Sinaloa have encouraged the state to seek flexible and business friendly solutions to problems and bottlenecks. The state Secretary for Economic Development, for example, has worked out agreements between the three levels of government, that have allowed a network of enterprise advice centres to operate throughout the state. These centres seek to bring one-stop-shop style services to local businesses and endeavour to reduce bureaucratic delays in matters like the issuing of permits, licences, etc. Similarly, the state administration supports a network of financial advice centres in Sinaloa, through which mentoring and business supports are provided to micro businesses. This network is now franchised out. The federal enterprise development programme CRECE is well supported in the state. This is a programme that applies to existing businesses (3-30 employees) and it offers advice, help with business plan preparation and ongoing support. It is 80% funded by the federal government and the remaining 20% is contributed in equal measure by CODESIN, the state (through the Secretariat for Economic Development), the municipality and the private business requiring support. Projects can work through the enterprise advice centres to avail of the supports provided by CRECE.

Councils and commissions are instruments commonly used by the state to work with the municipalities in Sinaloa and to involve civil society in the affairs of government. Councils may be permanent while commissions are created on an *ad hoc* basis to address specific tasks. These committees and councils are restricted to an advisory role only. Although these instruments provide instances of government working with people, it is also true that the membership and selection procedures of these committees and councils are still not fully open or transparent. While all citizens may apply, members are typically selected by the administration from sectors such as the artistic community, university staff, Chambers of Commerce, business people and property owners. Two examples of these councils are included in Figure 4.2. One is an educational council set up by the Sinaloa state administration two years ago to address issues of school quality in the state. Resources to pay for secretarial and office support to the president of the council is provided by the state. The mayors of the municipalities can give support to citizens on the council to attend meetings. While there is a huge willingness to do things and, indeed, there is much that must be done in relation to schools and school quality, this council is very much in its infancy and there is no evidence available as to what this council may achieve. Much the same can be said about the security council, that has been reconstituted by the current governor of Sinaloa to allow for citizen participation. It too is just beginning its work on issues such as policing, public security and the quality of public services.

Analysis and findings

As in other OECD countries, it is clear from the foregoing account that decentralisation and partnership models are being deployed to meet various challenges in a wide variety of settings in modern day Mexico. New horizontal and vertical co-ordination mechanisms involving all tiers of government have been put in place. Increased emphasis is being attached to integrated place-based strategies relative to traditional top-down sectoral approaches. The federal government is no longer the only significant actor and it is now increasingly active in its capacity as a co-ordinating facilitator, in a process that seeks to enable sub-national levels of government, the private sector and civil society to exert real influence on decision-making in relation to many spheres of life. These developments, which have been previously reported elsewhere (OECD, 2002) are corroborated by this investigation. The developments are quite recent and represent a contrast with the highly centralised system of government that has been characteristic of Mexico for many years.

However, even though decentralisation experiments are going on in many areas of public administration in Mexico, quantitative evidence relating to their impacts and effectiveness is rather scarce. Much of this experimentation is new and it is supported by a rhetoric that speaks about participation and access to local decision-making. A critical question is whether there is, at this stage, a capacity to take advantage of the new opportunities that this decentralisation can create.

Decentralisation to be really effective, as Bardhan (2002) points out, has to be accompanied by serious attempts to change the existing structures of power within communities and to improve the opportunities for participation and voice, engaging the hitherto disadvantaged or disenfranchised in the political process. After all, the logic behind decentralisation is not just about weakening the central authority, nor is it about preferring local elites to central authority, but it is fundamentally about making governance at the local level more responsive to the felt needs of the large majority of the population (OECD, 1999a and OECD, 2003). In this section we discuss how well the tools for local partnership and participatory planning described in the previous section address this challenge.

A common problem with many new social experiments or programmes for change is that it is methodologically difficult to evaluate the change process. Rarely are the basic ingredients of a good research methodology in place *a priori*. The most basic of these ingredients is that we have some form of a counter-factual framework that will allow the researcher to note and measure change. Successful cases of decentralisation in Latin America, where there is some evidence available on the "before-after" comparison of service delivery outcomes, have been reported:

> "One is the widely noted case of participatory budgeting in municipal government in the city of Porto Alegre in Brazil; the other is the less well-known but quite dramatic success of the post-1994 decentralisation initiative in Bolivia. In Porto Alegre, where assembly meetings of local citizens and neighbourhood associations in different regions discuss investment priorities, review accounts and elect representatives to a city wide council that allocates available resources across wards, impressive results have followed: between 1989 and 1996, access to basic sanitation (water and sewage) as well as enrollment in elementary or secondary schools nearly doubled, while increasing revenue collection by 48%. Although it is difficult from this study to isolate the impact of participatory budgeting reforms from those of other ongoing changes, it seems likely that there has been a substantial impact on the pattern of resource allocation across localities, particularly to poor ones. In Bolivia in 1994, the number of municipalities as well as the share of national tax revenue allocated to municipalities doubled, along with the devolution to the municipalities of administrative authority, investment responsibility and title to local infrastructural facilities. This change has been associated with a massive shift of public resources in favour of the smaller and poorer municipalities and from large-scale production to social sectors. It was found that public investment in education, water and sanitation rose significantly in three-quarters of all municipalities, and investments responded to measures of local need; for example, the expansion in public education spending was larger on average in municipalities with a lower literacy rate or with fewer private schools" (Bardhan, 2002).

With respect to the Mexican experiences we do not have the luxury of a quasi-experimental approach, thus any assessment of the effect of these experiences has to be guided more by principles and comparisons with experiences found in other OECD countries (OECD, 2002).

Local capacity and capacity building in Mexico are generally acknowledged to be weak. Strong local interests, familiarity and relationships with politicians and local *caciques* still shape the agenda and thrust of local development in many instances. One could argue that there are not enough social institutions to offer a view on a range of different issues; nor are there adequate resources to engage with all of society. Citizens' committees can, through the mechanisms of the COPLADEMUN, highlight the "demand" of local development but nothing more. Most local level projects are initiated by the centre and society is then "invited" to participate. There is no evidence, for example, of NGOs being active in the different municipalities. In fact there is no law that allows government to work with these types of organisations.

Nevertheless, experiences in León are encouraging. It is significant to note that the model of local development in León is not new. It has grown with the administrative institutions and capacity of the city over a period of years. Efforts at neighbourhood development have been integrated into the work of the Social Development Directorate and the Municipal Planning Institute. There are structures that involve neighbourhood committees and these have, in the words of the neighbourhood facilitators "led them to see a future in how to develop resources in their neighbourhoods". The FIDOC programme is evidence of the positive type of engagement that is taking place between the municipal administration and many of its poorer citizens.

Access to resources for local development is important and, as described earlier in this report, municipalities in Mexico have very limited budgets. Much of the discussion on decentralisation in linked with the fiscal federalism literature that typically assumes that lower levels of government both collect taxes and spend funds. The key features of Mexican fiscal federalism are discussed in OECD (2002). With only 5% of total tax income accruing to the sub-national level in 1999, Mexico is one of the least fiscally decentralised OECD countries, particularly when compared to other federal countries (OECD, 1999b). In León, for example, there is only one tax levied, it is called *predial* (real state tax) and is paid by any owner or possessor of an urban or rustic estate.

Bardhan (2002) in his review of decentralisation of governance and development issues makes the point that in many low-income countries the issues are really about providing centrally collected tax revenue to lower levels of government rather than about debates on how to empower lower levels of government to collect taxes. In the short run what matters in Mexico is getting an efficient use of transfers to state and local government. For local development to be successful, it is important to focus a good deal of attention on strengthening local accountability mechanisms. At the municipal level there is a lack of confidence in existing mechanisms that distribute resources.

At the federal level there is also a lack of confidence because of the poor feedback and evaluation mechanisms that accompany these transfers.

The laws that specify the mechanisms for resource transfers appear to promote complexity and poor transparency. In order to encourage new forms of co-operation and local partnership it is important to have strong accountability frameworks. "Weaknesses in the accountability framework harm commitment from those institutions most responsible, such as the public services ultimately responsible to parliament, and elected municipal officials. Strong accountability is a prerequisite for effectiveness in policy co-ordination and legitimacy of resource allocation decisions" (OECD, 2001). Accordingly, it may be preferable to work within existing structures and strengthen the existing units, i.e. COPLADE and COPLADEMUN, rather than set up new structures. Giving non-governmental organisations a voice is another possibility for strengthening local accountability. At the municipal level itself there are severe technical and professional deficits that cannot be overcome immediately. There must be support for developing capacity in local administrations. Local administrations themselves have already identified this training need, as reflected by the CATAM initiative.

The mechanisms of accountability can also be improved by "yardstick competition" whereby jurisdictions are compared to each other. To some degree this competition does exist as states and municipalities watch where they are located in statistical tables of economic performance, literacy, educational achievement, etc. Because there is a need to build new mechanisms and experiment with new institutions at the local level, there is merit in developing a programme of what may be termed "indicative targeting". The federal government could set out specific objectives and problem areas for potential projects at a local (municipal) level which would be guaranteed funding through, for example, a global grant. Potential projects would be ranked and monitored on some predicted performance indicators and on proposals for working through new participative and partnership structures. This combination of decentralisation and yardstick competition allows the opportunity to experiment with new mechanisms for local development and learning from other jurisdictions. There is a parallel here with the evaluation of PROGRESA that shows how knowledge and rigorous evaluation helps set a high standard for the design and conduct of social policy (Coady, 2001).

This argument also has relevance for the micro-regions programme. The challenge and opportunity for this programme, in operationalising integrated local development, is to move beyond the rhetoric of integration, and work out what its different elements mean (i.e. sustainability, bottom-up development, institution building, infrastructural facilities) and more importantly how these can be achieved in the identified localities. Central to this task is the strengthening of the strategic area-based development locus around which the different elements of integration can be focused and where sectoral polices are integrated at the point of implementation. The experience in other OECD countries suggests that the potential to co-ordinate policies at local level is limited by the degree of consistency across the policy objectives pursued by the various government departments at national level. In order to make partnership relevant and effective, the partners must aim at common or compatible objectives at national level which can be pursued more concretely and attained more efficiently in partnership at local or regional level (OECD, 2001). More formal structures, that promote a spatial consistency of objectives in the programming exercises performed at different levels of government and assist in the identification of common municipal objectives, are key elements in the OECD experiences with strategic frameworks for partnerships.

Local levels of government play active roles in promoting conditions conducive to local business development. States and municipalities have sought to build relationships with the business sector, which in turn has been willing to develop these links and to work in partnership with the political structures. The level and direction of this local co-operation varies and it can be linked to the industrial structure. In Sinaloa, where there is a strong economic dependency on agriculture, there is a business coalition dominated by owners of less mobile factors of production and a strong state/business relationship in CODESIN. In the city of León, there is the shoe and leather cluster and, again, a strong relationship exists between business and the municipality. In the state of Guanajuato generally there is not an identifiable business coalition and so the involvement of business in state economic planning is much less visible. If anything the economic strategy in Guanajuato is linked more firmly with FDI and so state economic planning is more about providing the infrastructures that will satisfy this highly mobile investment. For the smaller municipalities, local business development is a new activity.

Irrespective of the economic contexts, the challenges facing all levels of government in Mexico are to promote local competitiveness and business development. Federal economic development programmes appear to be numerous and thus provide lower levels of government with opportunities to step in and promote local approaches to enhancing their local economies. A partnership approach across the set of diverse policy instruments that are available can facilitate this task. Having a focus (e.g. to stimulate business investment in sectors of local competitive advantage) facilitates the implementation of the partnership model. The food producer groups in Sinaloa and programmes of development and support for the shoe sector in León are good examples of this focussed approach. OECD experience shows that partnerships are more efficient when strict principles are followed with respect to objectives, accountability and evaluation. The business sector itself favours a specific and pragmatic focus to systems of training and other forms of business supports and planning. Supporting local business development is a very new sphere of activity for municipalities. Key concerns at this level include the availability of credit schemes for new SME's and micro-businesses, of training opportunities that are flexible and relevant for new and existing enterprises and the need for technical resources that will enhance the capacity of the municipal administrations.

Conclusions and issues for consideration

It is clear from the evidence presented in this report that a certain amount of progress has been made in Mexico in recent years with respect to fashioning an approach to development that is more inclusive in design, more flexible, and more focused on priorities as perceived and identified by local stakeholders. Through participatory processes in the preparation of strategic plans at national and various sub-national levels, and through the decentralisation of functions and financial resources, national government is attempting to create an enabling institutional environment in the regions and at local level that has the capacity to be responsive to the wide variety of conditions and challenges that inevitably characterise a country as large and heterogeneous as Mexico.

The planning in respect of large-scale infrastructural projects that is done at the level of the meso-regions is one example of partnership in practice. In this case, a number of states work together, in recognition of the sub-optimal size of individual states as the most appropriate geographic scale for such activities. This model provides for the involvement of key stakeholders, including the federal government, in a search for more consensual solutions. It is a good example of the decentralisation of decision making that is taking place more generally in Mexico and in this respect it accords well with the principle of subsidiarity.

The decentralisation of responsibilities regarding expenditure of financial resources in areas such as education and health represents a parallel development in strengthening sub-national government. A serious shortcoming associated with resource transfers to the lower levels of government is that monitoring and evaluation safeguards are not always undertaken. While there are social agreements, there are no incentives to improve the quality of spending by state and municipal government. In schemes which decentralise government responsibilities to lower levels, the rules governing the division of spending and taxation should specify clear lines of responsibility which force sub-national governments to bear the costs of their decisions. Otherwise local governments have few incentives to improve the quality of spending decisions. Furthermore, decentralisation initiatives can often pass formidable responsibilities to lower levels of government without making provision for the requisite governance capacity through training and technical assistance (Markusen, 2002).

As mentioned before, COPLADE is a decentralised body of each state government and represents the primary mechanism for intergovernmental planning relating to public investment and services. Although these institutions are designed to be inclusive and to facilitate decentralised decision making, their effectiveness is questionable. For example, in the case of Guanajuato municipal actors were openly sceptical of the efficacy of the COPLADE and of the level of its responsiveness to their particular priorities. Municipalities access state resources, upon which they are heavily dependent, through the COPLADE, but these are provided only on an annual basis and in a form that allows for little discretionary spending. The COPLADEMUN is another similar body that functions at municipal level. Although it too provides for local participation and place based co-ordinated planning, there appear to be serious limitations regarding the extent to which these are accomplished. The absence of a tradition of participative planning together with a lack of the necessary capacities amongst large sectors of the population represent major obstacles in this respect.

Public-private partnership as in the case of CODESIN in Sinaloa is another interesting model of participatory government. It successfully overcomes a major weakness in municipal government associated with short-term planning horizons arising from the restriction on mayors serving for more than one term. It also addresses to some extent the dearth of professional and technical expertise available within municipal administrations. The continuity in policy and programmes afforded by it provides an environment conducive to investment and business expansion. Furthermore, it provides a vehicle for business people to be centrally involved in creating an enabling and attractive environment for entrepreneurship. It is, however, dominated by business interests with no representation from other social partners or from community and voluntary bodies. Councils and commissions are used extensively in Sinaloa and elsewhere to involve civil society, but they are usually confined to an advisory role and do not appear to be particularly influential or even well-known to the people whose interests they are supposedly representing.

At the lower end of the geographic scale the micro-region programme represents a positive intervention in the fight against poverty and social exclusion. In acknowledgement of the multi-faceted nature of the causes of poverty, the programme endeavours to co-ordinate policies across 11 ministries. By involving local actors in the definition of priorities and solutions it seeks to facilitate the adaptation of measures to local conditions. People living in these localities are less the object of poverty programmes and more the architects of solutions to their problems. This is a welcome trend that is apparent in several poverty programmes being sponsored by SEDESOL, but there is a very serious question relating to the extent to which the public is sufficiently empowered to pursue a self-help approach to the development of its own communities.

Partnerships may be a useful vehicle to improve living conditions through improved governance in a wide variety of situations. Partnerships, however, come in may shapes and guises. A useful typology in the current context is as follows: a) purely shell, in which partners are only nominally involved, b) consultative, where limited consultation of the partners takes place, c) participative, through which partners have increased often equal access to the decision-making framework and exert real influence, or d) autonomous, characterised by the partnership having an independent identity in which the partners are integrated and mechanisms exist to ensure genuine and sustained involvement on an equal basis (Smith and Beazley, 2000). Many of the partnership initiatives in Mexico appear to belong to the lowerlevels of this typology (rather consultative). This is understandable in the light of the short time-span during which the country has seriously embraced the transition to full democracy and to a system of governance that is participative as well as representative. In order to realise their full potential, it is imperative that the process of partnership is enhanced. Ironically, it appears that partnerships are weakest in the very many remote rural settlements, where the need for intervention is acute and where local area-based bottom-up initiatives represent the most promising development strategy.

This chapter reveals that a planned and co-ordinated partnership approach to development is being implemented in a variety of settings. Although several shortcomings are found to be associated with current practices, it is apparent that progress toward a more participatory model of society is being made and that this is gradually facilitating the accumulation of the social capital that is vital to enhancing the well-being and future prospects of all concerned. This form of capital encompasses those social relationships that facilitate collective action in the public good. Such relationships enable co-operation within and between groups and across institutional divides, between civil society and the state. These ties are of special import to under-represented social groups as their capacity for collective action usually represents their most important power base (Fox and Gershman, 2000).

A good governance framework enables society to solve problems more effectively through means such as facilitating co-ordination of policies and initiatives, enhancing the participation of civic society, in general, and the social partners in decision-making with government, and developing custom-tailored area-based strategies involving all key stakeholders. Governments in many OECD countries have supported the establishment of partnerships at regional and local levels in order to improve governance conditions.

Partnerships have been set up to address new policy challenges requiring greater efficiency in resource allocation and better co-ordination of actions. They have been deployed to tackle problems relating to economic development, employment, social cohesion and quality of life. A recent study extending across seven countries found that "partnerships have improved the ways society collectively solves its problems and meets its needs" (OECD, 2001). This has been accomplished in several ways: a) through stimulating the use of public measures by actively involving potential end users, b) through matching measures more closely to locally identified needs and c) through creating synergistic effects by combining measures in imaginative fashions.

The creation of good governance conditions, including ample opportunity for public participation, is vital to the accumulation of social capital and its exploitation as a development resource. Building an institutional framework that facilitates these twin objectives represents a key objective of public administration reform. Although it is acknowledged that the full potential of partnerships has not been realised in many countries, the further development of a partnership strategy in the pursuit of better governance is clearly favoured (OECD, 2001). It is concluded, in the case of Mexico, that the concept of partnership, as documented in the OECD study, is not widely applied and that the development potential of a partnership-based approach to governance is still not fully appreciated or exploited.

In enhancing partnership processes in Mexico, the four main recommendations emanating from the OECD (2001) study are apt. In summary, they call for a) co-ordinating policy goals at central government level in order to achieve full consistency among national policy objectives and the goals assigned to partnerships, b) adapting the strategic framework for partnership to the needs of the partners so that they can achieve their own objectives more effectively by pursuing them through the partnership, c) strengthening the accountability of partnerships by clearly defining mandates, appropriate representation mechanisms, responsibilities and related matters, and d) providing for flexibility in the management of public programmes so that they can be adapted to local needs and conditions.

Considering the wide variety of conditions and development opportunities that exist in Mexico's vast array of urban and rural settings, the vigorous promotion of a bottom-up, partnership-led local development programme, that is complimentary to top-down measures, is strongly recommended. Every local community needs to be motivated and organised to pursue a self-help development programme. In keeping with the recent transformation in economic development theory and practice reported from the United States (Teitz, 1994) and elsewhere, the enhancement of local communities' capacities to create and retain employment and wealth generating opportunities from within ought to be prioritised. The local development programme should also focus specifically on problems of social exclusion and deprivation.

Widespread and meaningful participation of local community members is essential in order for any programme of local development to succeed. Participation not only generates a sense of community ownership of the process but it also facilitates "learning by doing" or "action learning". The accomplishment of specific task objectives such as the preparation of a local development strategy, the provision of some social infrastructure, or the creation of employment opportunities represent the most immediate and tangible results of a local development programme. However, the ultimate goal is much less apparent and may be easily overlooked. It is the intrinsic merit of getting a local community to identify its own needs, the desirability of involving all segments of the community in a collaborative effort, the importance of participatory democratic structures, the nurturing of local leadership and the development of community capacity to function effectively on a self-help basis. This approach to development is fundamentally an educational process. Participants need to acquire a range of skills if the initiatives they embark upon are to succeed. The acquisition of these skills is a gain in itself, and a gain with a potential to multiply so that many observers attach great significance to the attainment of this goal in the overall process of local development (Commins, 1985; Ó Cinnéide, 1987).

Getting business people to work in partnership with the community at large in a strategic planning initiative at local level is of paramount importance so as to ensure a private sector stake in the whole process. This will help ensure that the process is grounded in economic reality and supportive of the establishment of viable private enterprises that are required to generate wealth and employment opportunities. Local political and administrative leaders also have a critical role to play in promoting and facilitating the local development process. These local actors need to be encouraged, empowered and facilitated by higher authorities to which they are answerable, including national government, development organisations and international bodies.

Getting communities to engage in a strategic local planning and development process is not an easy matter. Many people with much to offer to such a process may not participate because of feelings of apathy and powerlessness. This is particularly the case in poor communities, characterised by low levels of educational achievement, and who very often lack people with the necessary leadership skills and self-confidence to take part in the process. Many communities also lack a tradition of self-help and co-operative endeavour. These difficulties may be compounded by local political, administrative or business leaders who have a vested interest in retaining the status quo, lest the new open-ended approach may lead to a situation of diminished influence and control for themselves. Finally the process may flounder in the absence of a steering framework and sufficient support from higher levels of authority. To overcome these difficulties, the recruitment and training of local development agents, that would orchestrate and lead the process of local development within each community, is strongly recommended.

A highly participative or autonomous model of partnership is strongly desirable in devising and effecting the local development strategy in each area. This requires that attention is paid to such elements as the representative legitimacy of the partners, the extent to which they have a stake in the goals of the partnership so as to ensure willingness to collaborate for mutual benefit, and the degree to which they are empowered to exert equal influence on decision-making. Unless such factors are adequately addressed in the process of building partnerships, the reality of community involvement is likely to be subsumed in the rhetoric and although short-term gains in the form of specific task objectives may be realised, the long-term educational benefits arising from meaningful participation will not materialise.

The following measures are considered necessary for the successful implementation of a comprehensive programme of local development in Mexico: a) a policy framework which provides the necessary steering, technical support and flexible funding, within an adequate framework of public accountability and reporting; b) an information and training programme relating to strategic planning and management of local development, aimed specifically at local development agents, political leaders and other key actors, all of whom have a critical role to play in successfully implanting the process in their communities; and c) an education and training programme aimed at mobilising and organising local inhabitants and empowering them to prioritise and execute projects which they themselves recognise as important and manageable. Facilitating learning at the individual and community level by involving them in all stages of project planning and implementation is regarded as a key process objective.

Typically, communities are at different levels of preparedness to engage in a programme of local development. Natural resource endowments and potentials also vary from place to place. So too does the available social capital. Some communities have a long tradition of co-operative endeavour and therefore are well positioned to engage participatory development processes, whereas others may be in a much weaker position and in need of capacity building measures, in a first instance, to prepare them for the challenges of local development. An important aspect of any local development programme is to recognise that these differences exist and to provide custom-tailored interventions that addresses them (Keane and Ó Cinnéide, 1986). Targeting areas and communities of greatest need, as in the case of the micro-region programme, and providing them with additional resources, is commendable, but the promotion of local development is something that has universal application and ought to be pursued nation-wide.

In this respect, it is also of the utmost importance to pursue an adaptive management approach, that permits the flexible integration of local knowledge and formal scientific knowledge, as both can greatly compliment one another, as has been reported recently in an excellent case study of indigenous communities in highland Michoacán, Mexico (Klooster, 2002). Social scientists have a central role to play in this process as relevant social science knowledge and data are needed to face the challenges of planning, financing and managing projects, and also to help focus on the wider long-term consequences of different courses of action (Korten, 1980). Adult education courses focused on local development can make a valuable contribution in this respect (Curtin and Varley, 1986; Ó Cinnéide, 1987). The Local Employment Development Action (LEDA) programme of the European Commission, which aimed to contribute to employment creation efforts, by enhancing know-how relating to local development through the distillation of good practices from a wide range of experiences and settings, and by disseminating that know-how to relevant local actors (Ó Cinnéide, 1994) provides another possible intervention model.

Finally, Ireland has been to the fore in pioneering and promoting partnership led programmes of local development (Mosely et al., 2001). These initiatives have attracted a good deal of attention and favourable commentary They have been commended for a) their practical problem-solving approach, needs-driven and action oriented agendas, resulting in the provision of enhanced services of direct benefit to many poor and unemployed people, b) the alliances and networks they have created, to improve information flow and better co-ordinate employment and social programmes, c) the increased influence they have given disadvantaged groups in the determination of appropriate interventions, d) introducing a more open culture of thrust and responsiveness in public bodies, and e) pioneering innovative solutions to intractable problems associated with poverty and social exclusion, some of which have been applied universally throughout the country (NESC, 1999; OECD, 1996; Turok, 2001). They have also provided the inspiration for similar initiatives in other countries e.g. Finland (Ó Cinnéide, 2001). It is suggested that Ireland's experience with successive local development programmes can provide valuable lessons in designing and implementing an appropriate model for Mexico.

Notes

1. The COPLADE (Comité de Planeación para el Desarollo Estatal) is a decentralised body of each state government and is made up of a president (the state governor), co-ordinator (a civil servant nominated by the governor and generally head of a unit in charge of the planning and finances of the state), technical secretariat, an assembly and a permanent commission. The commission is composed of civil servants, municipal presidents and community representatives. The COPLADE's main functions are to co-ordinate planning measures between the federal, sate and municipal governments, prepare and update the State Development Plan, propose to federal and state government an annual investment plan for the state and municipalities and evaluate the programmes and actions agreed on by the federation and the state. The COPLADEMUN (Consejo de Planeación y Desarollo Municipal) is a similar body that functions at municipal level. Its main function is to co-ordinate the Municipal Development Plan with actions taken at municipal level by state and federal governments.

2. To complete the research made on the basis of literature and data provided by the federal, state and local authorities, a study visit to Mexico was undertaken in February 2002 to meet with representatives from the public, private and civil society sectors at local, state and national levels.

Bibliography

Bardhan, P. (2002), "Decentralisation of Governance and Development" in Journal of Economic Perspectives, Vol. 4, No. 16.

Cabrero-Mendoza, E. (2000), "Mexican Local Government in Transition: Fleeting Change or Permanent Transformation?" in American Review of Public Administration, Vol. 4, No. 4.

Cabrero Mendoza, E. and Martínez-Vázquez, J. (2000), "Assignment of Spending Responsibilities and Service Delivery", in Giugale, Marcelo M. and Webb, Steven B. (eds): Achievements and Challenges of Fiscal Decentralization, Lessons from Mexico, The World Bank, Washington, DC.

Canak, W. and Swanson, L. (1998), Modern Mexico, McGraw-Hill, Singapore.

Coady, D. (2001), "An Evaluation of the Distributional Power of Progresa's Cash Transfers in Mexico", International Food Policy Research Institute Working Paper.

Commins, P. (1985), "Rural Community Development: Approaches and Issues" in Social Studies, Vol. 8.

Corbacho, A. and Schwartz, G. (2002), "Mexico: Experiences with Pro-Poor Expenditure Policies", International Monetary Fund Working Paper, WP/02/12, Washington, DC.

Curtin, C. and Varley, A. (1986), "Adult Education and Community Development in the West of Ireland", in Community Development Journal, Vol. 3, No. 21.

Fernandez de Villegas, M. (2000), "Civil Society Participation in World Bank and Inter-American Development Bank Programs: the Case of Mexico", in Global Governance, Vol. 4, No. 6.

Fox, J. and Gershman, J. (2000), "The World Bank and Social Capital: Lessons from Ten Rural Development Projects in the Philippines and Mexico", in Policy Sciences, No. 33.

Fox, J. (1995), "Governance and Rural Development in Mexico: State Intervention and Public Accountability", in The Journal of Development Studies, Vol. 1, No. 32.

García, L. González (2001), "Decentralisation and Infrastructure for Poverty Alleviation", paper prepared as background note for the OECD mission to Mexico.

Hakim, P. (2002), "Two Ways to Go Global: the Differing Paths of Mexico and Brazil", in *Foreign Affairs*, Vol. 1, No. 81.

Keane, M. and Ó Cinnéide, M. (1986), "Promoting Economic Development Amongst Rural Communities", in *Journal of Rural Studies*, Vol. 4, No. 2.

Klooster, D.J. (2002), "Toward Adaptive Community Forest Management: Integrating Local Forest Knowledge with Scientific Forestry", in *Economic Geography*, Vol. 1, No. 78.

Lichfield, G. (2000), "Survey Mexico", in *The Economist*, October 28th, 2000.

Markusen, A. (2002), "Two Frontiers for Regional Science: Regional Policy and Interdisciplinary Reach", in *Papers in Regional Science*, No. 81.

Mosely, M.J., Cherrett, T. and Cawley, M. (2001), "Local Partnerships for Rural Development: Ireland's Experience in Context", in *Irish Geography*, Vol. 2, No. 34.

NESC (National Economic and Social Council) (1999), "Local Development Issues", The National Economic and Social Forum, *Forum Opinion* No. 7, Dublin.

Ó Cinnéide, M. (2001), "Fighting Unemployment and Social Exclusion with Partnerships in Finland", in *Local Partnerships for Better Governance*, OECD, Paris.

Ó Cinnéide, M. (1994), "Stimulating Local Development in Marginal Regions: the Experience of the European Community's LEDA Programme", in Wiberg, Ulf (editor), Marginal Areas in Developed Countries, CERUM (Centre for Regional Science), Umeå University, Umeå, Sweden.

Ó Cinnéide, M. (1987), "Adult Education and Community Development in the West of Ireland", in *Research in Rural Education*, Vol. 3, No. 4.

OECD (2003), *Decentralisation. A New Role for Labour Market Policy*, OECD, Paris.

OECD (2002), *Territorial Review of Mexico*, OECD, Paris.

OECD (2001), *Local Partnerships for Better Governance*, OECD, Paris.

OECD (1999a), *Decentralising Employment Policy: New Trends and Challenges*, OECD, Paris.

OECD (1999b), *Taxing Powers of State and Local Governments*, OECD, Paris.

OECD (1996), *Ireland: Local Partnerships and Social Innovation*, OECD, Paris.

Ros, J. (2000), "Employment, Structural Adjustment and Sustainable Growth in Mexico", in *Journal of Development Studies*, Vol. 4; No. 36.

Smith, M. and Beazley, M. (2000), "Progressive Regimes, Partnerships and the Involvement of Local Communities: a Framework for evaluation", in *Public Administration*, Vol. 4, No. 78.

Tamayo-Flores (2001), "Mexico in the Context of North American Integration: Major regional Trends and Performance of Backward Regions", *Journal of Latin American Studies*, No. 33.

Teitz, M.B. (1994), "Changes in Economic Development Theory and Practice", in *International Regional Science Review*, 16(1&2).

Turok, I. (2001), "Innovation in Local Governance: the Irish Partnership Model", in *Local Partnerships for Better Governance*, OECD, Paris.

Ward, P.M. and Rodriguez, V.E. (1999), "New Federalism, Intra-governmental Relations and Co-governance in Mexico" in *Journal of Latin American Studies*, Vol. 3, No. 31.

ISBN 92-64-01530-2
New Forms of Governance for Economic Development
© OECD 2004

Chapter 5

Czech Republic: Rebuilding Partnerships in a Society in Transition

by

Filip De Rynck,
Department of Business and Public Administration,
Ghent University College, Belgium

Czech authorities seek to enhance the participation of civil society and business in local economic and employment development. Reforms of the regional governance structure and public administration are geared at stimulating a new dynamism at regional and local level. The newly-established regional self-governments must build inclusive partnerships to succeed. Yet the full exercise of democratic rights and the transition to a market economy are still recent and pose significant challenges to partnership working. This in turn encourages partners to innovate further in the development of new forms of governance.

Modern public management is dominated by the search for effectiveness and efficiency and a renewed search for legitimacy. "Governance" covers the efforts to engage the private sector, NGOs and citizens in public policy activities. The shift from steering by hierarchy (the "closed shop" – government that looks to pursue its own programme) to more market- and network-steering (through partnerships) dominates the transformation of public administration in most western countries.

While western countries are shifting from government to governance, the Czech Republic is moving from its communist hierarchical heritage towards a stable democratic government structure. It is quite understandable that Czech politicians put priority on their own organisation in order to demonstrate the ability of government to tackle problems. Legitimacy of government has yet to be established. It is difficult to open up politics to governance and partnership if public administration still has to prove that it can make a difference and if there is general mistrust of people in "going public".

The main heritage is not institutional but mainly cultural: public administration was dominated by centralism, hierarchy and absence of choice and public accountability for decades. It is relatively easy to reform institutions but changing public attitudes is much more difficult. Decentralisation and regionalisation are part of that change: they can encourage people and institutions to take more responsibility and to develop a more pro-active attitude. But the cultural history is still present and is, in general, an impeding factor for partnerships.

A challenging economic background

This is against a challenging economic background. The economy and the economic policy are in a process of transition. The introduction of market principles has caused important problems in the regions dominated by industrial companies. The general expectation is that their further restructuring will enlarge the disparities between regions and increase unemployment.

The Czech Republic has inherited relatively small disparities from its past. The system of communist central planning managed to balance regional differences mainly through a policy of income redistribution and relocation of industry. The currently growing disparities are a result of the transition of the Czech economy to free market principles replacing the redistribution policy at

Box 5.1. **Territorial units in the Czech Republic**

Czech institutions widely use the territorial unit classification system (NUTS, for *Nomenclature des unités territoriales statistiques*) developed for the European Union (EU) by the European statistical agency (Eurostat). The territorial units of the Czech Republic are listed below according to this typology:

- NUTS I: Country.
- NUTS II: 8 "cohesion regions" (or groups of *Kraje*).
- NUTS III: 14 regions (*Kraje*).
- NUTS IV: 77 districts.
- NUTS V: 6 244 municipalities.

In addition, Czech institutions use the term "micro-region" for sub-regional areas smaller than NUTS III regions that correspond to voluntary groupings of municipalities.

Source: Ministry of Regional Development.

central level. Differences are also increasing at sub-regional level, both within regions and within districts (Government of the Czech Republic, 2000a).

However, the decline and restructuring of industry in traditional sectors has had a concentrated impact in some regions, for example in Ostrava with the restructuring of the metallurgical industry and in North-west Bohemia with the decline of coal mining. Most large industrial and formerly state-owned companies now suffer from a lack of financial resources and make investments from their own resources to a small extent only. Investments are largely made on credit at high interest rates. The capital market is underdeveloped and does not offer a significant alternative means of obtaining finance.

"The poor standard of technical equipment results in low labour productivity, poorly-valued labour, a low standard of innovation and a low value-added output level" (*ibid.*). The market environment lacks "cleaning mechanisms": badly-managed companies with large debts and poor perspectives still survive. The level of innovation is low. There is a constant decline in R&D expenditure with the closing down of many development centres in manufacturing companies accompanied by a decline of employment in R&D. The greatest growth in production among industrial companies is in those with foreign capital and under foreign control. Long-term objectives prevail in these companies and their market value is growing.

Though small business if sometimes considered as a hopeful, dynamic and developing sector (*ibid.*), policy has so far devoted too little attention to the conditions necessary to promote the creation of small- and medium-sized enterprises (SMEs). Various schemes to support the development of SMEs are being implemented by the Ministry of Industry and Trade and the Ministry of Regional Development, jointly with the Czech-Moravian Guarantee Bank,[1] although a lack of awareness hampers their results (OECD, 2002). The service industry is growing but the regional distribution is concentrated in the bigger cities and urban areas. Mainly composed of SMEs, is not in a position to offset rapidly the problems in the most afflicted regions.

In official documents the lack of a comprehensive national strategy to support SMEs has been emphasised. In this connection, it is striking that the financial and human resources devoted to R&D are declining. In many countries R&D is a fertile ground for the creation of new local economic initiatives as a spin off of R&D. Also, the tradition of large and state-owned companies has made a clear impact on the banking culture. Access to credit for local business initiatives is not easy for individuals and SMEs. A "risk-taking" culture, essential for setting up new SMEs, still has to be developed in society.

Research on economic development show that SMEs are dependent on the quality of their environment (*e.g.* quality of labour, level of education, banking facilities, support of local government) (see for example OECD, 1998). Policies towards SMEs, and complementary regional and local initiatives, should be closely linked, and aim to enhance, the quality of local development (Hull and Hjern, 1982). Poor attention is given to these considerations in the Czech Republic although, in some regions, a positive attitude to SME can be observed for instance with the support of local initiatives in tourism. Regional development, SMEs and local economic initiatives are interrelated: the regional level opens up opportunities for a more decentralised policy and better support for local initiatives. This could be part of the national and regional strategy to promote SMEs, which surely demands co-operation between the levels of government.

Several official documents focus on the problems of public infrastructure, "neglected to a considerable degree in the past" (Government of the Czech Republic, 2000a). In particular there is a lack of important transport connections "to support the growth of urban areas, to facilitate internal mobility and to provide fast connections with other European countries. Priority now is given to motorway, highway and transit railway corridor projects in regions which have close links with Prague, while connections with other regions, such as East Bohemia and North Moravia (the Ostrava region) to the national and international motorway network have been delayed, with all the consequences for the development of these regions".

The governance structure

During the communist period, there were "committees" (in reality, state administration) at each level of the administration (local, district, regional). Public administration and politics were dominated by the totalitarian authority of the communist party *apparat*. After 1990 the regional committees were abolished, the district became a state administration and municipalities regained their autonomy. These developments have been followed more recently by an ambitious regionalisation process and further changes at district level.

Municipalities: gaining autonomy

Local self-government was abolished after World War II and replaced by local committees. During the communist period the number of municipalities was reduced from 11 000 to 4 100. A number of municipalities have retrieved their jurisdiction since the velvet revolution (bringing the total now to 6 231).

Competencies

Municipalities are mainly responsible for infrastructures and environmental services: local roads and street lighting, water supplies, drainage, sewage treatment, refuse collection and disposal, parks and other recreational and cultural facilities, cemeteries, public transport. Housing responsibilities include the management and repair of publicly-owned housing. Municipalities also determine applications for planning permission. Land use plans must nevertheless be in accord across levels of government (the new act of regions gives the regions responsibility for land use at regional level and both levels legally have an equal status). Municipalities license business activities, and administer markets, libraries, fire protection, cultural centres, children's nurseries and sports facilities.

If some of the basic principles and procedures remain unmodified since the communist period, for instance for spatial planning, the situation is different for other, new, competencies, such as local development. There is only a very limited tradition in preparing local development strategies and their preparation is at the complete discretion of the respective municipalities. Consequently, "the structure, aims and quality of local development strategies differ enormously across areas" (Blazek, 1999). The biggest problems with local development strategies are related to their slow implementation and poor evaluation.

There seems to be little official support, advice and help for local governments in this field. Much depends on the municipalities' own initiative. This is of course a flourishing business for private consultants but this does not improve the capacity of local governments to respond to development problems. As it will be seen below, municipalities are often very weakly linked with the regional development agencies.

Coping with local fragmentation

Local government is fragmented. Ninety per cent of municipalities have less than 2 000 inhabitants and the majority is concentrated in rural areas. The current economic trends increase disparities with urban areas, as mentioned above. The large number of municipalities and their low critical mass cause two problems: i) a huge gap between their resources and the investment needs, and ii) very limited human resources ("many small villages do not even have the personnel to read new legislative texts", ibid.).

The fragmentation of local government is mitigated by a network of "arm's length" agencies for most public services (e.g. water supply, refuse collection, cultural services) working at a more appropriate scale. "In practice they (a group of municipalities) share the services of the various arm's length companies. Typically these serve a town and its surrounding villages, and have been largely supervised by the district or central town municipalities" (Davey, 1996). Most companies existed in communist times, were quasi-autonomous and led by central persons in the party, so their relations with municipalities were not one of a principal (local government delegating the implementation) and an agent (the semi-autonomous service responsible for the implementation). Now municipalities can choose how to organise their services as they are no longer compelled to use those companies.

Those agency companies are very uneven in the quality of their management. The traditional relationship was not geared to obtaining "value for money", and standard management tools (e.g. performance management, quality control) have rarely been implemented. The basic instruments for a good relationship between municipalities and those agencies are still to be developed (ibid.).

Statutory cities and authorised municipalities

The existence of the so-called "statutory cities" in the Czech Republic is worth noting. "These (16) cities have the right to determine their internal problems and the matters of management by a generally binding degree (the Statutes)" (Government of the Czech Republic, 2000b). These statutory cities have a broader range of powers than ordinary municipal authorities and "in the case of delegated powers (state administration), the authorisation of a municipality to execute state administration for another municipality or for several municipalities exceeds the territorial limits of the delegated municipality, which is not possible within the framework of self-administration". These powers are executed by the mayor. Execution of delegated powers for other municipalities is not only the case for statutory cities. In each micro-region, an authorised municipality usually executes delegated powers for neighbouring small villages.

The local fiscal system

Blazek (1999 and 2000) describes the local financial and fiscal system as a process of trial and error, which changes frequently. Different systems have succeeded themselves from 1990 to the present and yet a new system is planned.

An important change was introduced in January 2001, closely linked to the establishment of self-governing regions. This new system categorising municipalities according to their size of population and assigning each group with a coefficient (higher for larger municipalities and cities responsible for outlying areas) has the effect of promoting amalgamation to obtain a higher coefficient. While the strengths and weaknesses of this system are being discussed, a new change has been announced for 2002. The frequent and drastic changes of the local financial system hinder multi-annual investment plans, mainly in infrastructure, an urgent need in most micro-regions.

Blazek describes the continuing changes as a search to find a solution to the trade-off between the principles of solidarity and meritocracy. The new system results in an extensive redistribution of resources towards the bigger municipalities and hence favours solidarity at the expense of merits. "The incentives for municipalities to encourage employment creation and business support on their territories are extremely limited" (Blazek, 2000).

Capital investments

Municipalities recovered properties from the pre-communist period (before 1948 municipalities owned substantial quasi-commercial assets such as shopping centres, premises, dairies and laundries. "Faced with the prospect of subsidising loss-making enterprises, repairing crumbling buildings and finding capital to complete pretentious complexes (white elephants), many local authorities have sought to sell their newly acquired property as quickly as possible for whatever it will fetch" (Davey, 1996). Towns in particular sold their shares of regional energy companies.

The municipalities have allocated parts of these revenues to new and demanding infrastructure investments, which have become the priority. The central government also helped in offering significant grants for investments. The sum of investments of local governments has exceeded the investments of central government. This represents an important contribution of local governments to economic development, although at the expense of growing local debt.

A tool: *public-private partnerships* (PPP)

To develop and manage infrastructures, municipalities in western countries often make concessions to the private sector in the form of contracting relationships. Alternatively, they may set up a mixed organisation with the private sector for the autonomous management of infrastructure or services. Both techniques are known as public-private partnership (PPP).

PPPs need a solid legal framework to operate. The Czech legislation does not seem favourable towards local PPP. Municipalities can perform profit-generating activities as a legal entity, not subject to business tax (the State returns the tax paid by local governments). This provision is widely-used – and exceeds the amount of revenues generated by the property tax – but if municipalities set up a separate legal entity in the form of PPP or in a 100% ownership, there is no similar incentive. "This means that the legislation (...) restricts PPP to spheres where the profits can be reinvested: this is hardly acceptable for private firms" (Blazek, 1999).

The districts: only an administrative level?

At district level, state administration is fully executed by the district offices (law 425), headed by chief officers and consisting of individual departments. Their main activities are performing state administration in matters designated by special laws and supervising the decisions of the municipal authority and the municipal economy.

After the communist period, in 1993-2000, the district level was also political: there was a council composed of representatives of the municipalities. The chief activities of that district assembly included the distribution of appropriations among individual municipal budgets. The former situation but also the current competencies resemble the French practice of close networks between local politicians, local public officials and the state offices of the prefect. The French prefects (or district directors in the Czech case) are important intermediates or brokers between local policies and state policy. Of course, the qualities of networks at district level are contingent upon local and personal characteristics.

Although the former political structure of the district was abolished in 2002, the relationship between municipalities and the district officers has not disappeared. This may explain part of the attitudes of municipalities in the district-regional debate (see further on). Municipalities are more familiar with the districts, which offered concrete support and an entry to central ministries. The regions however represent a new political factor, and local politicians can use this also as a leverage to strengthen their position.

State administration

The districts are part of the state administration, at sub-regional level, but not all sub-regional state administration is part of the district organisation. A number of ministries have established their own branch offices at district level (financial services, land registry, police and justice), removing their responsibilities and their budgets from the direct control of the district office. They were not concerned by the abolition of the district administration.

The district authority in its present form is largely concerned with employment, education and social services. Economic development issues are not addressed by district offices (nor by any other de-concentrated or decentralised state administration at sub-regional level).

The district labour office

The state administration plays a strong role in the implementation of labour market policy at sub-regional level through the district labour office. These offices offer all the employment and social services for unemployed people and people with social needs (*e.g.* placement, counselling, training, social benefits, support for business start-ups and self-employed initiatives). The staff varies according to the size of the service area: from 100 staff members (in districts with 100 000 inhabitants) to 40 (smaller ones). Statistics on the use of measures are produced every month, and evaluation reports every six months.

"Consultation" belongs to the standard instruments of the districts to promote an effective use of its measures. Its use has been promoted by European pre-adhesion programmes. Each district office has a consultative committee (grouping together social partners, employers, schools, financial institutions), which is legally obliged to hold one meeting every month. The main task of the committee is the allocation of subsidies to the employers applying to the various schemes available. The district officer is free to set up further co-operation mechanisms.

One of the districts co-ordinates the other districts in NUTS III regions and an advisory committee of directors supports the co-ordination. Programmes on NUTS III level are subsidised from the budget of the national department (Ministry of Labour and Social Affairs).

The future of the districts

The district offices till now are legal entities with a relatively broad flexibility. Over the period 1993-2000, the districts financed their expenditures through a share of income tax. Since 2001, they receive transfers from the State budget. The Act on district authorities remained in force until

31 December 2002. Under the reform, the most important administrative functions of district authorities were officially taken over by 180 larger cities, by regions or by special administrative courts.

Education is an area where competencies were already transferred in 2001. Elected regional assemblies at NUTS III level have become the owners (managers) of the vast majority of schools (including practically all secondary schools). However, it is unclear if this task will be enlarged to a planning role. Meanwhile, the district authorities have taken on more administrative responsibilities in this field (financing schools, textbooks, student-aids, costs related to continuing education of teachers).

The new plans are still the object of fierce controversies. The regional restructuring goes to the heart of the administrative system. Such operations lead to long lasting administrative uncertainty that harm the effectiveness of public administration. A lot of energy is spent on the so-called "office-politics" (the battle of the bureaucrats). Although the regionalisation offers new opportunities for governance (see following part), it may also generate some damaging effects.

The regions: a complex programme

"Structural changes in societies have their spatial dimensions (…). The regional structure is remoulded by the societal changes and it is itself one of the elements in societal change (…). The regional structure acts as a moderator of societal change (…) and also defines developmental potentials, the relative advantages of different regions and, in this sense, is an active factor in the societal transformation" (Illner, 1995). We witness only the first stage of the Czech regionalisation process, mixed up with several other elements of transformation (e.g. the free market effects, the influence of the European Union, reform of taxation, political dynamics).

The processes of regionalisation and the creation of political and administrative regions for "self-government" have the "regional" element in common but they do not have the same ambitions. Regionalisation often refers to the elaboration of planning systems leading to a better adaptation of national policies to regional conditions. It is characterised by a "top-down" approach often supported by a well-structured dialogue between administration, trade unions and organisations of employers and by the de-concentration of administration. In part, this corresponds to the situation of the Czech Republic, especially symbolised in the approach for the first generation of programming for the European pre-adhesion programmes at NUTS II level (see further on).

The creation of a political regional level (NUTS III) in the Czech Republic also aims at stimulating "bottom-up" dynamics and changing the democratic and probably also the political structure of a country. It leads to debates on decentralisation, subsidiarity and autonomy. This is the story of constructing a democratic society, giving citizens and local actors responsibility for the general interest of their area. This is the second part of the Czech regional case.

Both parts of the case are inter-related: processes of regionalisation affect regional ambitions and dialogue between local actors, they can influence perceptions on scales and the regional potential and they can be the trigger for the political ambitions of an area. The Czech Republic demonstrates the close relationship between the two rationales.

Regional economic structure

The economic structure of the regions is heavily related to the country's heritage of communist policy. Illner (1995) describes the main features of the communist heritage of regional development:

- A redistribution towards the eastern parts of Czechoslovakia and the marginalisation of the regions along the German and Austrian borders.
- Socialist industrialisation strengthened the mono-structural character of industrial agglomerations, making them extremely vulnerable, creating social problems and environmental damage, especially in North-west Bohemia and North Moravia.
- Collectivisation of agriculture changed land use and the settlement system (rural settlements without function, losing residents and transformed in recreational villages).
- Priority for housing construction in city suburbs, remaining inner cities in urgent need of renewal.
- Infrastructure, transport and telecommunication, especially with the west, were neglected (considered as "non-productive" services).
- The sector-branch system and the big industrial services prevailed over the territorial organisation and the decision-making of self-government.

"Czech Republic entered the period of post-communist transformation with polarised regional structure, over-industrialised urban agglomeration, underdeveloped infrastructure, polluted environment and over-centralised territorial administration. The dynamics have been shifting toward the east part (Moravia) to the detriment of the west (Bohemia) part, that part (historically the stronger macro-region) acquiring the character of an 'old' industrial region" (ibid.).

After 1989, the societal transformation in the Czech Republic began to change the regional structure. The following factors came into play:

● Restoration of economic dynamism in the western part, due to the changing geopolitical position of border regions capitalising their proximity to western countries, the eastern part now becoming more marginal (also due to the split of the country).

● Changes in land ownership (price of land co-determined now by the market, sub-urbanisation, selective out-migration in former housing projects).

● Restructuring of economic activity is spatially selective (booming service sector in the cities, reduced production in mono-industrial regions).

This leads to the following typology of the regional potentials (*ibid.*):

● Development opportunities for border regions, mainly in the west.

● Deteriorating opportunities for regions with declining industries.

● Good opportunities for regions with diversified economic structures.

● Better opportunities for regions with privatised businesses.

● Handicaps for polluted regions (North-west Bohemia, North Moravia), potential for South Bohemia.

The driving forces of regionalisation

Scholars agree that the growing regional disparities and the economic decline in general are one explanation for the growing awareness of the need for a regional planning system. "Central Czech authorities only react in individual cases where intervention is inevitable because of a critical situation (high unemployment or extreme pollution) has arisen" (*ibid.*). The small interregional disparities as a product of the communist regime in the beginning of the 1990s explain the slow start. "There were regional disparities but the problems were not considered to be serious enough to stimulate the central government towards the establishment of a regional policy adapted to the problems of the different areas" (Brizova and Maryska, 2000).

When the need of a more pro-active system became urgent, the problems of an un-coordinated administration became clearer. This was an important stimulant for the administration to change in order to tackle the institutional fragmentation and the lack of horizontal co-ordination ("the main problem was the total lack of co-ordination between the central departments. And also the co-ordination with the other levels of government was unsatisfactory", *ibid.*).

If the first reason to establish a regional system was mainly economic and institutional, the second one was more political: the urge for re-establishment of democracy and promoting local and regional initiatives (Blazek, 1999). The bottom-up pressure to tackle economic problems prompted national government to act in a more pro-active way and to strengthen public responsibility. "The objective of these changes is an effort to make the public administration more democratic by transferring some of the State functions to self-governing bodies on the one hand, and by bringing administrative decisions closer to taxpayers on the other hand" (Government of the Czech Republic, 2001a).

A third reason has to do with geopolitics. Interviews revealed how influential the European Union was for administrative structures and culture in one of the states wishing to become member of the Union. Although the European Union may not be the main factor, it certainly played a role of trigger for the transformation of the regional system.

A corollary: the development of RDAs

The growing regional problems (mid-1990s) first resulted in the creation of regional development agencies (RDAs), mainly on the basis of private local initiatives (chambers of commerce) and the support of local government. The activities of the RDAs are: collection and data processing on the region, support for investors, organisation and assistance of projects for industrial estates, technical advice for companies, support for governments in economic planning, promotion of the region. As only in a few cases supported by the State, most RDAs have suffered from a lack of resources, experience and qualification of staff, as well as of respect among local actors. However, this analysis varies across areas and depends on local circumstances: "the position of the RDA in Ostrava is much stronger due to its backing by the self-government authority of the large city dominating the whole region of Ostrava. On the other hand, the position of the RDA in Most (North-west Bohemia) is much weaker, partly because of the competition from several cities of approximately equal size" (Blazek, 1999).

A major impetus for the creation of new RDAs recently was the anticipation of the creation of the 14 regions and surely the preparation for the European pre-accession adhesion funds.[2] In many cases, RDAs have been involved in the design and implementation of programmes and projects funded through these schemes. Now "at least one RDA is operating in each of the 14 regions" (ibid.). Some of the RDAs built up their first planning and field experiences with the programmes of the European Union. This is a power-resource, for instance in relation to the new regional administration (see further on).

The EU impulse

Following the Czech Republic's application for EU membership, the European Commission stated that the Czech Republic had no regional policy, there were no co-ordination mechanisms at national level, no effective instruments and financial resources for regional development, and no legal, administrative and budgeting framework for integrated regional policy (Government of the Czech Republic, 2000a). The judgement was sharp. The structures had to be prepared to fit the requirement of European regional policy: regional and sectoral planning and programming documents, support frameworks and co-finance systems, organisational institutions and regional committees, applying the principles of subsidiarity and partnership.

The EU influence had probably its most important effects on the restructuring of the national level, on the emergence of a new level of institution and on new types of consultation structures established at regional level:

- Creation of Ministry for Regional Development (MRD) and a supporting Centre for Regional Development at ministry level (1996).

- Implementation of EU pre-accession support: creation of a National Programming and Monitoring Committee for Economic and Social Cohesion at national level; creation of the eight cohesion regions at NUTS II level and establishment in each region of a partnership structure, the regional management and monitoring committees (RMMC), to help with planning and programme implementation.

- Creation of regional co-ordinating committees (RCCs) to prepare regional development plans (RDP) in the new 14 NUTS III regions (*Kraje*), ahead of the election of self-governments.

- Enactment of the Regional Development Act (basic documents: 235/8-4-1988 and 248/2000) on 1 January 2001.

The regional management and monitoring committees (now abolished) at NUTS II level consisted mainly of the tripartite partners in the regions (key politicians, trade unions, entrepreneurs). Representatives of the NGOs participated in a different way according to their regional position and strength. The RMMCs were the first "official" partnership structures based on the European Union model. Although top down structures, the RMMCs stimulated the regional planning processes, depending on the characteristics of the regions. They offered the first officially-recognised framework for discussion on regional priorities and gave legitimacy to the processes.

The regional co-ordinating committees (also abolished, due to the election of regional assemblies) at NUTS III level were mainly composed of representatives of state administration, municipalities and social partners. In some regions the elaboration of the regional development plans (RDP) was dominated by technicians and the members of the committee, in other regions the public debate was more open and interactive (see the case of the region of Vysocina in Part II). The committees opened up the minds for strategic planning and installed the concept of partnership, although the concept itself was in most regions mainly interpreted in a more formal way (consultation of interest groups for the elaboration of public programmes dominated by public authorities).

The current planning system

The official planning system based on the Regional Development Act can be described as follows, at three levels of action: national, NUTS II and NUTS III.

National level: the Ministry of Regional Development. The Ministry of Regional Development (MRD) created at national level has the following duties. It: i) sets forward the goals of regional development and the criterion for selection of regions; ii) builds up a Regional Development Strategy, co-ordinates and ensures monitoring of regional development activities; iii) approves the regional development programmes at NUTS II and NUTS III level; and iv) establishes a Management and Co-ordination Committee (MCC) at national level.

NUTS II level: the cohesion regions. The eight "cohesion regions" (at NUTS II level) have a regional council, securing the implementation of programmes and responsible for effective usage of such means. The council collects data and ensures evaluation system. In the five cohesion regions with more than one NUTS III region, the council is elected by the boards of representatives of the NUTS III regions. In cohesion regions coinciding with one NUTS III region, the function of the council shall be fulfilled by the boards of representatives of the NUTS III region under transferred authority.

The council of the cohesion region has competence for: i) the pre-accession programmes and structural funds (the council is the managing authority); ii) establishing the regional development committee, the selection commissions and the executive section; and iii) proposing to the Ministry a deputy to the MCC.

The regional development committee, installed by the council of the cohesion region, monitors and evaluates the implementation of aid provided from the funds; and submits to the council proposals for solutions and further steps to be taken. Representatives of NUTS III regions, municipalities, administrative offices, entrepreneurs, trade unions, NGOs and other partners are members of the committees.

NUTS III level: a new level of representative democracy. The new regional administrations came into force on 1 January 2001, soon after the first regional elections took place, in November 2000. The elected assemblies of the new self-governing regions (*Kraje*) support regional development in co-operation with other authorities at central and local level (ministries, district offices, municipalities). They design regional development programmes, to be submitted first to the council of the cohesion region. Act 129/2000 concerning the regions summarises the competencies of the regions. Regions are allowed to:

● present proposals to the national parliament;

● approve spatial planning plans;

● co-ordinate educational, social and health-care services;

● administer roads (second and third class) and traffic policies; and

● design policies in the field of environment.

Regional controversies

The new regions are the result of a fierce political debate. We summarised above the main driving forces and official motives for setting up the regions. Major objections were also made, by fear of increased bureaucracy and of a new dualism between the two historical lands (Bohemia and Moravia).

Both concepts of "region" and "land" are present in Czech academic literature: "while lands (Bohemia, Moravia with Silesia) ceased formally to exist in 1949, they partly survive as cultural entities and also in the memory of parts of the population. Moreover, there is pressure to re-introduce them as political and administrative entities" (Illner, 1995). Davey notes that particular regions in the Czech Republic have aspirations for a quasi-federal status, "a product both of historical identities and of the proximity of the German model" (Davey, 1996).

The number and scale of the 14 regions reflect a political compromise. "There is some doubt for some regions, but in general we can say that the NUTS III regions coincide with the *natural* scale of the city centres dominating the regions" (Brizova and Maryska, 2000). Not all the people interviewed in this study subscribe to this view. And the reverse question remains open: can the new political elite create a new regional identity and social capital? Is the scale suited for effective public policies and to build up administrative capacity?

The public interest for the first regional elections was low (32.2% of the electorate), raising the issue of the compatibility of scale and regional identity: "one of the most important obstacles towards regional planning is the lack of sympathy and interest of the people and the non-existing regional identity of citizens" (*ibid.*). Citizens, however have to be convinced by products and outputs. So it is far too early to conclude that there is a lack of belief in the region.[3]

The creation of the cohesion regions was made necessary due to the fact that NUTS III regions were considered too small for the efficient implementation of European programmes. The creation is also considered by some as a tool for central ministries to maintain regional influence. NUTS II regions are sometimes viewed as bargaining platforms between the regional politicians and the central ministries.

The "third sector": a new major player

The history of non-profit activity goes back to the Middle Ages and for centuries was closely connected with the Catholic Church. The Church lost much of its power (18th century) and non-profit activity became secular. The main impulse for development came with the National Revival (19th century), culminating in the establishment of an independent state (1918) and the "Golden Age" of civil-society associations before the Second World War (Fric *et al.*, 2000).

The communist take-over in 1948 severely limited independent activity. All legal organisations were federated in the National Front and in the Communist Party at different levels. Trade unions and professional associations received generous state subsidies in return for strict control by the Party. A wide range of organisations in the area of culture, sport, hobbies got support. Critical organisations were oppressed and there were no independent organisations.

After 1989 the number of NGOs exploded (44 378 organisations with approximately 6 660 000 members in 1995) (*ibid.*). New non-profit organisations play a more independent role and some of them also function as a civic opposition to the party-political system. Today, NGOs cover a wide range of organisations, from very specialised ones (conservation of monuments, professional training) to organisations with a wide scope and a more general goal (related to the development of a region or the civil society), from the traditional neo-corporatist organisations to organisations working in the alternative cultural spheres.

NGOs and legitimacy

Politicians in the Czech Republic often prefer to keep their distance from the NGO world. Research suggests a number of arguments for this:

- Old and new organisations work in the same sector with different modes of operations, different perceptions of their role in society. Sometimes the relation resembles the Cold War atmosphere, as battles are waged for resources and influence within the sector.
- There was a lack of professionalism and there were a number of abuses. NGOs only recently started to set up a system of self-regulation (code of

ethics, separation of administration and governance of the NGO). Up to very recently, less than half NGOs had a board of directors.

● There used to be no effective umbrella organisations at the different levels of administration, so there was no legitimate representation. But "in the last two or three years there has been a process of integration. As a result there are now several effective umbrella organisations for example in the areas of culture, the environment and social services as well as seven community coalitions throughout the country" (ibid.). Old organisations are not engaged in those new co-ordination structures and they maintain their traditional networking activities.

In recent years, the following steps can be seen as positive: a national structure of NGOs, a structured form of representation at regional level (with regular conferences) and representation of (some) NGOs in the regional development institutions. These new modes of organisation however are restricted to the new NGOs.

Policy for NGOs

The European influence and its partnership concept (projects designed in partnership are generally privileged with regard to financial support from EU institutions) combined with the creation of the Ministry for Regional Development have increased the official attention on NGOs. The participation of NGOs in regional and sectoral plans is now made obligatory.

One per cent of the revenues from the operation of privatisation must be attributed to NGOs. But for years NGOs have been neglected by government policy. "While the commercial and public sectors have enjoyed considerable attention and significant financial support from all sectors of society during the transformation process, the non-profit sector has been given little consideration and its development has been severely under-financed" (ibid.). This situation has gradually improved during the past few years, with new legislation and more financial support. The situation is better for those NGOs active in "visible" sectors to the public, such as environmental protection or conservation. To some extent, those NGOs are executing public functions and work in a quasi-contractual relation with government.

Approximately 55% to 60% of financial support for NGOs come from the State. "State funding for NGOs has remained essentially unchanged since communist times. It is a very centralised system with less than one sixth of funds allocated via regional and local bodies. Funding sometimes depends on the size of membership and on the discretion of individual public officials. Payments are made on an annual basis and delays are frequent. Sports and recreational organisations obtain the lion's share of support (there is no distinction between organisations that work for the benefit of society and those that serve mainly their own members" (*ibid.*).

Local governance in practice

This section analyses more in depth the partnership experience in a representative sample of three areas of the Czech Republic: *i)* the cohesion region of North-west Bohemia (NUTS II), and more particularly its district of Most (NUTS IV) in the region of Ustí nad Labem (NUTS III), *ii)* the region of Vysocina (NUTS III) and *iii)* the micro-region of Přerov (region of Olomouc).

The case of North-west Bohemia: facing highest economic challenges

North-west Bohemia was, and still is, dominated by heavy industry. It has been severely damaged by the brown coal industry. The dramatic environmental situation was a major problem for the European Union adhesion, which provided a strong incentive to tackle those problems. In some areas, such as the district of Most, there has been a remarkable reconversion, with significant land recovery operations supported by massive state intervention (*e.g.* hippodrome, vineyards, car-racing circuit). The dominant concept of partnership in this industrial district refers to more traditional tripartite coalitions, as illustrated by the economic and social council (ESC). The industrial character, the massive problem of unemployment and the prominence of the ESC are determinant for partnership relations in the area.

Box 5.2. **Region of Ustí nad Labem: some statistics**

Population: 827 000 inhabitants (1999).

Urbanisation: 40% of inhabitants live in cities (nation-wide: 10%).

Agriculture and forestry: second lowest percentage in the country, industry and building sector are above-average, service sector living up to the nation-wide average.

Industry: dominated by brown coal.

Unemployment: 15.3%(20% in the district of Most) in 2000.

Source: Ministry of Regional Development.

In the region of North-west Bohemia (NUTS II), and more particularly in the district of Most (region of Ustí nad Labem), the concept of partnership is used for:

● The economic and social council: a network of the most important actors of the district, social partners mainly.

Map of Czech Republic

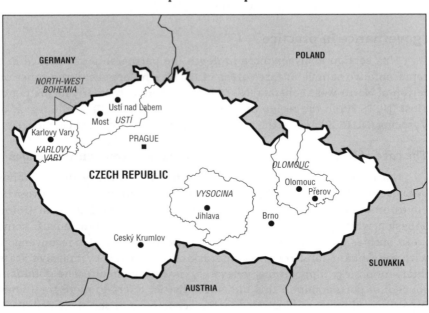

- Projects by NGOs carried out in co-operation with the district labour office.
- Local economic initiatives: the Business Centre of Litvinov (a business incubation managed by the chamber of commerce and municipality, with the support of the State).
- An educational project of the chamber of commerce, implemented in partnership by entrepreneurs, schools, the district labour office and municipalities, aiming to identify and fulfil needs for skilled labour force.
- The inter-municipal co-operation in the Ore Mountain micro-region, aiming at developing tourism activities.
- An independent private school offering tailor-made training programmes in co-operation with local private companies (run without support of public authorities).

The RMMC impact

The regional management and monitoring committee operating in North-west Bohemia no longer exists (2000), but made a useful development plan for the implementation of pre-accession funds. The ESCs' workings in the region still operate within the framework of this plan. The plan puts emphasis on public infrastructure, restructuring of industry and investment in new businesses, attracting foreign investors, new industrial estates, water-management and public health infrastructure. It is an example of a traditional development approach led by the most powerful actors: trade unions, large state-owned companies, chambers of commerce, supported by the mayors of the most important cities (such as Most).

The RMMC period has had positive effects: putting people together in a structure, stimulating the strategic planning process for the area, directing the central budgets to a set of priorities. In particular, the RMMC provided an incentive for NGOs to enter the economic arena and it stimulated their self-organisation, as NGOs organised conferences to elect their representatives in the RMMC. Thus, although the RMMC was a structure created from the "top", it activated planning processes and bottom-up initiatives.

The RMMC was abolished in 2000 and the tasks were officially taken over by the two new regional assemblies, as well as to the regional council and the regional development committee that assemblies set up. Due to the organisational weakness of the regions at their inception, the planning process was in practice taken over by the dominant network of the ESCs at district level.

The ESC: a win-win solution to prevent further loss

The economic and social councils are tripartite organisations at district level, united in the regional council at NUTS II level. In Most, the ESC is run by a staff of four people (two with an academic degree). Members of the council are: cities, companies, trade unions, State administration, chambers of commerce. The council works with several committees (e.g. education, investment, infrastructure). As one achievement, the council created a fund, sponsored by Chemopetrol and Coal Mining, both state-owned companies, which allowed the development of a number of reconversion projects. Chemopetrol is engaged in an important process of restructuring with a possible loss of 1 000 jobs for low-skilled people.

The chairman of the ESC of the district of Most is senator Falbr, a central figure in the tripartite networks and at the central political level. His role cannot be underestimated. This resembles a classic phenomenon: much depends on one or two key figures who make use of their networks to help the local agenda to make progress.

ESC and RDA: working apart together

There are three regional development agencies in North-west Bohemia: in Karlovy Vary, Most and in the city of Ustí nad Labem. The RDA of Most has a total capacity of 18 persons. The RDA played an important role in the preparation of the European programmes: the RMMC was the programming committee but the RDA did the preparatory work. The relation between RDA and ESC seemed to be more antagonistic than co-operative. The ESC is based on a large participation of important actors and acts as a "parliament" of the district. The council activates projects, provides money, based on voluntary engagement.

The RDA is run like a company: it sells services (to municipalities, districts, companies) on a profitable base. It uses its experience with European programmes as a power resource in the relation with the ESC, less equipped to manage those programmes. Being the officially-appointed management unit of the European programmes is an important source of power and income for the RDA. All those elements explain the impression that for ESC key persons, the RDA is an "unwanted but inevitable secretary".

The envoy: a tailor-made institution for a priority region

In 2000, the central government installed the "government envoy", a new de-concentrated service of the Ministry of Regional Development, with a staff of 10 people, in North-west Bohemia, one of the two priority areas. The activities of the envoy are oriented towards infrastructure projects (roads, railroads, waterways, industrial zones, management of water systems).

The added value of the envoy is the more direct relation between the region and the central government, generating more means and better co-ordination of national policies in the region. Apart from this latter impact, the envoy has no clear impact on local governance. The envoy is mainly engaged in the large infrastructure projects. There is no evidence of any organic bottom-up partnership being assisted by the envoy, nor of involvement of representatives from civil society or private sector in the strategic orientations defined, nor of any relation with employment and social policy. The role of the envoy in relation to the regional level is an open question, also due to the recent start of the region. The agenda is, for the moment, clearly dominated by central government.

NGOs: no open relation with other actors

The NGOs often have contacts with the district labour office for projects they carry out, on creating jobs for young unemployed and unskilled people. However, subventions for social projects are degressive (after one year, they decrease by half). NGOs lack the financial capacities to compensate this reduction.

The NGOs of this area find it hard to establish constructive relationships with the labour office. The general evaluation by NGOs of the labour office is often negative: bureaucratic, rule-oriented, centralised, defensive style, poor management capacities, expensive costs for training courses (organised in Prague). The labour office picture of the NGOs is not flattering either: lack of openness of NGOs, misuse of funds, no financial responsibility, lack of management. The perception by NGOs of municipalities is also rather negative: not an open attitude towards co-operation, a "we are elected" – culture. The perception on NGOs on behalf of the mayors is similar to those between the labour office and NGOs.

In the region of Ustí nad Labem, nearly 5 400 NGOs are active and the RDA helped them create a centre to network the NGOs. While this project (a cross-border European project with a Dutch province) is a source of income for the RDA, it does not lead to comprehensive networking between RDA and NGOs. The sample of NGOs met as part of this study were not aware of this project.

Conclusion

In this area dominated by severe economic problems, the partnership concept is related to tripartite consultation, bargaining and personal networks. The will to co-operate dominates the relationship between municipalities, trade unions and entrepreneurs. The programmes and plans are inspired by a traditional economic approach mainly based on public initiative, infrastructure and inwards investment.

Under the impulse of European programmes, steps are taken toward more comprehensive strategic planning as new partners are integrated in the process. Yet more needs to be done. Only the bigger municipalities are engaged and even they lack the capacity to take a leading role.

The relation between RDA and ESC hinders the efficient combination of the potentials of both organisations. The ESC has potentials in networking and bringing together resources. The RDA has potentials in the field of planning techniques, expertise in European programmes and experience with advice for companies. Yet their governance attitude totally differs: the ESC is based on general interest and voluntary engagement, the RDA is dominated by a profit-oriented management style.

The partnership concept is weakly developed in the field of employment and social policy. There are some examples of co-operation between the public administration (labour office) and NGOs but those types of co-operation are formal and there is no open dialogue between the two partners. They need each other's resources but they co-operate "face off". It is merely a relationship based on service delivery, not on co-ordination and strategic planning.

The case of Vysocina (Jihlava) region: an open culture for strategic planning

This large region has been created somewhat artificially and renamed, from Jihalava to Vysocina. It consists of five districts, which share differences in culture and identity (some districts are parts of historic Bohemia and some of Moravia). One of the open questions is the relation with the powerful Brno NUTS III region in the common NUTS II region Vysocina. Centralisation at NUTS II level is a danger but it is also possible that this brings the partners at NUTS III level (in Vysocina) closer together.

Box 5.3. **Region of Vysocina: some statistics**

Population: 522 486 inhabitants (1998).

Economic structure: while there has been a sharp decrease in the number of farm and forestry workers, agriculture still remains the region's strongest economic sector. Food processing and leather manufacturing are other strong sectors.

Gross domestic product per capita is lower (80%) of national average and average monthly salary is the lowest among all the regions.

Unemployment: 7.5% (2001).

Source: Ministry of Regional Development.

Apart from the identity issue, many questions surround the start of the new self-government region: the financial means and the tax competencies, the relation with the district reform and with the autonomy of the municipalities for their self-government activities. One of the interviewees summarised the financial issue as follows: "regions have no money yet, districts have no money anymore, municipalities never had money." This lack of own resources forces the region to build up legitimacy by involving other actors in the design of plans and programmes.

The regional administration is very small for the moment: 80 staff members for the combination of self-government and administration. This is an extremely modest capacity for a region of approximately 500 000 people. As a comparison, the district labour office in Přerov (the third case, see below) alone works with 80 staff members. The transfer of new competencies could of course lead to a rapid increase in the number of regional officials.

During the activities of the regional co-ordination committee a strategic planning process was set up, supported by a private consultancy, prepared with 70 partners (e.g. state administration, municipalities, chambers of commerce, NGOs). This seems to have stimulated partnerships and improved co-ordination in joint efforts. The regional development plan (RDP) was seen as a focus for directing minds and activities on the regional dimension of economic development. In effect the production of the plan was a process of partnership development in itself, which has then been taken on by the regional council. Some of the key persons involved in the RCC are now active members of the political regional elite.

In Vysocina, the concept of partnership is used for:

- The preparation of a strategic plan for regional development prepared by the former RCC as guideline for the activities of the new regional authority (NUTS III).

- Concrete projects implemented in partnership derived from that strategic plan: social projects involving the district labour office, NGOs and municipalities; investment projects involving municipalities and chambers of commerce.

- Working methods developed by the new region in view of better governance: mixed committees (statutory committees of the council) with the former partners of the strategic planning process.

- Specific projects based on the engagement of NGOs for health care, youth policy, social policy for disabled people, the management of ecological zones.

A partnership for strategic development: the RCC

A partnership, the RCC, was set up in 2000 and tasked with the design of a strategic development plan for the region. It agreed on four strategic objectives: i) improving the competitiveness of the regional economy, ii) developing human resources, iii) improving infrastructures (including communications and IT) and iv) fostering sustainable development. Thirteen working groups of the RCC were then created to elaborate the plan. For example, the group for human resources (mainly focused on training skills) was composed of NGOs, mayors, chambers of commerce, chamber of agriculture and individuals.

The planning project stopped in the stage of putting forward operational goals. The regional assembly, which inherited the process in 2001, is responsible for developing and implementing concrete projects along the lines agreed, and to define indicators and methods to monitor and evaluate the performances and results of the process.

NGOs: sceptical but prepared to take responsibilities

Regionalisation has had an impact on the development of NGOs in Vysocina. Because NGOs have been thoroughly involved in the regional strategic planning process, they have developed good co-operative relationships with other actors. NGOs have formed their own regional umbrella organisations. A less tripartite culture than in Most and a greater socio-economic diversity may have contributed to this.

The district reform affects the immediate financial needs of NGOs: the cut of district budgets, not (yet) replaced by regional budgets, has an important influence on their planning. As a result of the present uncertainty and confusion of competencies, NGOs do not know where to apply for funding.

The NGOs see positively the relationship being established with the new regional authority. However, they are concerned that regional politicians still do not understand the essence of a dynamic civil society. They are preoccupied with the fact that the partnership concept might be used in establishing legitimacy for the regional level. The NGOs seems to have more intimate relations with the municipalities, although the same "we are elected" – culture is present at this level.

Another problem lies within the representation of NGOs. Despite the fact that they set up umbrella organisations, it remains a challenge to unite all NGOs. Of the 1 300 NGOs operating in the region, only 70 have participated in a conference organised to elect NGO representatives to participate in the strategic planning process.

The RDA: standing on the sidelines

As in the district of Most, the RDA in the district of Jihlava supports the development of projects on a commercial basis, similar to private consultants. However, it lacks the experience of the RDA in Most with implementation of European funding, due to the different characteristics of the region (less industrial restructuring). This has an important impact on the role of the RDA in the region. Its relationship with other partners is less antagonistic in Jihlava than in Most, but the RDA is also less involved in the design and implementation of the regional development strategy.

The district labour office

The director of the district labour office in this area illustrates the impact of personality on the quality of networking. He is the prototype of the pro-active manager engaged in close networking with NGOs. This confirms that dynamic leaders can, to some extent, compensate for weaknesses in governance frameworks. Formal centralised or decentralised characteristics of the administration are always moulded by characteristics of the civil servants involved.

Conclusion

The creation of the new region is met in Vysocina by enthusiasm, as shown by a new generation new politicians and public servants, some of them formerly active in NGOs or in the RCC.

The strategic planning process initiated by the RCC in Vysocina was of a rather classic type. Yet partnership is not only about planning methods. It is also about trust and confidence, it brings people together, eager to support the construction of a renewed civil society. This is the "public spirit" that could lead the region to create a new atmosphere, bringing democracy closer to the public.

The follow-up of the strategic process, led by the new regional government, represents an ambitious attempt to achieve this connection as it tries to combines representative with participatory democracy, decentralisation with partnership. The new regions are elected but, since they have no taxing power yet and properly speaking no budget, to achieve anything they must establish effective communication channels below (to the local level) and above (the national level), and the strategic planning they conduct must involve all relevant actors. The present weaknesses of the region could be the strong points of this new level: building up platforms in society, breaking up the government style into a new governance culture.

The case of a micro-region: Přerov

Přerov (region of Olomouc, in central Moravia) is an industrial city, dominated mostly by the pharmaceutical and chemicals industries. In addition to these sectors, the region has some significant economic potential in business tourism. It also faces some problems, particularly the decline of agriculture. The Přerov case is situated at a micro-regional level: it concerns both the city and district of Přerov.

Box 5.4. Přerov, city and micro-region: some statistics

Population of the Přerov micro-region: 137 500 inhabitants (2000).

Agricultural lands: 68% of the territory.

Negative migration ratio, unfavourable age structure.

Economic sectors: Industry: 32.5% of employers, agriculture: 8.2%; trade: 13.2%; transport and telecommunication: 10.1% (2000).

Unemployment: 14.4% in 2001 (10% in 1997).

Source: Ministry of Regional Development.

The city administration is on its way to modernisation: a more professional communication culture, a more open functioning of commissions, the design of a strategic plan for the city, putting forward ten key priorities dominated by infrastructure issues: development of industrial estates, transport, logistic centre, road infrastructure, housing availability, city promotion, training facilities, development of the educational system, water supply, leisure supply. Hence, the strategic process is dominated by the priorities of the municipality. In this context, partnership is for an important part devoted to public-public co-operation, rather than with enterprises, NGOs and voluntary associations.

In Přerov, the concept of partnership is used for:

- A more open culture of the municipal government (more information, consultation of citizens in an urban civic commission, apparent openness for suggestions).
- Involvement of actors in the elaboration of a strategic plan led by municipal authorities.
- Public-public partnership (involving state departments, district offices and municipalities).
- Improving dialogue between public authorities and NGOs at district level.

A partnership led by NGOs

NGOs took the initiative to create a socio-economic platform in the district of Přerov. Official members are: the city of Přerov, the district labour office, NGOs, chambers of agriculture and commerce. The main goals are to improve communication and co-operation, and promoting the interests of the district. The organisation is based on voluntary engagement. In practice it depends mainly on the input of the main NGO figures. The organisation has no staff of its own and has no implementation competencies.

Four cities quit the partnership recently. The engagement of the city of Přerov has become crucial but its goal is unclear: there is some mistrust and scepticism. The dominance of NGOs, the lack of implementation capacity and the strategic ambitions and programmes of the city itself seem to be the main reasons for this. The district partnership is not focused and there are no clear goals.

The role of the district labour office

One important participant is the district labour office, which in this region seems to have the real potential to play a major role in the partnership. Eighty staff members work for the labour office, 12 of them on the implementation of active labour market policy. The office benefits from a significant degree of autonomy from the central level, with which it negotiates quantitative targets. It then uses the budget allocated in a relatively free way. The municipalities play a marginal role in the implementation of labour market policy. However, the labour office searches for potential partners to help it implement policy in the best possible way. The service has the capacity, the financial means and the formal legitimacy to do so.

Conclusion

The case demonstrated the potential of local government to strengthen communication with citizens. A strong local government does not automatically lead to better partnerships. The government puts forward its priorities and looks for partners to participate in the implementation of those projects. It is also quite understandable that the most important partners in this stage are other public authorities, which often pursue similar policy objectives.

The district case illustrates that partnership needs to build up confidence and trust. The ambition of NGOs and sometimes their negative attitude towards public initiative undermines the willingness of public authorities to participate in partnerships. The framework of the partnerships should enable and even support public authorities to achieve their policy objectives so that their engagement opens up possibilities for more local co-operation. This mutual respect is a basic condition for effective partnerships (as shown in OECD, 2001) and the Přerov case illustrates some problems on this point. It was difficult to make a judgement on whether or not the fact that a NGO takes the lead is accepted in the present situation. It could explain some resistance from the municipal administration.

Perspectives for partnerships and local governance

Partnerships: what is in the name?

Many people in the Czech Republic see a partnership as any new co-operative relationship: formal consultation of citizens, dialogues engaging social partners in tripartite organisations, projects of NGOs using public funds, improvement of intergovernmental co-operation. The concept of partnership covers all these ways of working.

Although there is a difference between a local government opening up its communication to citizens, two public administrations working closer together and the co-operation of public and private actors in a re-training project, all these represent attempts to improve governance. In promoting participation and co-operation and bringing together tools of public administration, civil society and private actors, partnership is a tool to improve governance.

Of course improvements in governance can be marginal when consultation is purely formal, when co-operation is led only by personal networks or when partnership is dominated by one partner, potentially leading to biased priorities, as the first phase of the OECD Study on Local Partnerships clearly showed (OECD, 2001). All these cases have been observed in the Czech Republic, where partnerships are still at an early stage of implementation. Partnership in the Czech Republic also often refers to mere contracting relationships between public services and NGOs for the provision of specific services, with unclear consequences for the quality of governance since in these cases decision-making and strategic planning remain fully in the hands of public authorities.

The concept of partnerships that emerge from the cases refers to the specific "co-operative networks of autonomous organisations" based on a process of negotiating and bargaining, building up a common interest, focused on specific operational goals and implementation of projects based on the input of resources of the different partners.

Politics and partnerships: first things first?

The political and administrative restructuring of the country is a determinant for the development of partnerships. It opens up new opportunities to improve governance (self-governing regions, better local government, new regional planning system) but it also contains factors of uncertainty (abolition of districts and the "administrative war", reduction of financial means for NGOs, ambiguous relation between NUTS II en NUTS III regional levels).

From our perspective, the following priorities should be of major political concern in order to create the stability that is necessary for improving governance through partnerships:

- A firm political statement on: decentralisation and core business of each administrative level, decentralised fiscal responsibility, improving intergovernmental joint implementation, a legal framework for partnerships.

- A middle-term perspective for the legal competencies of the new regions: decentralisation of planning and development competencies for regional economic employment, SME, spatial planning, education (life-long learning, professional skills, training of unemployed).

- A policy for local government: a framework for modernisation, a fiscal system based on incentives to stimulate co-operation (or amalgamations), reinforcement of the leading role of cities.

- An elaborated policy towards NGOs (see further on).

The search for the legitimacy of politics may hamper real partnerships. There is a tendency to over-stress the primacy of politics and a reluctance to relinquish political control and responsibility. Many examples of partnership have the official features of partnership, however further investigation reveal that control is very much in the hands of the political authority with very little co-ordination over priority-setting and sharing of responsibility. There is no simple advice to solve this problem: changes of public culture need time. But incentives to modernise government and a policy of decentralisation can reinforce those cultural changes.

Partnerships have specific aims and objectives and a lifespan to achieve them. They have their pragmatic logic: why set up a partnership, what is the partnership going to do, how long will it take, what is needed to manage partnerships, how communication will be organised, how are results evaluated, what are the goals on short and middle term? This "management agenda" is, in the cases examined, marginalised by the political agenda.

The NGOs: a complex world

The NGO concept covers a broad range of organisations. This notion creates unity of purpose where very little exists. There are community organisations, voluntary organisations, enterprises pursuing social goals, semi-commercial organisations, organisations with a very localised sphere of action, organisations with national ambitions. All those types of organisations have different expectations from partnership. The use made in the Czech Republic of the general concept of NGO to represent this array of organisations covers up realities and hampers clear discussions. It neglects the wide variety of types and relations with public administration. Being more specific, linking types of organisations to specific types of partnerships, can foster the search for more tailor-made techniques and strategies. Big organisations formerly supported by the communist regime still receive important subsidies and defend their position while new organisations try to get official support for their work.

In western countries, NGOs often have close relationships with the public sector due to a long history of private initiative and of public involvement of private organisations. Those NGOs do not belong directly to the public administration but they sometimes fulfil public tasks and are subsidised and controlled by the public administration. NGOs also often participate in strategic planning exercises and collective decision-making in their fields of action. Those relations are supported by close networks dominated by a culture of trust and confidence that offers the basic conditions to handle conflicts, the interdependencies and the respective roles.

In the Czech Republic, the involvement of NGOs in partnerships is merely about informing and consultation, with some exceptions in the field of social and employment policy, where they participate in implementation on a contractual or subsidised basis. The involvement of NGOs is not always welcomed by other partners. NGOs represent their own views and not those of the people they serve, and some of them are politicised. More generally there is a general mistrust towards "going public", either in politics or in NGOs.

Mutual mistrust reflects the battle of subsidies, positions and official recognition, typical for elitist conflicts. The representatives of NGOs and the public administration have in fact a common problem: changing the attitude of citizens, building up a public forum and debate, encouraging people to rebuild a new belief in politics and public involvement.

The process of regionalisation clearly offers new opportunities for NGOs: the regions are a new platform for dialogue and for public debate. Thus, regionalisation is a strategic opportunity to support the involvement of citizens and NGOs.

To make further progress government policies on NGOs should:

- Provide general frameworks in central and regional legislation making it possible to integrate NGOs in public policies (following the example of environmental policies).

- Encourage self-regulation and public evaluation by legislation. (Evaluation mechanisms currently being developed by the Ministry of Labour and Social Affairs in close co-operation with NGOs may provide a good model for similar efforts elsewhere).

- Decentralise funds to the regions and encourage regions, including through financial means, to establish dialogue with NGOs.

One of the consequences of this is that the appointment of the representatives of NGOs (elected by the NGOs themselves) in regional development structures should be the responsibility of the regions. The regions should ensure that NGOs are well-represented in their own strategic planning exercises and commissions.

The attempts to organise the NGOs in regional and national conferences can be useful to support a more transparent national and regional policy and system of subsidies. Policy of subsidies should be based on a more ring-fenced system targeting different types of organisations and supported by different umbrella organisations to assist the sectors of the complex NGO world.

We did not find examples of significant resources being directed toward capacity building and community development. If NGOs are to be directly involved in strategic planning and service delivery, this should be the absolute priority of regions and municipalities. Regions and municipalities should encourage citizens to voice their concerns and propose initiatives, even if this means that citizens become more critical to the way regions and municipalities function. That civic attitude is the cornerstone and driving force of partnerships.

The impact of the Europe Union and regional planning

RMMCs and RCCs were active before the directly elected regional government was installed (2001). They involved public administrations, politicians and civil society. Although this representation was mainly formal and the establishment of those institutions was a "top-down" initiative, this has been one of the main drivers for partnerships on the level of the planning system. In the Vysocina region, for example, a process of strategic planning was set up integrating a range of organisations on different policy fields. People taking responsibilities in that process entered the new political level as public officials or politicians. Among the impacts of this process are a greater cohesion among regional actors, increasing pressure for bottom-up policies, better co-ordination and more consultations of civil society. This example illustrates that bringing together different actors (even in formal and top-down structures) can improve governance.

The European pre-adhesion funds, mainly for infrastructure and led by public-public co-operation have played a central role in these developments. They have contributed to the improvement of the intergovernmental relations and to establishing the strategic planning framework. However, the effect of these programmes on wider partnerships involving NGOs, private and public sector in projects seems rather marginal.

Overall, a new type of administrative culture is fighting its way through bureaucratic traditions. Progress has been made since an earlier evaluation carried out in 1999, referring to a lack of co-ordination, a lack of a proper system of financial management, a lack of a suitable system for co-financing the EU programmes, a lack of qualified people and lack of high-quality projects (Blazek, 1999). There are now frameworks for consultation and planning. The learning process has just started, and the various actors still have to learn their roles and how to co-operate. There is an obvious lack of capacity, maybe in terms of personnel, but surely of financial means. However, the entry of a new elite supports the modernisation. The creation of regions is important in that perspective. It can speed up the modernisation process.

The creation of a planning structure through legislation and administrative organisations (e.g. the Ministry of Regional Development, cohesion regions, regional development programmes) offers some stability and a common referential framework; it provides opportunities to re-organise the system. Every country has to build up its own capacity to evaluate the former system and introduce a new generation of regional planning systems. The Czech Republic has yet to build up its capacity to evaluate the first generation of regional planning and to prepare the following one.

The role of regional development agencies

Most regional development agencies in other countries are part of the interactive development discussion. In many countries partnerships evolve in and through the structure of the RDAs. In the Czech Republic the RDAs are dominated by a market-oriented attitude: it is our conviction that this, for the moment and in this period, is not the best choice. This is a choice more suited to a situation with a well-established culture of partnership and a satisfactory level of economic development.

There is an apparent lack of expertise in local development and partnership in the Czech public administration, at both regional and local level. The RDAs have a potential know-how that could more directly benefit regions in need. A RDA network of specialists could well provide the support needed in the design and implementation of projects in partnership. However, their commercial attitude hinders an efficient use of their expertise by municipalities and regions. It surely hinders partnerships because partnership demands some public energy and financial investment, especially in the stages of creation and development. Looking to other actors from an exclusive commercial viewpoint means in fact neglecting the real needs of new partnerships involving a broader range of actors. Sometimes the initial cost is wasted, sometimes the investment leads to success, rarely however to quick commercial profits. That is a risk that cannot be avoided. To become a real partner for local and regional development, the RDAs should integrate in their mission the priorities established by partnerships involving the public and private sector as well as the civil society. This would be in line with the OECD "strategy to improve governance through partnerships", which recommends to make the objectives of the main partners consistent with the goals assigned to partnerships (OECD, 2001). This may mean that RDAs should themselves become broader partnership organisations, involving all these actors.

The regions and the reform of public administration

The general situation of the new regions can best be described as unstable and unclear: a lot of uncertainty, a lack of basic legal instruments, the search for a balance with local self-government especially in the relation with the leaders of the bigger cities. We mentioned that the regional battle (between districts, municipalities, ministries and regions) could harm the effectiveness of public administration. The actual capacity of the regions (financial resources and personnel), compared with regional structures in the western countries, is extremely modest.

But there is more than doubt and scepticism. We also encountered enthusiasm: people with a great belief that the region could make the difference. Some regional elite officials were active in the regional planning processes and try to continue that spirit in the new political structures. The region is organising the public debate about the priorities for the area. Other actors are adapting their structure to the regional scale: chambers of commerce, trade unions but also NGOs.

So regions can change the communication channels and have influence on the structure of social and political networks. Regions, as we stated earlier, are the result of societal changes but they, in turn, can also influence society. Overall, the creation of the new regional political level enhances the potentials for good governance.

A more responsive employment policy

The district labour offices are accountable to the Ministry of Labour. The tension between centralisation and decentralisation is present and can be a problem (for example, in the case of a central-oriented attitude of the district director), but can also create new opportunities for partnerships (due to relative autonomy on the use of financial means). Overall, the organisation of the employment service at district level appears positive to partnership development: there are substantial financial and personnel means; effectiveness and local appropriateness are central priorities; there is a formal consultation structure with public and private (potential) partners.

Moreover, the Czech labour administration provides a high degree of combination between employment services and social policy. Clients are served by the same public service. While problems in the application of the combination of social help and employment actions occur (e.g. reduction of the social benefits after one year), many of them can be solved by adaptation at district level of the central regulation and budgets.

On a second level of analysis, much depends on the quality of the district officer and the public officials responsible for employment policy. That observation means that the degree of partnership-oriented attitude could be part of the assessment qualities of new directors. The current system of monitoring and evaluation encourages the district officials to achieve projects, for instance in terms of meeting the targets set. Improvements in the degree of adaptation of employment policies to local needs, and of co-operation with other partners, could also be the subject of performance evaluation frameworks. This would encourage them to be more responsive to other organisations as their personal evaluation would depend partly on the success of cross-cutting activities. These characteristics of evaluation (in terms of governance outcomes), would be positive to good governance and help make partnerships more effective, as recommended by the OECD Study (OECD, 2001).

This prospect brings on two crucial points: a need for a more strategic approach of employment policy at regional level, but also the need for the maintenance of an efficient implementation service. The first element could indeed be a point of criticism derived from the cases: the approach of the employment services in the cases surveyed was mainly implementation-oriented, i.e. following national targets and setting up programmes for target groups. A regional strategic or middle-term approach is often missing. Nevertheless, pursuing a strategic approach always needs concrete input and experience from the field: thus, even if regions become responsible for employment policy planning, there should be a close link with the implementation level (labour offices).

Creating those links seems to us a good example of the most promising way of constructing partnerships in the Czech Republic, combining the tools and core business of each public actor, together with the expertise of private and community partners, and thus improving governance of the Czech society.

Notes

1. There are three major national programmes in the Czech Republic: a guarantee programme, a credit programme and a small-loan programme. These schemes are complemented by a number of smaller programmes to assist firms on business plans, marketing, co-operation, consulting and design. Information on these programmes can be found in OECD (2002).

2. There were three instruments assisting the applicant countries until they joined the EU: PHARE: consolidation of institutions, participation in EU programmes, regional and social development, industrial restructuring and development of the small-business sector; ISPA (Instrument for Structural Policies for Pre-Accession): development of transport and environmental infrastructure; SAPARD (Special Accession Programme for Agriculture and Rural Development): modernisation of agriculture and rural development.

3. The Czech parliament rejected a recent proposal (2002) to reshape territorial units according to the wishes of some municipalities to shift from one region to another, such as those in the Moravska Trebova-Jevicko micro-region (OECD, 2002).

Bibliography

Blazek, J. (2000), "Systems of Czech Local Government Finances as a Framework for Local Development", draft research paper, Department of Social Geography and Regional Development, Faculty of Science, Charles University, Prague, Czech Republic.

Blazek, J. (1999), "Local and Regional Development and Policy in the Czech Republic in the 1990s", in: Hudak, V., H. Huitfeldt, E. Meegan (eds), Regional Policy Goes East, The East-West Institute, Prague, Czech Republic.

Brizova, M. and Maryska, I. (2000), "Dezentralisiering in der Tschechischen Republik – neuere Entwicklungen", draft research paper.

Davey, K. (1996), "The Czech and Slovak Republics" in: *Local Government in Eastern Europe*, MacMillan: London, United Kingdom.

Fric, P. *et al.* (2000), "A Proposed Strategy for the Czech Third Sector", paper presented at the Donors Forum, June 2000, Prague, Czech Republic.

Government of the Czech Republic (2001a), "Consequences of Public Administration Reform for Self-Governing Territorial Units and District Authorities", informal note by the Ministry of Regional Development, Prague, Czech Republic.

Government of the Czech Republic (2001b), "Common Provisions of the Statutes of Regional Councils of Cohesion Regions", Prague, Czech Republic.

Government of the Czech Republic (2000a), "Regional Development Strategy of the Czech Republic", General Document, Ministry of Regional Development, Prague, Czech Republic.

Government of the Czech Republic (2000b), "Local Government Authorities in the Czech Republic", Ministry of Interior, Prague, Czech Republic.

Government of the Czech Republic (2000c), "Act no 548/2000 on Support to Regional Development", Prague, Czech Republic.

Hull, C. and Hjern, (1982), B. "Helping Small Firms Grow: an Implementation Analysis of Small Firm Assistance Structures", in *European Journal of Political Research*, No. 10, Amsterdam, The Netherlands.

Illner, M. (1995), "Regional Structures and Post-communist Transformation: the Case of the Czech Republic", in: Faltan, L. (ed.), *Regions and Self-government European Integration*, Institute of Sociology, Bratislava, Slovakia.

OECD (2002), "Review on the Development of Rural Regions, Local Development Issues, Regional and National Policy Making: Moravska Trebova-Jevicko Micro-region Territorial Review", Official document, DT/TDPC/RUR(2002)9, Paris.

OECD (2001), *Local Partnerships for Better Governance*, OECD, Paris.

OECD (1998), *Fostering Entrepreneurship*, OECD, Paris.

ISBN 92-64-01530-2
New Forms of Governance for Economic Development
© OECD 2004

Chapter 6

Slovenia: Building Regional Capacities for Economic Development

by

Murray Stewart,
University of the West of England, Bristol

More than a decade after its breakaway from Yugoslavia and the transition to a market economy, Slovenia enjoys strong economic conditions and a healthy democracy, and has now a free access to the European Union market. Authorities are concerned that further economic development should remain sustainable and benefit all regions, and hope that business and civil society will take part in joined strategic planning exercises. Yet regional infrastructures are fragmented. More efforts are needed to build regional capacity and find the appropriate mechanisms of co-ordination, adaptation and participation.

Introduction

Much attention has been given in recent years to the role of partnerships in addressing the complex problems confronting local governance (OECD 2001).* The second phase of the OECD Study on Local Partnerships has sought to focus on local governance in practice, with a particular emphasis on the need to assist in the development of effective interorganisational working, to improve local capacities, and to inform national and European governments about the potential for exploiting cross-sectoral partnership working to achieve both competitiveness and cohesion. Across Europe one of the most important challenges to building effective partnerships for local economic development lies in resolving the dilemmas of scale. On the one hand greater efficiency is often achieved by generating economies of scale allowing local economies to become more competitive in a global environment. On the other hand an effective economy can also be dependent on the exploitation of local strengths and a locally-driven response to economic circumstances and needs. These dilemmas of scale are often reflected in debates about geography and space. What is the most appropriate spatial scale at which to undertake which particular economic activities? In many countries this resolves itself into a debate about regionalism. Is there an appropriate, or even necessary, level between state and municipality at which local economic development can be supported?

In Slovenia, as in many other countries, the region provides an important focus both for its immediate role in supporting Slovenian accession to the European Union and for its potential contribution to long-term sustainable growth. There are general lessons to be learned even if the differing age and maturity of the institutions of regionalism, together with their specific application to the geography and history of Slovenia, make comparison with other countries hard.

Following this introduction, this chapter falls into three parts. First the Slovenian governance context will be presented through a brief outline of some of the issues confronting Slovenia as it entered the European Union, a cameo presentation of the socio-economic circumstances of the country and a description of the existing structures for local and regional development. A

---

* The author wishes to thank Brian Morgan, Cardiff Business School, for his contribution to this chapter.

second section will describe some of the local economic development activities in three different parts of the country and make some empirical observations of the Slovenian local economy and its programmes of support for business and employment. The third section will analyse these results and address some key issues for the future of regional economic development capacity, including the role and function of the region and the practice of partnership working. This will be followed by a conclusion.

Central to the whole discussion are the challenges to regional economic development in Slovenia of a new governance of multi-sector collaboration, networking and partnership. Accession has posed a number of challenges, but this chapter highlights two in particular, first the need to develop intermediate regional structures and capacity between the state and the (very small) municipalities, and secondly the need to enhance partnership working and to develop structures which engage public, private, voluntary and community sectors.

The Slovenian governance context

The accession to the European Union

The accession of Slovenia to membership of the European Union has been a dominant feature of economic and administrative life over recent years. Accession provides a further impetus to the processes of modernisation which have characterised economic management, but which, within a larger economic community, add political and economic obligations wider than those which have hitherto been experienced by many Slovenian institutions. It is not that Slovenia lags behind the social and economic standards of the rest of the Union. Indeed Slovenia is economically the most advanced of the 2004 accession countries (see Table 6.1 below), and with a 2002 GDP running at 69% of the EU (15) average exceeded Greece, and almost equated with Portugal.

Table 6.1. **GDP, international comparison, 2002**

	GDP	
	Bn EUR	Volume per head EU-15 = 100
Slovenia	23	69
Czech Republic	78	62
Hungary	69	53
Poland	202	41
EU-25	9 613	91
EU-15	9 169	100

Source: EUROSTAT, News release, 36/2004, 11 March 2004.

Accession brings challenges, however, and for Slovenia these are reflected in decisions about how best to conform to EU requirements for the use of structural funds but at the same time to make the most effective use of what is likely to be once and for all support. Whilst it is not possible to predict accurately either the future form and levels of cross-national support nor the eligibility of different countries or regions for that support, it is reasonable to suppose that Slovenia may cease to be eligible for the widest (*e.g.* Objective 1) support in the medium term.

In addressing these challenges, although facing many of the same obstacles as other accession countries, Slovenia presents a distinct, perhaps unique, picture. The country is relatively small geographically (20 000 km^2) and in terms of population (just under 2 million). The density of population varies widely between the central Ljubljana region and the remainder of the country where, with only a few exceptions, urbanisation is less advanced and population more sparsely distributed. Despite the relatively small size of the country there is considerable regional diversity. The European NUTS 2 classification of regions makes a distinction only between the capital (Ljubljana) region and the rest of the country, but from beyond the country there are often seen to be five differing regions of the country – a central capital region surrounding the capital Ljubljana together with four other major areas each bordering on other countries – a northern Alpine region (with Austria and Italy as neighbours), a western Adriatic region (with Italy and Croatia as neighbours), an eastern region (with Austria, Hungary and Croatia as neighbours), and a southern region (again bordering Croatia). Whilst such broad regions should not be confused with the twelve statistical regions which are discussed later in this chapter, they capture some of the characteristics of a country land-bounded on all sides except for one small Adriatic coastal strip. Slovenia has lain at the borders of the European Union and the Balkan states, but with its economic focus shifting ever northwards as trade and commerce with the European Union has grown. The shift from dependency on Yugoslavian markets, has led, through economic restructuring, towards a stronger relationship with Europe (especially Germany and Austria).

Substantial foreign investment inflows have occurred since the mid 1990s in the wake of the privatisation programme, with direct investment totaling EUR 3.85 billion at the end of 2002. Initially merger and acquisition activities drew foreign investors to take an equity share with Slovenian partners. In addition, there were the sales by the Development Fund of troubled local companies to foreign investors. More recent investments in the manufacturing sector have included Goodyear, and in the area of financial services, the Bank of Austria and Creditanstalt have been the most important players.

Independent since 1991 following the break-up of Yugoslavia, Slovenia has not only achieved economic success but also recreated, indeed reinforced, an autonomous national identity built on a natural and cultural heritage and history. It faced accession with some optimism, but entry into the European Union poses a number of problems. On the one hand there is a threat of excess bureaucratisation as the country faces a battery of EU processes and procedures, the possible introduction of a regional tier of administration, and the demands of complex inter-sectoral partnership working. On the other hand there are the tensions and potential imbalance between the central capital region and the more peripheral rural and mountain regions. There may also be a tension between strong economic growth which, with mobility of capital and labour, may lead to the centralisation of economic activity, and the balanced development which supports a more widely, evenly distributed, but possibly slower, rate of growth. Unlike some accession countries, however, the relative strength of the Slovenian economy and its institutions allows at least some discussion of redistribution as well as of growth and efficiency.

Some key socio-economic characteristics

The population of Slovenia, numbering almost two million, is ethnically homogeneous with 83% Slovenian, and small numbers of ethnic Hungarians, Italians, and Roma. 6.5% of the population settled from other parts of the former Yugoslavia. The ethnic affiliation of the remaining 10% is unknown. The key characteristics of this population in economic terms are an increasing life expectancy, a declining birth rate, and the consequent ageing of population structure. The proportion of the population aged 65 and over is increasing (from 14.5% in 2002 to an expected 15.4% in 2005), whilst the proportion of those aged 0-14 is falling (15.4% to 14.8%). Old age dependency is also increasing with the consequence of a reduction in the proportion of the population able to work, which is expected to fall after 2005. This will have implications for the size and structure of the workforce, but also for health care, social protection and social services which will inevitable make heavier demands on resources.

Demographic trends vary across the country. Life expectancy at birth is shorter in the eastern regions than in the western to the extent of 2.7 years less life expectancy for men and half a year for women. Mortality rates are also high with the north eastern Pomurje region having the highest standardised mortality rates of the whole of Slovenia.

If population is growing only slowly, household formation remains high as the size of household decreases, from 3.0 persons per household in 1991 to 2.8 persons per household in 2002. Households often include more than one family but Slovenian household size exceeds the European average 2.4 in (1999-2001). Internal migration within Slovenia, however, has been significantly lower than in the majority of EU countries, although increasing slightly in the second half of the 1990s. In 2002 61% of those employed were employed within the municipality where they lived. Similarly 61% of the unemployed found work in the municipality where they reside, although there is daily movement for work from neighbouring municipalities into the larger urban centres. This low level of mobility is related to tradition and culture, but also to the nature of the housing market. Relatively high levels of private ownership, allied to low levels of social and not-for-profit rental housing inhibit mobility. Nevertheless there is considerable movement of younger populations and a major issue for local economic development is the retention of younger and more qualified labour within the local economy.

These demographic trends are reflected in the workforce and its structure. Although women form the majority of the overall population, activity rates are higher for men than for women with the result that the active workforce is still male dominated and there are more male jobs that female jobs. Nevertheless the numbers of unemployed are roughly equal for men and women.

Table 6.2. **Population and workforce 2003 (thousands)**

	Total	Men	Women
Total population	1 996	976	1 019
Workforce	962	523	438
Persons in employment	897	490	407
Unemployed persons	64	33	31
Inactive persons	739	301	438

Source: Statistical Office of the Republic of Slovenia, Labour Force Survey.

In terms of age the workforce, whilst dominated by those in the 24-49 age bracket also draws in significant numbers from the 15-24 and 50-64 brackets and indeed retains a small proportion of workers aged 65 years and over.

The Slovenian economy displays a number of strengths – balanced public finances, favourable corporate tax rates, a balanced structure of industry by size, a strong export base, a relatively high share of GDP invested in research and development.

The main industrial sectors are in Slovenia are automotive, electronics and electrical, ICT, metal processing, tool-making. The major service sector activity focuses on financial services and logistics – largely because of Slovenia's position as the land road and export link between Eastern Europe to EU. There are important sectoral developments through, for example, the Slovenian automotive cluster and the Slovenian transport logistics cluster.

Figure 6.1. **Structure of workforce, by age, 2001**

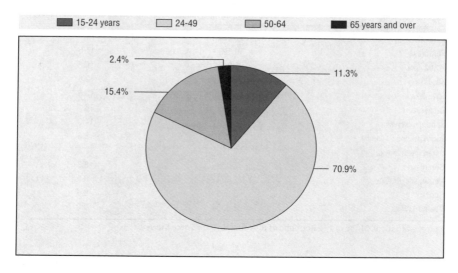

Source: Statistical Office of the Republic of Slovenia, *Rapid Reports*, No. 178.

Nevertheless Slovenia retains too high a share of economic activity in the traditional textiles, clothing and steel sectors and is argued to have a low level of technological and organisational know-how in companies and a low level of co-operation between enterprises. By and large, however, and increasingly in recent years, the economic base has responded to the availability of wider European markets and to the possibilities offered by inward investment. The major challenges revolve as much around the distribution of growth across the regions of the country as around the creation of growth itself. Unemployment varies between the more prosperous regions and those experiencing economic difficulties at a time of economic transition.

Institutional capacity for local and regional development

Since 1999 regional policy in Slovenia has aimed to promote balanced economic, social and spatial development, to reduce the impact of economic restructuring, to counter demographic change (especially in peripheral areas) and to respond to the coming demands of EU regional policies. The 1999 Law on Balanced Regional Development gave force to these aims and encouraged the development of regional capacity building through the establishment of partnership working, the creation of Regional Development Agencies and the generation of a range of development initiatives, building especially on EU supported cross-border work. This legislation allowed the 192 municipalities

Table 6.3. **Regional unemployment, 2003**

Statistical regions	Registered unemployment number	Registered unemployment rate
Slovenia	**97 674**	**11.2**
Pomurska	9 593	17.5
Podravska	22 217	16.2
Koroška	4 050	12.6
Savinjska	15 578	13.5
Zasavska	3 235	16.1
Spodnjeposavska	4 520	14.9
Jugovzhodna Slovenija	5 279	8.6
Osrednjeslovenska	17 116	7.8
Gorenjska	7 025	8.3
Notranjsko-Kraška	2 004	8.8
Goriška	3 258	6.4
Obalno-kraška	3 800	8.3

Source: Statistical Office of the Republic of Slovenia, Labour Force Survey.

to come together to form regions comparable to the EU NUTS 3 statistical regions with the aim of promoting balanced growth, diminishing structural problems, preventing negative demographic trends, and adapting to EU regional policy in terms of institution building and systems of financing. In its early years regional development in Slovenia has been established administratively as a cross-cutting government function, designed to engage all ministries in contributing to regional economic growth within principles of subsidiarity. A Ministerial Council for Structural Policy (a co-ordination body of nine ministries) establishes priorities for regional development and formally approves Regional Development Programmes. The National Agency for Regional Development (NARD), a body under a Minister without departmental portfolio within the Ministry of Economy until June 2003 and subsequently a public agency under the supervision of the Minister for Regional Development and Structural Policy, integrates the activities of the several sectoral ministries. Several ministries themselves have decentralised structures. The Ministry for Labour, Family, and Social Affairs is the most significant in relation to management of regional and local labour markets, whilst the Ministry of Economy has sponsored significant programmes for the development of entrepreneurship and the creation of small businesses. This was done through the establishment of the Small Business Support Network (SBSN) and the founding of a further network of local and regional business centres. This policy initiative has since evolved through the establishment of Regional Development Agencies (Ministry of Economy/Small Business Development Centre 2002).

The Employment Service of Slovenia operates under an Administrative Board which regulates the activities of a central office which itself manages twelve regional offices and fifty-nine local offices. The Service has the objectives of reducing unemployment and increasing employment, of facilitating the career development of individuals, of guaranteeing social security for those eligible, and for ensuring the quality of employment services throughout the country. Its activities range widely across job mediation and careers advice, the implementation of unemployment insurance legislation, employment policy measures and programmes, the issuing of work permits for foreigners, national scholarship programmes for young people, provision of labour market information, and the formulation of strategic material on the basis of monitoring and analysis of labour market trends. Central to these activities is working with the unemployed through provision of information, job placement, counselling, assertion of insurance rights, and provision of opportunities for active employment. The Employment Service has also begun to be engaged with partnership working with Chambers of Commerce and of Crafts, with Regional Development Agencies and in relation to European programmes.

Slovenia has a long tradition of local democratic government, and there are 192 municipalities across the country, the majority of which are small. Given a national population of two million the average size of municipality is 10 000 people. With a number of larger towns, however, the median size falls outside the largest cities and towns (Ljubljana, Maribor, Kranj, Novo Mesto, Celje and Koper). The smallest 50% of municipalities (with less than 5 000 residents) hold only 12.5% of the total population. Nevertheless the municipalities are a significant focus for local influence and power, with mayors ever concerned to foster the economic fortunes of their locality. The use of planning powers to prepare and release land for development and thus to attract enterprise to their area represents a major area for civic entrepreneurship, and mayors jealously guard their right to autonomous action in relation to the stimulation of economic activity. Municipalities have begun, however, to act collectively through their involvement with Business Development Centres and Regional Development Agencies, are represented on the boards of the latter, and indeed contribute to the funding in some areas. Nevertheless the creation of a regional capacity for economic development can represent a threat to the mayor, and working in partnership with the private sector and with community and voluntary associations is a way of working not yet familiar to all mayors.

Supporting the local and regional economy: evidence from the field

The diversity of Slovenia's economy, and the differing history and circumstances of different regions are illustrated by the experience of three sub-regions – South Primorska, Celje and Ptuj. These display different characteristics – of the Adriatic western seaboard, of the older industrialised centre, and of the more peripheral and still heavily agricultural and self employment based north east:

- South Primorska in the southeast, borders Croatia and Italy and provides Slovenia's only port outlet a well as offering Adriatic tourism development.
- Savinska in eastern/central Slovenia takes in the labour market regions of Celje and par of Velenje, and borders Austria to the north and Croatia to the south.
- Ptuj, further northeast than Celje, adjoins the second city of Maribor and also borders Croatia to the south.

South Primorska in the Obalno-Kraška Region

South Primorska plays an important role in the Slovenian economy. Dominated by its access to the Adriatic, and by its borders with Croatia and Italy, the coastal area (Slovenian Istria) is one of high population growth and relative prosperity. Strongly export oriented (with over a quarter of its net income from trade with foreign markets), the economy of the coastal area has an above average share of a large service sector, with economic activity dominated by trade, transport, real estate, business services and tourism. This reflects the importance of Koper as a major city, indeed Slovenia's only port city, together with the growth of tourism on the coast. Koper is a thriving logistics center and gives the region huge development possibilities in the fields of transport and distribution. It is linked to Ljubljana both by rail and the motorway, with a planned rail link to connect Koper and Trieste (less than 10 kilometres separate the two cities).

By contrast, in the rural hinterlands of Karst and Brkini the service sector is proportionately smaller, with greater reliance still on industry and agriculture. The municipality of Ilirska Bistrica (accounting for almost one third of the territory of South Primorska) lies in the central region otherwise dominated by Ljubljana, but as a border area, has been included in much of the development planning of the region.

The coastal area – the three municipalities of Koper (48 000 population), Piran (17 000) and Isola (15 000) – accounted for 80 000 of the area's total population of 118 000 in 2001, with the remaining five municipalities accounting for the remaining 38 000 (of which Sezana and Ilirska Bistrica

Map of Slovenia

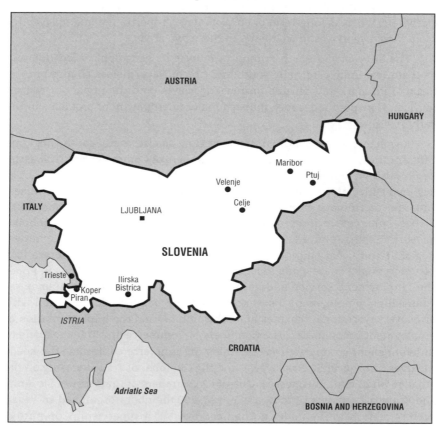

account for 12 000 and 14 000 respectively). Population grew by 11.5% 1981-2001, but this overall rate masked a decline in population in the hinterland areas and a more rapid growth in the coastal region (of 15.5% in 20 years). As elsewhere in Slovenia, there is outward migration to Ljubljana, with a loss of higher qualified and graduate people. Even so unemployment amongst highly qualified workers is high, a consequence in part of the fact that the region has a higher number of students per head of population than Slovenia as a whole.

Despite the dominance of the coastal areas, the Sezana Local Employment Office incorporating the inland Karst area, recorded the lowest unemployment rates of the region (5.8% in August 2003). Koper also experienced unemployment below the regionl average of 8.1% (itself 2.7 percentage points below the national average) but the coastal areas of Izola and Piran saw higher than average rates – even in August – the tourist season.

Ilirska Bistrica also experienced unemployment above the regional aveage. Unemployment rates for women were much lower in Izola and Piran than elsewhere, whereas long-term unemployment (proportion of unemployed for more than a year) was much higher in these two areas.

The buoyancy of South Primorska reflects its geographical location and its historical links externally south and north. Nevertheless changes in the focus of its markets from the former Yugoslavia (and the impact of war on tourism, transport and trade), induced major unemployment problems in the early 1990s.

Key actors in the South Primorska region, as elsewhere, are the Regional Office of the Employment Service, the Chambers of Commerce and Trade, the Regional Development Agency (RDA) and the municipalities. The Koper Regional Office of the Employment Service operates through six local offices. Four are coterminous with the municipalities of Koper, Piran, Izola and Ilistra Bistrica, one covers the remaining four municipalities of South Primorska based in Sejana, and a sixth based in Postojna covers two municipalities. Regional and Local Employment Offices throughout Slovenia operate to a common model but respond to local needs and circumstances. Thus in Koper the Employment Service addresses issues of job placement, employment counselling, employment insurance rights and benefits, co-operation with employers, vocational schemes and scholarships, and the implementation of employment programmes. The Chambers of Commerce and Trade respond to different client groups with the Chamber of Commerce addressing the needs of larger firms (over 50 employees), and the Chamber of Trade focusing on the smaller, often craft, businesses. One of 62 Chambers of Craft across Slovenia, the Koper Chamber of Trade has over 1 300 members organized in seven sectors and operating under a Chamber director, a supervising Committee, and an overarching elected Assembly of 29 members. Membership is compulsory for the vast majority of Slovenian businesses and the Chamber offers a number of licensing, counselling, training, information and networking services. Threatened by the possible decline of the traditional craft base of its membership, and in competition for members with the Chamber of Commerce, the Chamber of Trade nevertheless feels it has much to offer to economic growth, with the small firm base providing the foundation for expansion of activity and employment.

The municipalities also play an important role – as partners in economic initiatives, and as funders of local development agencies. The agencies of Koper (with Izola), of Piran, of Ilirska Bistrica and of Sezana (incorporating the Divaca, Komen, Sezana and Hrpelej Kozina localities) are all supported by municipalities, and together form the structure of the South Primorska Development Agency, with the mayors of the eight councils forming the Council and taking the chair annually in rotation. The Council works with a wider forty-four member Programme Committee drawn from municipalities, national ministries, employers and employees, providing guidance on the Regional Development Programme.

The region has three other business centers but the Koper one gained the status of lead organisation for the South Primorska Regional Development Agency. The RDA now performs a range of functions which include:

- Regional development tasks (managing and monitoring the Regional Development programme, supporting the establishment of a regional information centre for north and South Primorska, cross-border cooperation and international programmes, implementation of the Rural Development and Village Regeneration programme).

- Business stimulation (managing the regional Guarantee Fund, publishing a monthly newsletter for business in N. and S. Promorska), running a voucher based counseling service for business, participating in IN-PRIME, organizing seminars/conferences for business).

- Human resource development (managing the concession system for workers and students, organizing information workshops).

- Environmental protection (establishing an environmental information system, participating in MASP Mediterranean Action plan for sustainable development).

The RDA is engaged with a wide range of initiatives supporting the development of the economy across Western Slovenia. Two of these programmes are described briefly here – the IN-PRIME innovation programme of Primorska, and the Regional Development Programme of South Primorska already referred to above.

The Phare Cross-border Co-operation Programme, Slovenia/Italy has supported a range of initiatives within the fields of cultural exchange, human resources, spatial planning, tourism, and above all the establishment of regional development networking. One project emerging from this development of networks was IN-PRIME, a programme supporting innovation and technological development across the whole of western Slovenia in the three statistical regions of Goriska, Notranjsko-Kraska, and Obalno-Kraska. The programme addresses the fear that western Slovenia will continue to experience lower levels of technological capacity than its neighbouring cross-border regions (Friuli-Venezia Giulia and Austria), and might thus become a low-level production center for the needs of those strong economies. This might lead to the out-migration of qualified workers, to the weakening of educational establishments, to the disappearance of innovation, and to an inevitable cycle of lower level of growth. The eleven-year 2003-13 IN-PRIME programme supports breakthrough, a supportive environment, innovation networks, and links with international innovation programmes. Engaging a range of partners it is implemented through a Steering Committee, to which a programme manager reports, with programme working groups and sub-programme managers (such as the Koper RDA), project managers and project working groups. External experts advice, together with a programme administration, coordinates applications for funds to a range of national and international programmes.

Most significant in the period 2001-02 was the preparation of the regional development programme of South Primorska 2002-06. Setting out 33 sub-programmes within 13 programme areas, and relating to five priority action fields, the development programme sets a challenging development agenda for action over four years. Equally it sets a challenging agenda for institutional development, and the programme itself sets out (as one of the five Action Fields) a programme of institutional strengthening and co-operation in regional development. This programme aims to raise the motivation of local and regional players, to encourage closer co-operation between municipalities and other players, and consequently to increase the efficiency in the use of funds for joint working. To do this the programme aims to strengthen professional and organisational support for the implementation of the Regional Development Programme through organisational consolidation and the enhancement of professional competence.

South Primorska illustrates graphically the complexity of the administrative arrangements which appear to the external eye to surround local economic development in Slovenia. Primorska is the larger region of Western Slovenia within which lie two statistical regions: Goriška (North Primorska) and Coast Karst (South Primorska). The Coast Karst statistical region is made up of seven municipalities and joins with an eighth – Ilirska Bistrica to make up the South Primorska development area. Ilirska Bistrica is in a different statistical region. Whilst the area of Primorska and its three constituent statistical regions are broadly similar to two Employment Service regions – Nova Gorica and Koper – the Koper Employment Service region includes part of the central statistical region – not only Ilirska Bistrika, but an additional local office based in Postojna. The Nova Gorica Employment Service region excludes some parts of the North Primorska statistical region, which are included in the Ljubljana region. Whilst each function may have a logic of its own relating to activities and catchment areas, the consequence is a web of overlapping structures, the effectiveness of which may not be realised because of the fragmentation of the various parts.

The institutions of South Primorska have addressed a wide range of issues relating to the role, functioning and effectiveness of local economic development in the region. There has been stimulation of a mixed economy of traditional agriculture, and heavier port related working, allied to the development of new sectors in manufacturing and in tourism. There have been attempts to link the education and training sectors to the needs of a changing economy. There have been constructive cross-border relations. There has been the development of a support system for small business. There is also recognition of some of the tensions of economic growth – the tensions, for example, between economic and environmental interests and the appropriate balance between industrial and commercial expansion and that of leisure and tourism.

Operating within a web of inter-institutional networks, many of which have overlapping areas of activity in both functional and geographical terms, the impact on an organisation such as the Koper RDA is significant in both technical and organisational terms. The RDA has become engaged in – and indeed facilitates – a number of activities which are complementary but not totally integrated – business support, human resource development, stimulation of innovation, environmental protection, programme and project management. Technically this range of programmes stretches the capacity of the agency across a broad range of activity. Organisationally the call on the networking skills of the Agency represents a drain on its time and energy.

Celje

The Regional Development Agency at Celje responds to the economic needs of that part of Slovenia lying between the central Ljubljana area and the more eastern and less developed region of Podravska. Like South Primorska, the region also borders two neighbouring countries – Austria to the north and Croatia to the south. The area accounts for 8.3% of the country's territory and, with a population of just under 200 000, for around 10% of the national population. The region is characterised by decreasing population although in terms of age structure it still has a younger population than the national average. There is outward migration of those with qualifications and also students, who seek employment and career opportunities elsewhere – often in the central region. Educational levels are falling and whilst primary and much of secondary education standards are satisfactory, the region is losing many of its prospective graduates. The higher education network is weak, the proportion of the population attending university is amongst the lowest in Slovenia, student drop-out rates are high, many graduates who study elsewhere do not return to the region in response to the lack of acceptable job prospects. The region is consequently less attractive to inward investment. Nevertheless the two major centres – Celje and Velenje – remain buoyant centres of economic, service and administrative activity, and attract much inward movement for daily work. 40% of the workforce in Velenje, for example, come from other municipalities and regions.

The Celje area provides some 10% of the nation's labour force and again just over 9% of those employed. Unemployment, however, is above the national average with Celje generating 12.6% of the numbers of unemployed. The pattern of unemployment matches that nationally, although Celje has an above proportion of unemployed aged under 26, of women, and of those unemployed for over a year. By contrast the proportion of older persons unemployed is below that of the national average.

The local economy is reliant on some 9 000 businesses of which about a third are registered companies and the remainder single person businesses. As elsewhere in Slovenia (and the EU as a whole), the small number of larger companies generate considerable economic activity and resultant employment. Historically the region has been dependent on a strong primary and secondary industrial base – mining, metals, wood, energy – sectors which are now in decline, are subject to competition and are certainly less employment intensive than hitherto, but again as elsewhere SMEs dominate in terms of the share of companies and of employees. Three quarters of the self-employed traders are engaged in craft activities.

The statistical region of Savinska is made up of two sub-regional units, Celje and Savinjsko-Salesko, with Celje and Velenje as the major towns respectively. There are thirty-two municipalities in the region, nine in the Savinjsko/Salesko region and 23 in the Celje region. The area is covered by the Employment Service Celje and Velenje Regional Offices, although the latter also covers areas beyond the north east boundary of the Savinska region in Koroska. There are two Chambers of Commerce – the Celje and Savinjsko/ Salesko Chambers – and the Celje Chamber is broken down into six administrative areas covering different parts of the region. There are local Employment Service offices in the same six towns. The Regional Development Agency however, covers the whole area of the statistical region.

The Regional Development Agency, established as an Entrepreneurship Centre in 1996 now operates to offer a range of organisational, developmental, technical, and financial support. It has a Director and fourteen staff, and is owned by the municipalities (major stakeholder), banks, and local companies. The Celje RDA pursues both strategic planning activities with a view to increasing the competitiveness of the region as well as specific projects for clients and business partners. The latter projects include the preparation of business plans, of investment documents, and the initiation and later development and execution of projects. The RDA assists in the promotion of the region to inward investors and gives support in the preparation of projects bidding for funding from the relevant EU structural funds and community initiatives. Through the creation of a regional information system and the provision of monitoring and evaluation services the Agency fulfils a comprehensive role in supporting economic development across the region.

The Agency is organised around five thematic areas of activity within each of which there is a number of projects:

- The *entrepreneurship* programme involves the development of a network of technological parks and incubator centres, the establishment of industrial and business zones as inward investment attractors, the facilitation of a "toolmakers of Slovenia" cluster, and the management of a regional development and risk fund.

- The *human resources* programme involves the development of centres for learning, vocational training, a regional higher education centre dedicated to as a human resource incubator for technology, and the organisation and management of a regional schools network.

- The *environment and physical planning* programme involves the preparation of a regional spatial plan, support to the development and implementation of regional infrastructure projects, and the application of alternative construction methods and alternative energy sources for ecologically based development.

- The *agriculture and countryside development* programme comprises forest cleaning and wood processing towards a woodbased heating system, the development of ecological production and the marketing of ecoproducts, the development of regional co-operatives, and the restructuring of 10% of the land area to more ecologically efficient use.

- The *tourism and cultural heritage* programme involves the revitalisation of the cultural heritage in terms of tourist marketing and the development of an eco-tourist centre network.

In each of these five areas the RDA uses a project management approach to programme delivery with a central project office supplying integrated management, co-ordination and a global overview of the RDA activities. The project office supplies organisational and technical support and co-operates on the development of regional information systems. An additional cross-cutting theme is that of EU programmes which support a number of the theme areas. The Agency works through its manager to six activity boards and to a large programme committee of owners and partners.

The CELJE Regional Development Agency has developed a major programme of work and is now stretched between regional visioning and strategic planning on the one hand and project development and management on the other. The need to generate funding for the activities of the Agency and to retain the expertise of staff complicates the question of the future role and direction for the agency. There are two competing cultures underlying its role and function. Historically a small-business, entrepreneurial development agency, the staff retains skills suited to the needs of supporting local business, growing the local economy from indigenous resources and operating as the engine of local business growth. This is probably what the Agency is best at. At the same time – as in Koper – the regional development role which has emerged in the last few years has demanded both new strategic planning skills as well as reinforcement of pre-existing skills in project management, supervision, monitoring, and information management. These are important functions for regional development but ones which demand a different organisational style from that needed for traditional local business support. A growing work programme involving strategic planning as well as initiative management poses a threat to the effectiveness of the Agency. The ever-increasing institutionalisation of the regional development role, and the bureaucracy involved in acquiring, and managing external funds (from the European Commission or elsewhere) might, despite the best efforts of Agency staff, lead to fragmentation of effort and lack of focus.

Ptuj

Located to the northeast and bordering Croatia the Ptuj region (population 87 000) accounts for 4.4% of the population of Slovenia. Its two Local Employment Service Offices (Ptuj and Ormoz) provide the standard range of services – job placement, support for the unemployed, vocational guidance, social insurance and benefits management, student bursaries). Ptuj has 4.4% of the Slovenian population, 3.6% of its employment, and 5.5% of its unemployment. Strongly agricultural, the region has 20% of the country's farmers with a third of the population engaged in farming (compared to 7.3% nationally. Economic trends have been favourable. Employment has risen in the last six years by 4%; unemployment has dropped (as it has throughout Slovenia) with a decrease of the number of unemployed in the region of 1 500. Amongst the unemployed, the share of workers made unemployed through the redundancy of their companies has dropped significantly as has the share of young (under 26) workers. But the share of women and of first time job seekers in unemployment has risen, as has the share of older workers over the age of 50.

The Scientific Research Centre Bistra Ptuj evolved from its beginnings as a strategic technological bureau established jointly by the Slovene Ministry of Science and Technology and the local Ptuj community, into a more broadly based interdisciplinary research institution. Identified as a local Business Support Centre in 2001 and as the Regional Development Agency for nineteen municipalities, Bistra Ptuj is now also the regional office of the national association for organisations for technical culture. Together with the Maribor Development Agency and the Maribor Economy Institute the Bistra Ptuj centre is a member of the national RDA network. Its current role as a Regional Development Agency similar to that in other regions is extended by its commitment to research, to knowledge transfer, and to supporting the links between universities and institutes into practical application. The links are also backwards from enterprise and business into the scientific community in order to stimulate creativity and innovation. The philosophy of Bistra Ptuj is to use its position as an RDA to consolidate the linkages – domestically and internationally – between business, universities and the local community. Its activities involve a range of projects financed by ministries and by companies, many related to the exploitation of local culture and materials. In addition to its role as RDA with strategic planning, business support, information exchange, project management, Bistra continues to emphasise the promotion of social and technological research and has a handsome publications list as evidence of this specific strength and focus. In development terms its activities stretch from the translation of ideas into practical projects (for companies, local communities and NGOs), to the business and financial feasibility planning for these projects, and to assistance with project implementation. Many of these projects build on local heritage, employ local skills, and have sustainable local impacts – clay-based pottery, tourism and waste management represent different aspects of the Bistra generated economic development programme.

Elsewhere in Ptuj, but in a more traditional rural and environmentally focused part of the region, the HALO Local Development Agency provides business support services (business planning, development research, study circles), employment information services (skills bank, job club) and tourism support (tourist office, visitor information, facilities and attractions). The Haloze sub-region, historically reliant on agriculture, viticulture, and fruit growing, has suffered population loss as younger people migrate, with higher wage working work in Ptuj and Maribor attracting the labour force away from traditional jobs. The HALO agency aims to exploit the natural resources of the area to develop its capacity as a tourist area, and to encourage local business to be more open to the needs of visitors – walking, cycling, riding, fishing.

Key issues for local economic development

Such brief cameos of the institutions and the initiatives in three regions of Slovenia highlight the variety and richness of current arrangements for supporting the local economy. They reflect the commitment both to generating investment and employment opportunities and to building the capacity needed to manage a range of employment related initiatives at a number of spatial levels. The circumstances and responses in the three regions are very different reflecting their historical development, their geographical locations and their economic prospects.

Regional Development Agencies

Nevertheless the experience of the three regional development agencies in Koper, Celje and Ptuj is in many ways similar. All face major challenges in terms of competing demands for time and resources. All face the proliferation of possible functions. All must build new relationships and partnerships with other agencies. All have complex structures of funding and accountability.

Each, however, operates in a slightly different manner and has evolved to address new roles in a particular way. The Koper RDA remains woven into a complex web of relationships in a region where dynamic growth in some sectors is balanced by the slower growth of traditional sectors. The RDA is active across a range of activities and draws together a range of partners in different ways, but its style of operation seems to illustrate best an organisational style, which might be termed "network facilitator".

The Celje RDA faces similar challenges, but offers a model of a local development agency as "hub", sitting as it does at the centre of a ring of economic activities. With a significant staff and a group of associate consultants the agency is stretched between at least three major areas of interest and activity. These involve the traditional and well established support for local development through small business start up and advice, the emergence of a strategic role in information management, analysis and strategic vision building for the region, and a project management role for the growing volume of external funding brought to the region – much of it from the efforts of the agency itself.

Both Bistra Ptuj and the HALO agency illustrate a more free-standing and less dependent form of development organisation. Bistra, resting in part on its historical but continuing foundations of science, research and analysis appears to have a clearer vision of the contribution it can make to local firms and to the local economy. Equally in the Haloze, there is a very clear vision of how to move forward through exploitation of the natural environmental resources of that part of the region. Investment in nurturing these resources, in creating a more sustainable economy, and in marketing local its goods and services to visitors provides a clear focus for economic development activity.

The varying experience of the RDAs nevertheless illustrates a general problem – that the capacity of the development agencies initially set up to establish small business support and subsequently expanded to provide the capacity for strategic planning, is now unequal to the ever increasing tasks confronting regional economic development. Some of the RDAs have successfully developed their ability to move from informal networking arrangements towards a more focused, practical, problem-solving approach to regional constraints. However, there are also weaknesses in the regional partnership framework that need to be recognised – this is partly a reflection of their internal organisation and the relative newness of the organisations involved at regional level. For example, despite their practical knowledge of local conditions the RDAs have had difficulties developing an integrated approach to regional development and have not been able to provide area-based solutions to the skills deficit and some of the other constraints holding back local SMEs.

Whatever their considerable achievements to date, the capacity necessary to undertake effective regional planning and implementation in Slovenia can, for two reasons, no longer be assumed to be possible through the expansion of the responsibilities and resources of the RDAs. In the first place such expansion diverts the RDAs away from what they are best at – development of and support to small enterprises –, and in the second place the future demands of regional strategic planning require new institutional arrangements engaging a wider range of stakeholders and partners than hitherto.

The Employment Service

If the new governance of regions demands a rethink over the role of Regional Development Agencies, so also does it imply changes in the working of the national Employment Service. As described briefly earlier in this chapter, the Employment Service of Slovenia has played a central part in creating new employment opportunities, as well as in developing initiatives to engage the long-term unemployed and otherwise under-represented groups – Roma, women, people with disabilities, young people – into an active labour market. The Employment Service is active in the regions, with twelve regional offices and fifty nine district offices within regions, and it is from the Employment Service that much of the information about labour market working – employment trends, unemployment levels, activity rates across age groups, qualifications – comes. The Service is also actively engaged in partnership working, and is moving from a predominantly reactive role and culture, in which the main task was simply the response to unemployment or underemployment, towards a more proactive role in stimulating local and regional economic growth. The Employment Centre offices in Koper, Celje, and Ptuj are strongly engaged with the PHARE programme, with human resource planning and with educational and training provision. Nevertheless the evidence suggests that an even more proactive approach towards collaboration is needed, not simply from the Employment Service, but also from a range of state-managed departments and agencies. As in many OECD countries, organisations operating through a hierarchy of national, regional and local offices, and operating furthermore to a set of guidelines set nationally, will inevitably lack the flexibility to respond sufficiently to local issues or to working with local partners. The employment services of many countries are quite reasonably geared towards the achievement of targets set for the reduction of unemployment or the creation of employment opportunities (Giguère, 2003). Such a centrally-driven, performance-managed, system must be mediated by discretion to regional and local levels to adjust national programmes to local needs. The Slovenian system of decentralised regional and local offices allows this to some degree. As yet, however, the emphasis in partnership working for the Employment Service appears to mean working jointly with others towards running the programmes and meeting the targets of the service. Making sure that an enhanced employment service can make its full contribution to a new regional capacity for local economic development means reshaping organisational culture towards the values of genuine joint working and extending and enhancing the skills base within the Service to foster collaboration across agencies.

The role of business

Such a change in culture and practices would involve establishing different relationships with local business. Programmes to raise the levels of new business creation and to support the growth of small business have been, for over a decade, a major focus for local economic development in Slovenia. Their success is well documented, with business incubators supporting the formation of new enterprise from the enormous resource represented by self-employment. Examples of documented business/economic activity support include the Small Projects Fund, the public works programme of the Employment Service (and its links to the role of voluntary, community and municipal projects in what is perhaps the equivalent of a social economy), the Small Business Network, the Small Business Development Centres, and of course the emergence of local/regional business centres and thence RDAs.

In Slovenia business is generally represented at the local level through Chambers of Commerce and Industry on the one hand, and Chambers of Craft or Trade on the other. The boundaries between the two overlap, and indeed there is some competition for membership. Chambers of Commerce and Industry are engaged with the representation of the medium and larger enterprises in strategic planning, in the provision of infrastructure, and in the provision of education and training. Craft Chambers have closer linkages with, and representation of, smaller enterprises, especially those reflecting the traditional agricultural and craft trades and industries of Slovenia. There can be some tension between the interests of the two Chambers with the Chambers of Commerce and Industry offering a more strategic role in the future development of the locality and the Chambers of Trade reflecting the interests of the smaller firms and the self employed. This distinction is not always helpful, however, since whilst it is the large firms that may be the largest employers, it is from the Craft Chambers that much of the small business growth and development may emerge.

NEW FORMS OF GOVERNANCE FOR ECONOMIC DEVELOPMENT – ISBN 92-64-01530-2 – © OECD 2004

Small businesses remain the dominant sector but a new stage of development confronts business development. First there is a clear need for greater information about the numbers, scale, activities and problems confronting business at the local level. Whilst there is obvious commitment to representing the needs of small business in the Chambers of Commerce and Industry (and a drive to recruit smaller firms), the information base around which small business policies can be developed appears fragile within both sets of Chambers. Nor is it simply the needs of small business to which attention must be given. As the economy grows, so the needs of medium-sized and larger firms will become more important. Indigenous business will become more significant as the generator of continuing growth with less dependence on inward investment. The links between medium-sized and smaller businesses need to be recognised and exploited as a growing local economy provides the basis for economic clusters. There is little evidence as yet of supply chain analysis, of buyer to buyer linkages, of formalised sub-contract arrangements, or of other approaches to increasing the interdependence of local firms one upon the other.

Nor is there extensive evidence yet of business involvement in partnership working at local or regional levels, although in Celje, for example, there was a clear picture of business engagement with some of the RDA activities. Throughout Europe it is recognised that encouraging business to take part in partnership dialogue is a difficult task. The style of much partnership discourse involves different stakeholders using different language, removing stereotypes about attitudes and behaviour, getting to know each others' positions, and agreeing shared positions.

The public – private split is important here. Although the Chambers, both of Commerce/Industry and Trade/Craft have direct links with the enterprise sector there there is often the tendency for linkages to be established with the developing public sector and community sectors as much as with the business sector itself. Closer links with the major private sector employers, the banks, property developers and the corporate sector, including international companies are a crucial ingredient of successful regional partnership working.

Social inclusion

Ensuring that the benefits of a growing economy are shared by all is a major objective of national policy. The Slovenian "Fight against Poverty and Social Exclusion" (Ministry of Labour, Family and Social Affairs, 2002) identifies a range of measures across all government departments and functions which can contribute to the relief of exclusion and begin to integrate marginal and disadvantaged poorer groups into the mainstream. The focus is upon the reduction of poverty differentials, with the emphasis on the role of national policy instruments relating to wages, pensions, social protection, and access to health and welfare as drivers of social inclusion. It is at local level, however, that much of the application of national policies takes place, and there is a role for the region (as for the municipality) in ensuring that the most marginal groups or individuals are identified, that programmes of inclusion are targeted on need, and that the activities of a range of agencies are integrated. As elsewhere the evidence is that the factors producing exclusion are cumulative with poor housing, low health status, unemployment, and low educational achievement reinforcing one another in generating potentially permanent exclusion from labour and housing markets and access to both public and private services.

The Public Works programme has been one of the major vehicles for supporting initiatives which assist the socially excluded, but there may be a more active role for the Employment Service than in the past. There is scope for more sophisticated analysis of labour supply blockages, development of more responsive and targeted outreach programmes, potential for growing joint activities between statutory and voluntary/associational sectors. Labour market information already points to the disadvantaged position of some groups in terms of the gender or age distribution of opportunities. Municipalities and local voluntary associations have played a major role in developing and implementing the Public Works programmes, and it is at the very local levels of neighbourhood or municipality that the outreach necessary to identify the most disadvantaged can be carried out. Solutions to problems of unemployment and poverty, however, can seldom be found at the most local level, and it is often only in the wider sub-regional or regional context that the routes out of exclusion can be found. Regional development strategies increasingly need to make the links between economic competitiveness and social development.

Capacity building for regionalism

Capacity building for the Slovenian regions must respond, therefore, to four distinct pressures. These include the need to establish a clear role for Regional Development Agencies, the need to extend the functions and operational culture and functioning of the Employment Service, the need to engage business interests more fully and more constructively in regional development, and the importance of ensuring that regional development programmes respond more effectively to the inclusion of marginalised groups. These pressures cannot always be easily reconciled and the design of appropriate regional structures is dependent on two crucial considerations. The first is that of the function of the region in a system within which the region co-exists with state centralism and municipal localism. Secondly successful regional capacity depends on the emergence of a genuine practice of partnership.

The function of regions

The existence of overlapping boundaries and areas of administrative jurisdiction described in the earlier part of this chapter presents a number of problems for the development of an effective regionalism in Slovenia. One challenge is simply geographical. Slovenia is a small country, and to fit a regional tier of government or governance, between nation and municipality is difficult. There needs to be a sufficient separation between different tiers of government in order for citizens and firms to distinguish between the state, the region, and the municipality, and in a small country the administrative as well as the geographic space can become overcrowded.

It is even more important in these circumstances to be clear about the role and function of the regional level. Different stakeholders – central government, regional agencies, municipalities – have different hopes and fears about the emergence of an active regionalism, and in Slovenia as elsewhere, there are a number of scenarios for the future of the region.

● *Decentralisation.* The region as the basis for decentralised functional delivery of a range of state functions, with central state activity organised on the Employment Service model but without significant local autonomy over resources or decisions. Control is largely retained over policy, with little discretion to regional bodies and few departures from national standards and norms.

● *Devolution.* The region as the focus for devolved decision making over policies, activities, resources. There is some autonomy and flexibility over resource allocation for local stakeholders and greater sensitivity to local needs with more discretion over the application of national policies.

● *Aggregation.* The region as the focus for the exercise of the collective voice of more local – municipal – interests. Power and control at regional level are not exercised by regional bodies *per se*, but by assemblies or delegates from the lower tiers of government. There is a tendency to share out resources and benefits amongst the assembly of small bodies rather than concentrate on key regional priorities.

● *Representation.* The region as the focus for an inclusive debate across all sectors – public, private, associational – about the future of the region, its activities, and its priorities. This role can be highly influential with central government in setting its regional priorities, and can also the exercise of influence over its constituent members (the regional partners) to bend their activities to meet the collectively recognised priorities of the regional assembly. A purely representative role, however offers few resources.

Whilst such roles and functions are not necessarily mutually exclusive, the existence of very varying interpretations of which role or function should be dominant is likely to lead to institutional ineffectiveness at regional level. The essence of partnership working is recognition of the collaborative advantage, which can be gained if different stakeholders come together to achieve mutual gain (Huxham, 1998). Such collaborative advantage, however, can be dissipated if the processes and procedures which are designed to bind together the regional stakeholders become ineffective. If partners are not committed and engaged, partnership meetings descend into simply talking shops. Friction and fission replace joint working. Effective local and regional development must be grounded in the practice as well as the principles of partnership.

The experience of partnership

Great emphasis is laid on partnership working and the OECD itself is committed to supporting good practice in partnership working (OECD, 2001). There has been extensive learning about the application of partnership principles and the early PHARE programmes supported the development of, for example, cross-border partnership working. RDAs themselves provide backing to partnership working and, in all the documentation of Slovenian local economic development, partnership is regularly cited. But the term "partnership" can be used to describe any two agencies working together and as yet there is only modest evidence of formalised partnership working as opposed to joint projects, mixed funding, or shared membership of programme teams, management committees or task forces. There is a need, therefore to address partnership working more systematically and to assess the skills and knowledge needed to make partnership working a reality. The evidence from European Union programmes to date is that whilst effective partnership working can exploit shared interests, generate synergy and provide added value, there are also many examples of partnerships which generate high transactions costs without realising the hoped for benefits. It is important to note the distinction between "networking" – the informal relationships through which agencies and organisations communicate – and "partnership", which takes on an organisational form with the rules and protocols which govern formalised systems.

Relatively absent in the capacity of regions in Slovenia to date appears to have been a strategic capacity, with limited investment in the skills needed for strategic regional economic planning – analysis of trends, identification of local/sectoral opportunities, skills in packaging and managing complex funding packages. Regional Development Agencies have carried this role, and in some cases with significant success – the strategic activities in Koper and Celje provide valuable examples. Nevertheless investment in strategic capacity is a priority. There is here a possible role for Chambers of Commerce/ Trade and Crafts where there is an obvious need to think beyond the prospects for particular sectors and to engage small and large business in strategic thinking about their localities. This might concern, for example, the emergence of industrial or service-based clusters of activity, the relationship between small and large local business, and the potential for collaborative research and development or marketing.

Given this complexity it is perhaps unsurprising that RDAs have established neither the authority nor the capacity to broker the cross-sector networks needed to improve the flow of information between the various functional authorities in the region, such as the Employment Service, in order better to co-ordinate national programmes for enterprise development and employment growth. In part this is a function of the membership of the emerging networks and partnerships which characterize the new socio-economic management of Slovenia. One way forward might be to give local SME managers and entrepreneurs more direct say in the way that SBSN programmes are developed and resources allocated.

Where new relationships at regional level are being formed, and where as yet the function of regionalism is neither universally agreed nor understood, it is crucial to develop unambiguous and shared meanings of what good partnership practice might imply. Thus every attempt must be made to remove uncertainty over membership and the obligations which membership of a partnership implies. This is especially the case where partnerships are designed to be widely inclusive of a range of interests (with a membership of thirty or more), as opposed to a more efficient, but perhaps exclusive and closed membership of perhaps a dozen. Arrangements for joint resourcing and budgetting must be clarified, especially as far as the core costs of partnership funding are concerned. Most partner agencies are willing to contribute to the joint costs of programmes or projects. Few are so committed to the funding of the basic core activities upon which good partnership practice depends. Accountability structures must be clarified to ensure a balance between the accountability of partner organisations within their own respective public, private or voluntary sector systems, and the shared accountability of partners to the partnership itself. In the Slovenian regions, as elsewhere, the arrangements to be built for collaborative partnership working will involve organisations with differing power relations. Those organisations with resources, often the statutory organisations or those (including the European Commission), with influence and control over resources, tend to take most power in partnership working, and it is important to recognise that true partnerships involve recognition of those with weaker power positions and few resources. Working in partnership can be likened to playing in an orchestra. Each player has an instrument, but harmony can only be generated if players recognise the contribution of all, play to the same score, and operate under the influence of a sympathetic conductor (perhaps the chairman of the partnership). Equally, good partnership performance requires rehearsal. Those who have less experience need to learn to play together. Chambers of Commerce or Crafts and also voluntary associations, have been less engaged in partnership working than many public organisations and are less practiced in the new styles of joint working. Finally partnership practice may be inhibited by the lack of skills – the absence of appropriate strategic, analytic and organisational development skills for partnership working as opposed to the project development and project management skills which in many Slovenian regions are becoming better developed within the RDAs and other organisations.

Most important, however, is clarity about role and function. What seems to be needed at regional level is a robust strategy to introduce new ways of thinking into the public sector that will bring about a change in the organisational culture of the business support networks in ways that will make them more responsive both to SME needs and to the local constraints to growth. The area-based approach needed to have a significant impact on regional development will mean taking the concerns of entrepreneurs and corporate managers more seriously and addressing the issues they face through integrated policy-making in which the Employment Service Regional Offices, the SBSN, the Chambers and the RDAs work more closely together to deliver "joined-up" government. In regional development terms, the success of most reforms and innovations will depend on their ability to connect together the economic development side of the sub-regional agenda with the labour market policy side. As with most regional agencies across Europe, mechanisms need to be developed that allow greater consultation with local firms about their labour market needs and how these needs can be better addressed within a regional partnership model than relying entirely on a single functional agency.

The existing, but still fragile, web of partnerships must respond to the changing circumstances brought about by Slovenia's access to the EU by broadening the agenda of regional development to a wider range of economic and indeed social issues. One pressing need will be to develop strategies that will address the low levels of productivity in the SME sector in ways that will not unduly exacerbate the employment concerns of the workforce and lead to higher concentrations of unemployment. Successful solutions will need to be based on a combination of investment in both human and physical capital and will require an integrated approach.

The danger is that the scope of the embryonic regional partnerships that are developing may be too limited. Partnerships should not be restricted to a predefined agenda or to the delivery of a narrow set of services. Such a limited role would confine the potential capacity of regional partnerships potential to influence national policy and to draw together the private and public sector actors. RDAs should encourage and support greater involvement in policy issues in order to create a needs-driven agenda for regional growth and to more effectively develop a flexible, broader co-ordinating function. This will be vital if the partnerships are to be given an enhanced role and encouraged to develop the institutional capacity of existing networks.

Reducing the possibilities of inefficiencies in joint working depends, therefore, on the strength of the collaborative arrangements established at regional level. In addition to defining role and purpose, practical considerations include defining agreeing membership, establishing protocols for joint working, ensuring power sharing, supporting community-based organisations, developing skills, and investing in structures of communication and accountability.

Against the principles of democracy which underpin the European Union there is a need to map out a clearer relationship between the elected local authorities and the regional development partnerships. Although the mayors of the municipalities are often the key signatories to the partnerships there remains some ambiguity as to who is responsible within the region for the allocation of the resources which come to regions from the centre. Mayors must continue to participate in arrangements for territorial collaboration above that of the municipality itself. There must be recognition that effective stimulation of the local economy must be generated through joint action across neighbouring municipalities. This means that the release of land in one area may benefit other areas, that the provision of housing in one municipality may allow a region to retain qualified workers, or and that land use planning and the phased release of land must be co-ordinated across municipal boundaries. Indeed to reinforce RDAs co-ordinating function, much clearer links need to be developed with the municipal authorities.

The links between local democratic organisations and regional development partners funded by the public purse will need to be made more transparent in order to ensure accountability and coherence and to avoid overlap. This will not only help to avoid duplication of effort, but it will also offer some opportunities for rationalisation. Scrutiny and accountability will need to be focused and enforced to ensure that the partnerships formed by the RDAs remain inclusive but yet effective organisations.

Whilst the region may be the focus for economic and social development the central state has a crucial role to play. The National Agency for Regional Development (NARD) will need to respond positively to partnership agendas by deploying resources in ways that support an area-based approach to local problems. The objective now should be to reduce some of the uneven experience of the RDAs across geographic areas. The regional framework is still relatively new and has limited expertise in mobilising mainstream resources. Consequently, central government has not yet had much evidence of the benefits that can stem from closer co-operation between local partners.

The most important of these for the centre is probably the more efficient delivery of local support services, but this can only follow when mainstream resources are more effectively allocated at the regional level. Despite some recent improvements in co-ordination between the centre and the regions there are still too few reporting systems in place to communicate examples of best practice at national levels. Incorporating the lessons of the RDAs and the regional programmes into the policies of the main functional authorities, like the Employment Service, will require greater support from national level.

Because of these constraints and limited expertise of forming alliances within the new framework, some of the partnerships have been less strategic in their approach than others. As a result a range of sometimes loosely connected projects have been delivered by the RDAs against a background of operational pressures and a rationing of resources. As the system beds down, more should be done to develop a shared vision for the future for the RDAs and to persuade the more powerful agencies, like the Employment Service, to respond to the development priorities on a larger scale and in a more durable way than the Regional Development Programme partners can manage with their own limited budgets. Indeed there is a clear need for rethinking on the part of the regional offices of state departments (and in particular the Employment Service) towards a broader based approach to collaboration.

To strengthen the commitment of NARD to the regional partnerships and to raise the profile of this activity at the centre, we suggest that a regular policy forum be introduced on an annual basis that brings together the relevant departments of government and regional actors to evaluate the success of current programmes and suggest amendments and introduce innovative activities. Greater collaboration between NARD and the RDAs on their respective policy agendas will improve partnership development at a sub-regional level and help identify the supporting roles to be played by the other partners. At the centre, an inter-ministry structure that allows for greater consultation on regional development and the creation of new initiatives could serve this purpose. More active and practical interactions between the centre and the RDAs would allow targets to be set that could strengthen strategic focus and also reinforce partnership accountability. The targets might also facilitate greater decentralisation of resources and decision making to the RDAs in response to them meeting certain key performance criteria. This could then lead to the RDAs being given a formal consultative role in the strategic planning and budgeting by other regional organisations. However, if more resources and powers are devolved then more attention should also be given to the performance management and to process evaluation. RDAs should be subject to monitoring and evaluation on their administrative and delivery mechanisms as well as outputs. Ultimately, the success and economic impact of the regional partnership organisations will be determined on the one hand by the level of commitment by NARD and other ministries but on the other hand by their ability to secure the commitment of the regional and national offices of the Employment Service and the municipalities.

Decentralisation may be less of an issue in Slovenia than in other larger EU countries because of the scale of the country and the geography of economic activity. The focus is as much on the better integration of the initiatives already being undertaken at the sub-regional level as on the establishment of totally new institutional structures. For this to happen a longer-term planning approach may need to be introduced to ensure that efforts at the regional level have a broader relevance for national policy targets. This will involve the local partnerships being able to re-direct the resources and budgets of national agencies on the basis of a recognised local need. In addition, regional agencies will require control of their own resources in order to encourage key players from the private sector to engage with the development planning process. In strengthen delivery mechanisms the emphasis should be placed on transforming the RDAs from largely advisory institutions into more outward looking, co-ordinating budget holders. Another strengthening mechanism would be the establishment of a network for RDAs to exchange information about progress and best practice on integrating and co-ordinating local initiatives.

An earlier section of this chapter pointed to the alternative functions of the region in a system within which the region co-exists with state centralism and municipal localism – decentralisation, devolution, aggregation and representation. Analysis of the Slovenian context suggests the need to support a regionalism which incorporates and reconciles all four functions within an institutional structure which builds collaborative capacity through partnership working.

Conclusions

The Slovenian example of the emergence of a capacity for regionally-based economic development offers helpful lessons both for recent accession countries to the European Union and others addressing the question of the appropriate institutional arrangements between state and municipality.

As elsewhere, however, Slovenia faces a number of challenges in generating an infrastructure appropriate to the circumstances of membership of the European Union but still retaining the strengths which have given rise to its current economic vitality. Some of these challenges stem from the geography of the country. Eleven of the twelve statistical regions have borders with other countries and cross-border, and as a consequence many of the linkages upon which successful labour and trade markets rely are also cross-border. Some of these linkages are now with countries within the European Union; others remain with countries still outside the Union. The effectiveness of the Slovenian economy and the success of its regional policies and programmes, therefore, will always to some extent be a function of the effectiveness of external relations – the connections with the neighbouring sub-regional economies of Italy, Austria, Hungary and Croatia. Membership of the European Union reinforces the significance of such cross-border economic activity, and Slovenia has already benefited from the support of a number of EU cross-border programmes. Slovenia, however, also has a rich tradition of regionalism built upon the identity and of individual towns and cities, and upon a regionalism which is inherently closer to the local than to the national. Internally, therefore, there is much competition between what are small regions for economic growth and the creation of local employment opportunities.

The evidence is, however, of a regional infrastructure, which remains fragmented. Such fragmentation thus allows the continuation of the strong localism which emphasises the "local" in local economic development but also encourages the competition both between agencies and between individual municipalities and regions.

This competition can, and should, be mediated by the state. There is always a role for national policies and programmes to foster employment growth and combat unemployment. There is the need for national welfare policies to address issues of poverty, ill health, and social cohesion. In Slovenia, there appears to be the need for a more coherent and co-ordinated national housing policy to address issues of key worker housing and mobility as well as those of affordable housing for lower income groups or emergency and temporary accommodation for those without a roof over their heads. In addition national government sets the limits to the powers of self-governing municipalities, and must decide the boundaries between municipalities and any new regional structures. Yet exploitation of the potential for economic growth, and more importantly the need to distribute the benefits of that growth across the regions of Slovenia demands an active regionalism.

In a relatively small country, where external connections are important, it is essential that the internal relations between state, region and municipality do not create complications for those enterprise which seek to grow on the basis of both external and internal markets. The need then is for as simple an internal regional structure as can be managed, with the arrangements for strategic planning, infrastructure provision, and business support clear and understood by all. Partnership working between public and private sectors needs to be governed by definite protocols; duplication and competition between municipalities and regions minimised.

The immediate pre-accession years saw the emergence of a new regional capacity in Slovenia. There has already been considerable progress in local economic development through business support schemes, cross-border relations, regional development plans and programmes, and early strategic regional economic planning. Creating a sustainable capacity to take forward regional economic development at times of economic downturn, in the face of political tensions, and in a manner which retains partner interest and engagement without generating partnership fatigue and burnout on the part of the smaller players is more difficult. Given the still fragmented and fragile nature of institutional arrangements established in the late 1990s and early years of the twenty-first century, there remain improvements to be made towards more robust regional structures. An extension of the activities of the Employment service at regional level, the stronger engagement of business with partnership working, a closer relationship between the policies for economic competitiveness and those for social inclusion, and a reassessment of the demands placed on Regional Development Agencies would all contribute to capacity building. For all stakeholders an investment in more sophisticated and thought through practices of partnership working are a prerequisite.

Some of the challenges to Slovenian regionalism stem from accession to the European Union and without doubt many of the procedural requirements of the Commission arising from the economic requirements of EU membership will appear cumbersome. In accession countries, the pressures to improve competitiveness through investment and job creation are strong. This inevitably increases the pressures towards economic and administrative centralisation, however, and exacerbates the tensions between central regions and the rest of the country. Imbalances between income per head may increase, some geographical spaces may become isolated, even redundant, social inclusion for more vulnerable groups may appear a more distant target. Slovenia, however, as one of the more advanced and relatively less deprived of the new accession countries has the possibility of resolving these tensions through capacity building and a more ordered and systematic approach to regionally based partnership working.

Bibliography

Giguère, S. (2003), "Managing Decentralisation and New Forms of Governance", in OECD (2003), Managing Decentralisation. A New Role for Labour Market Policy, OECD, Paris.

Government of Slovenia (2003), "Joint Inclusion Memorandum", Ljubljana.

Huxham, C. (eds) (1998), "Creating Collaborative Advantage", London: Sage Publications.

Ministry of Economy/Small Business Development Centre (2002), "Report of the Small Business Support Network of Slovenia", Ljubljana: Ministry of Economy/SBDC.

Ministry of Labour, Family and Social Affairs (2002), "The Fight against Poverty and Social Exclusion", Ljubljana.

OECD (2001), Local Partnerships for Better Governance, OECD, Paris.

ISBN 92-64-01530-2
New Forms of Governance for Economic Development
© OECD 2004

Chapter 7

Spain: Towards an Integrated Approach to Economic and Employment Development

by

Hugh Mosley,
Social Research Centre (WZB), Berlin

Spain leads a wide variety of experiments to improve local governance. This chapter surveys two of them: sector-based patterns of co-operation (Andalousía) and more systematic integrated approach through area-based partnerships (Catalonia), in a context of a wide-ranging process of decentralisation to regions. The lessons show that benefits can always be reaped from a more co-ordinated and strategic approach, especially within a complex governance framework. Narrow mandates are likely to deliver successes in the short term mainly.

This chapter examines the experiences of local development partnerships in Spain based on two case studies: Barcelona and Almería.* It analyses their local context, their composition, their management framework and their programmatic focus. Their strengths and weaknesses are assessed in terms of their contribution to improving local governance, i.e. a) policy co-ordination; b) adapting policies to local needs; and c) fostering participatory strategic planning for local development. In Barcelona the initiatives are a territorial employment pact (TEP) in the county of Vallès Occidental and the subsequent adoption of this approach throughout Catalonia. In Almería there is a very different, more traditional pattern of sector-based co-operation. The two case studies also illustrate the impact and challenges of decentralisation for local governance in Spain.

The economic and governance context

The Spanish labour market

Since the mid-1990s economic and employment growth have been strong in Spain and unemployment has fallen sharply from a high of 20% in 1994 to 11% in 2003. Maintaining real GDP growth of 2% in 2002, Spain has been less adversely affected by the economic slowdown than other Euro zone countries, although the unemployment rate is still one of the highest among OECD countries (OECD, 2003a).

In addition to still high unemployment, the Spanish labour market is affected by several structural problems (NAP, 2003; European Commission, 2003; Ruiz, 2003):

● There are large differences in the unemployment rates by gender, region and by age. Thus the female (15.8%) and youth (22%) unemployment rates in 2003 were far above the national average (11.2%), and the unemployment rate in the province of Almería (8.5%) is less than half that of the region in which it is located (Andalusia 18%) and much lower than that in Spain as a whole. Regional disparities in unemployment rates have actually increased during the upswing since the mid-1990s.

---

* The author wishes to thank Xavier Greffe, Université de Paris I, for his contribution to this chapter.

- Labour market participation rates are low (59%) in comparison with the EU (70%). This is principally due to the large gap between female and male labour force participation rates in Spain (49% vs. 70%).

- The rate of part-time employment (8%) is low in comparison with the EU as a whole (18%) and is one of the principal reasons for the low level of labour force participation of women.

- Spain has an extremely high rate of temporary employment contracts (31%) in comparison with the EU (13%). High turnover in Spain means not only job insecurity but is also associated with low investment in training and lower levels of qualification.

Immigration is an increasingly important social and labour market problem in Spain. Immigrants still constitute a rather small, but rapidly growing, share of the Spanish population.[1] A number of factors have lead to increased immigration: a) the relatively robust employment growth in comparison with other European countries; b) the geographical proximity to North Africa; c) the lack of a language barrier for central and Latin American immigrants; and d) Spain's relatively liberal immigration policies, in particular the several massive waves of "regularisation" of undocumented immigrants. Noteworthy is the shift towards immigration from countries outside of the EU: natives of Morocco (the largest immigrant group) and of Latin America (Ecuador, Peru, Columbia, etc.) now account for a majority of the foreign population. Since 2000 a new administrative quota system ("Contingente") has been introduced with the aim of better controlling immigration and adapting it to labour market requirements at the provincial level. In 2002, the foreign population is heavily concentrated in a few regions: Madrid (22.5%); Catalonia (19.3%), Valencia (15.2%), Andalusia (10.7%) and the Canary Islands (7.2%).

Devolution of powers to the autonomous communities

The formerly highly centralised Spanish state has undergone a far-reaching process of regionalisation since 1979 and is now one of the most decentralised OECD states. Responsibility for many domestic policy areas has been devolved to the 17 "autonomous communities". These regional governments now account for about one third of public expenditure and employ more than twice as many civil servants as the central government. The share of the central government in total public expenditure has declined to around 52%, which is comparable to or less than that in older federal systems like those in Germany, the United States and Switzerland (OECD, 2003a). In summary there has been a very meaningful devolution of competence and resources to the regional level. This process is ongoing and not without tension and conflict over the scope and limits of regional autonomy.

The division of powers between the central state and the regional administrations falls into three categories: 1) powers exclusive to the autonomous communities: their government structure, territorial organisation, promotion of regional development, regional planning, agriculture, tourism, social assistance urban policies, health, education, culture, etc.; 2) shared powers: in these fields the powers to be transferred are defined in enabling legislation by the national state and the Autonomous Communities assume responsibility for implementing them by regional legislation (*e.g.* labour legislation and employment policies, environmental protection, public works, public safety, etc.); and 3) powers reserved to the central state: international relations, defence, foreign trade, monetary policy, etc.

Among the policy areas with which we are most concerned in this paper, local economic development belongs to the exclusively regional and active employment policy to the shared powers that are implemented by the Autonomous Communities within the framework of national legislation. Shared powers, and the dual responsibility that they entail, are sometimes a source of ambiguity or even conflict between the central government and the regions about the powers and responsibilities of different levels of government. Moreover, the 17 autonomous communities differ in the timing and manner in which they have assumed regional legislation responsibility for different policy domains.

Decentralisation in labour market policy

Until recently employment policy was primarily a responsibility of the central state, managed and implemented by the public employment service (*Instituto Nacional de Empleo,* INEM). INEM is an autonomous public agency under the jurisdiction of the Ministry of Labour and Social Affairs. The INEM central office carried out its responsibilities through over 600 local employment offices and training centres. Its territorial management structure is organised into provincial directorates throughout the country. In the past INEM was exclusively responsible for the core functions of labour market policy: placement services, active labour market programmes, including training and employment promotion, management and payment of unemployment benefits. Now, as a consequence of the decentralisation process, the autonomous communities and local authorities implement active policies related to employment and training, within the framework established by the national administration. Basic labour legislation, including labour market regulations and the social protection system, remain a national responsibility. Regional governments apply labour legislation and develop active policies adapted to their own needs. INEM remains exclusively responsible for the administration of unemployment benefits. Initially, the management of vocational training was transferred and, beginning in 1996, other active policies. As of 2004, 16 of the 17 autonomous communities have established their own employment services (Ruiz, 2003; see Ministry of Labour and Social Affairs, 2002, for an overview).[2] Under the Employment Act of December 2003 the National Employment System comprises the INEM and the public employment services of the autonomous communities.

Although the governments of the autonomous communities have a certain flexibility, they are required to spend the funds they receive for active policies for specified purposes (i.e. training, or employment for the handicapped) and in accord with the applicable state regulations for these programmes. National funds for activite employment policies are allocated to the autonomous communities in six programme funding blocks, and there is at present only limited discretion to shift funds between programmes. Conflicts that arise are resolved by the Sectoral Conference for Labour Affairs.[3]

Decentralisation in economic development

Responsibility for industrial policy has also shifted from the central government towards the autonomous communities. Instead of national policies implemented by central government the local development agencies (Agencia de Desarrollo Local), which are organised primarily at the level of the municipalities, now play a central role, adapting policies to the specific needs of local industries and enterprises. Central government's role is now largely limited to that of the co-ordination of industrial policy at the national level and with the European Union, and the design of framework programmes that are implemented at the local level. Since European competition rules place narrow limits on subsidies to enterprises, industrial policy has focused increasingly on promoting competitiveness, with a special emphasis on SMEs (Aguado, 2002).

Another major actor in regional development in Spain is the European Union through the European Social Fund and other regional funds. Spain has been a large recipient of EU funding for the maintenance and creation of employment and economic development. Their impact has been enhanced by Spain's general approach of integrating ESF activities for human resources with those of the other Funds as part of an overall regional social and economic development strategy.

The experience of partnerships in Catalonia

Vallès Occidental is a county ("comarca", a subregional unit) in Catalonia outside the city but within the metropolitan area of Barcelona. The county comprises 23 municipalities in a relatively densely populated and industrialised area with a number of major industrial plants. The unemployment rate of 8.6% is relatively low for Spain but somewhat higher than that of Catalonia as a whole (6.6%).[4] A former centre of textile production that has been undergoing restructuring, Vallès Occidental, has experienced better than average employment growth in recent years with economic activity concentrated mainly in the metallurgical, chemical, textile and foods industries. It has a growing population and has been the destination of many immigrants from within Spain and from the foreign population that has sought employment in the Barcelona area. Foreigners are currently 2.8% of the population and are expected to represent 8% within 10 years. The two largest cities are Sabadell and Terrassa, each with over 160 000 inhabitants. The total population in 2002 was 731 000, with a per capita income of EUR 8 641, slightly under the average for Catalonia (EUR 9 406), but higher than that of Spain as a whole and above the EU average.[5]

Catalonia, the Spanish autonomous community in which Vallès Occidental is located, is one of the most modern and economically developed regions in Spain. It is a region with a distinctive language and cultural traditions and the regional government (Generalitat) has assumed a large degree of autonomy within the limits of the Spanish Constitution and was one of the first Spanish regions to assume responsibility for active programmes by setting up its own employment service.

Economic development and labour market issues enjoy a high priority and are supported by a dense social infrastructure of public and private organisations. The Centre for Innovation and Business Development (CIDEM) is an autonomous body attached to the Department of Labour and Industry of the Catalan Government, committed to "providing Catalan companies with the methods and tools to increase their competitiveness." Initially, special attention was paid to quality as a key competitive advantage, thereafter CIDEM shifted its focus to the need for companies to internationalise their operations, and for the past three years innovation has been at the core of CIDEM's concerns. With a staff of over 100, it provides business consulting services to promote Catalonia as a location for foreign investment and to assist business start-ups and existing SMEs to grow and diversify. Its activities are based on the assumption that innovation is crucial for companies to remain competitive and grow. CIDEM's "Innovation Plan" for the 2001-2004 period is organised along five lines of action: managing innovation, developing the technology market, encouraging the entrepreneurial spirit, promoting digital technology in business and achieving logistical and production excellence. It has an additional programme budget of EUR 130 million per year to finance innovation in Catalonian enterprises. However, CIDEM does not consult on personnel policy and employment issues.

Within the context of the Spanish National Action Plan, the Catalonian government has developed its own General Employment Plan, which is also the basis for priorities set for the local employment pacts (Catalonia

Department of Labour, Industry and Commerce, 2003). The Catalonian employment plan offers a labour market diagnosis and proposes strategic goals.

Among the central elements are the following:

- The need to increase the already high Catalonia labour market participation rate. The activity rate is currently 72.5% in Catalonia in comparison with an EU average of 68% and the relatively low overall Spanish rate of 67%. The strategy calls for focussing efforts to reduce the gap between the male and female activity rates (84% vs. 61%) by focusing in particular on increasing the activity rates of women aged 45 and older, whose activity rate is especially low, and on reducing premature withdrawal from the labour force.

- Furthermore Catalonia has adopted the European target of a 70% employment rate by the year 2010 (currently 65% in Catalonia vs. 58% in Spain and an EU average of 64%). In achieving this goal there is a particular focus on increasing the employment rate of older workers (those aged 55 to 64) from the current 42% to 50%, and of women from 55% to 60% (both goals are also EU targets).

- Increasing the stability of employment is a major objective in Catalonia as in Spain as a whole. Whereas over 85% of employed persons in the EU have permanent employment contracts, this is the case for only 68% in Spain and 77% in Catalonia in 2002. The employment plan calls for focussing in particular on augmenting employment stability for women and, especially, on youth, for whom the rate of permanent contracts is only 42% in Catalonia (compared to 35% in Spain and 62% in the EU).

- Another principal goal is to close the gap between the unemployment rate for women, which is almost twice that for men in Spain, and that for older persons (45 and plus) to the level of the overall unemployment rate.

- Combating long-term unemployment by offering long-term unemployed jobseekers a labour market measure before they reach 12 months of unemployment.

- Promotion of part-time work, which like in Spain as a whole is a very low percentage of all employment in Catalonia (7%) and one of the principal reasons for the low activity rate of women.

- Increasing the participation of adults in education and training, which is only 5% in comparison with the EU average of 9%, by promoting continuing life-long learning.

- Promotion of labour mobility and social integration of immigrant workers.

Territorial administration in Catalonia

According to the Constitution of 1978 the Autonomous Community of Catalonia comprises the four provinces of Barcelona, Girona, Lleida and Tarragona. Catalonia has, however, traditionally regarded the division of the region into provincial units – reintroduced by the Franco regime in 1949 – as inimical to aspirations for unity and autonomy.

The territorial administration in the relatively large region of Catalonia (31 895 km^2) is subdivided into different administrative units, which are determined by laws enacted by the Parliament of Catalonia and consequently differ somewhat from those in other Spanish regions.

The 1979 Statute of Autonomy provides that the *Generalitat* shall structure its "territorial organisation in municipalities and counties" and "may also set up larger administrative districts". The two basic local government entities are then the 946 municipalities and the 41 *comarques* (counties) into which the municipalities of a local area are grouped.[6]

The municipality is the basic entity in the territorial organisation of Catalonia, and it is also the most important path through which citizens participate directly in their local community since the county and provincial administrations are only indirectly elected by the municipal councils. The municipalities are governed by town councils (*ajuntaments*), which are composed of a mayor and the councillors. The responsibilities of the municipality depend in part on its size.[7]

The county is a territorial entity made up of a group of contiguous municipalities which has its own legal personality and full capacity and independence to act to accomplish its aims. By law the counties must coincide with geographical areas reflecting the basic structure of the economic activity of Catalonia, and municipalities with common social and historical characteristics must be grouped together. The government and administration of the county is the responsibility of the county council. Its members are councillors of the municipalities and must reflect the results obtained by each party or electoral grouping in the municipal elections.[8] The county council has powers over: territorial and urban planning, health, social services, culture, sport, education, public safety and the environment.[9]

The county of Vallès Occidental is located in the Barcelona metropolitan area north and west of the city, but within the province of Barcelona. Despite the ambiguous status of the provincial administration in Catalonia, the Barcelona Provincial Council (*Diputació de Barcelona*) also plays an important supportive role for local authorities in local economic and employment development. Its 51 indirectly-elected members are chosen from mayors and councillors from the 311 municipalities in the province. Like the county councils, its political composition reflects the results of the municipal elections.

Map of Spain

The Provincial Council is a service and consulting body for local governments in the province. In addition to local employment and economic development, it is engaged in supporting a variety of cultural activities and educational activities throughout the province (*e.g.* local festivals, local museums, the local library network) and provides technical and financial support to the municipalities to improve social services. In the area of local development and employment the Provincial Council's Economic Development Service promotes good practices by providing a consulting instrument designed to facilitate "the detection, analysis, dissemination and exchange of local active experiences in the fight against unemployment and the creation of jobs." This "practical guide" also provides a methodology and guidelines for preparing synthetic reports that serve to disseminate local experiences. Local good practice reports, based on the guidelines, are collected and published on the agencies.[10]

The Catalonian territorial structure based on counties is an alternative to the traditional provincial structure, but at the risk of duplication of the supra-municipal territorial organisations (province and county). Catalonian law regards the provinces and provincial councils as provisional "so long as the legal conditions do not exist which would make possible the integration of the provincial government and administration into the *Generalitat* and the consequent elimination of the division of Catalonia into provinces."[11]

Vallès Occidental: early co-operative experiences

Vallès Occidental had a tradition of co-operative industrial relations between unions and employers' associations even prior to the establishment of the territorial employment pact (TEP) of Vallès Occidental. There had also been several previous projects for the promotion of employment in the county with an innovative and co-operative approach, mainly promoting the employment insertion of youths and creating employment in the area of new emerging activities (ECOTEC, 2002). These initiatives are the following:

- *1995: District approach.* Assisting unemployed youth with training deficiencies to enter the labour market and facilitating the exchange of experiences in the county and nationally.

- *1995-1997: Youthstart I – orientation of young people with training deficiencies in Vallès Occidental.* Establishing a nexus of relations between school and work for young people, prevention of school drop-outs and sensitising society towards the problem of youth unemployment.

- *1996-1998: European Regional Development Fund (ERDF) programme – Niovallès.* Creating jobs around new employment opportunities, promoting county-wide co-operation and experimenting with new ways of intervening in order to create employment in business and personal services and the environment.

These county initiatives were a basis for developing new projects, which after March 1997 were carried out within the framework of the territorial employment pact of Vallès Occidental. It thus can be described as "an old partnership performing a new function" (ECOTEC, 2002).

The EU territorial employment pact in Vallès Occidental (1998-1999)

The Vallès Occidental pact was one of six Spanish pacts established under the EU pilot programme for the creation of territorial employment pacts in 1997-1999.[12] Altogether 89 territorial employment pacts proposed by national government were established in all 15 EU countries. For each pact, EUR 200 000 in funding for technical assistance was provided, which in practice covered start-up expenses and some co-ordination costs but not funding for programmes. Funding for pact programmes comes largely from the role they are able to establish in co-ordinating or implementing other EU and national programmes. The county council was responsible for the management of the original Vallès Occidental pact, a function which it still maintains.

The first action plan of the TEP covering the period 1998-99 was based on a partnership agreement between the *Generalitat*, the county council of Vallès

Occidental, representing the 23 municipalities in the area, two labour unions (*Comisiones Obreras*, CO, and *Unión General de Trabajadores*, UGT) and two business associations (the Business Association of the Sabadell region, CIESC, and the Business Association of the Terrassa region, CECOT) (ECOTEC, 2002).

After conclusion of an official partnership agreement in March of 1997, the first action plan of the pact was agreed in January 1998. Relatively prosperous, it was the only one of the original six Spanish pacts to be located in an Objective 2 rather than an Objective 1 region.[13] Thus, in contrast to other Spanish pacts in Objective 1 regions, Vallès Occidental is a region with relatively good economic conditions. It was historically an important centre of the textile industry now undergoing a process of transitions and diversification. Originally employment issues were at the centre of the pact's concern but the actual spectrum of projects became much broader, encompassing a wide range of social, environmental, industrial relations and economic development issues (Pacte per l'Ocupació, 2000).

The EU-wide evaluation of the first generation of pacts found the Vallès Occidental pact to be very effective in implementing the basic elements of the EU pact approach, which can be defined as follows:

- focus on employment;
- bottom-up approach;
- formal, broad-based partnership;
- integrated strategy based on diagnosis of strengths and weaknesses;
- innovation; and
- appropriate spatial scale.

It cited Vallès Occidental as a success story especially with regard to the role it assumed in co-ordinating labour-market and related activities (ECOTEC, 2002).

During its initial 1998-1999 period as a pilot EU territorial employment pact, the total expenditure for its 18 project areas amounted to EUR 29.4 million. Funding sources for pact programmes in the first period were as follows: 50% came from the EU (ESF and ERFD), 39% from the Catalonian regional government, 8.5% from local authorities and 3% from private sector contributions (Pacte per l'Ocupació, 2000). Of the EU funding circa 40% (EUR 6 million) is classified by the pact organisation as additional funding leveraged by the existence of the pact organisation, together with matching funds a substantial addition to pact resources.

Pacte per l'Ocupació del Vallès Occidental (2000-2003)

The 2000-2003 Second Action Plan of the Vallès Occidental TEP comprises 21 municipalities within the county. The two principal cites in the area,

Sabadell and Terrassa, have their own separate organisations during the current period. The new pact is a continuation of the previous 1998-1999 pact experience, which had already developed formal and professional structures for designing planning and carrying out, and controlling its actions. As in its previous phase, the parties to the pact were the regional government (*Generalitat de Catalunya*), the county council of Vallès Occidental, which again serves as the managing body for the pact, 21 of the municipalities in the area, two labour unions (CO and UGT) and two business associations (CIESC and CECOT).

Projects being carried out under the current Action Plan (2000-2003) encompass a wide spectrum of concerns, with a strong emphasis on the integration of labour market problem groups and the prevention of social exclusion. The *Employment Vallès – Equal Community Initiative* is addressed to 1 200 persons, largely women, at risk of social exclusion; *Vallès without barriers* serves 250 handicapped people and aims at achieving a reintegration rate of 33%. The pact also supports and maintains a *County network of job market observatories for continuous* diagnosis of the socio-economic situation of the county and produced a 2001 *Report on training needs* in Vallès Occidental. Other projects are directed toward persons in employment or enterprises. For example, *Concerta* promotes work health and safety, quality and environmental awareness in small and medium sized enterprises and *Promotion of job opportunities for women* provides an internet-based guide to companies for good practice in favour of the *female worker*. A *Databank on collective negotiation and employment and support for an Arbitration* Centre address the particular concerns of the social partners. *Urban Vallès* aims to improve the urban environment through over 40 neighbourhood projects in towns in the county and *Natural Vallès – Stage II* extends the existing 100 km of footpaths in a local park area "Vallès Natural". Other projects address the social and labour market concerns of immigrant workers or offers training for local social services in dealing with people with special problems. Only one project has a clear focus on local economic development: the *County network for promoting local urban* shopping, which also supported the establishment of a local shopkeepers association.

The Vallès Occidental pact's governing organs, which are jointly chaired by the representatives of Department of Employment of the Generalitat and the Vallès Occidental county council, are:

- *Executive Committee*: takes all the decisions and approves all the actions and financial management. Included in this body are representatives from: the Vallès Occidental county council, the Generalitat (Department of Employment and Department of the Interior), the Barcelona Provincial Council, the two largest cities (Terrassa and Sabadell), representatives of 5 other municipalities, trade unions (CO, UGT) of Vallès Occidental, Terrassa

County Business Confederation (*Confederació Empresarial Comarcal de Terrassa*), Intersectorial Council of Entrepreneurs of Sabadell and County (*Consell Intersectorial d'Empresaris de Sabadell i Comarca*) and an association of non-profit organisations in the county which fight against social exclusion.

● *Permanent Commission:* conducts the day-to-day business of the pact and makes proposals to the Executive Committee. It oversees relations with the collaborating and co-financing bodies that implement the pact's programmes and proposes and monitors pact financing. This smaller body includes representatives of the county council, the Departments of Employment and Interior of Catalonia, union and employers organisations, and local chambers of commerce.

In addition to these governing bodies, the pact maintains technical and consultative bodies and commissions for the development, management, and execution of its projects. The Permanent Commission is served by "co-ordinators" charged with responsibility for linking and co-ordinating pact activities and the "technical offices" that they head. The latter prepare and develop the projects and actions on a county basis, provides technical assistance, work with the different agents of the pact on the projects carried out locally and facilitate the joint management of the pact. There are in addition specific "work groups" made up of technicians from the member bodies of the pact, who define, carry out and follow-up pact activities. There is in addition a consultative plenary organ to which bodies linked with the economic and social development of the county belong. It makes non-binding proposals to the pact.

Supplementing the original pact agreement and initial action plan, co-ordination and accountability within the pacts is codified in several key "co-ordination tools", documents and data bases that are continually updated. These include:

● The so-called "framework document", a diagnosis of the socio-economic situation and a description of the priority lines of action which must be carried out in the employment field. This document is intended to serve as a strategic basis for drawing up new programmes within the framework of the county pact.

● The "co-operation manual" describes the working mechanisms for the co-ordination of active policies for employment in the territory. It is drawn up with the active participation of the local, social and economic agents who are in charge of the planning, development and follow-up of the county pact.

● The county map of employment services provides a collection and description of all the actions which make up the county pact. It includes all the actions planned by the different local, social and economic agents for the promotion of employment and equal opportunities and business competition. The identification and classification of the actions is intended to facilitate coherence and avoid duplication in developing projects.

In summary, the organisation and management of the pact itself and its projects are highly professional with transparent and clearly defined decision-making structures, explicit allocation of responsibility for projects to different participating organisations, and careful auditing of implementation against targets, with some effort to monitor results with descriptive statistics. The pact organisation also maintains an exemplary web page,[14] a detailed system of reports and publications (in Catalan, Spanish and English), for both internal co-ordination and monitoring as well as external presentation and dissemination. Insofar as information is available, its evaluation activities can be best described as intelligent monitoring against targets.

Mainstreaming pacts in Catalonia

After the positive experience with the EU Vallès Occidental pact, the Catalonian regional government decided to extend the pact approach to the entire Catalonian region. The pact approach appears to have been conceived as a new model of territorial intervention in the Spanish governance context, which has become more decentralised but also more complex as a result of regionalisation, which primarily transfers more responsibility and resources to the regional government without addressing the problems of vertical and horizontal co-operation at the local level.

The pacts are the creation of the regional government and it monitors their activities in connection with recognition of the pacts and approval of matching funds for eligible purposes. The mission of the territorial pacts in the view of the ministry is twofold: 1) to participate in the development of the Catalonia employment plan and in the formulation of the annual work plan; 2) to analyse labour market problems and to develop in concert with the principal local actors suitable proposals and strategies.

The principal policy goals are the insertion of women and of labour market problem groups, qualification of workers in new information and communication techniques and the creation of quality jobs in new areas of employment, the implementation of employment programmes in a locally co-ordinated manner, and facilitation of employment growth through local co-operative agreements (Generalitat de Catalunya, 2003). These priorities are based on the Catalonia Employment Plan, the regional equivalent of the National Employment Action Plan, as seen above.

The Catalonian pacts must include the local authorities and the most important employers associations and trade unions. Other employment-related organisations may also participate. Prior to the formation of the new territorial pacts the responsible regional Department of Employment entered into a framework agreement on the new programme with the Catalan Association of Municipalities and the Federation of the Municipalities of Catalonia. Over the period 2001-2006 EUR 30 000 000, from Objective 2 ESF funding, are being allocated to support the local pacts. The local authorities that act as co-ordinating bodies for administering the pact agreements receive 50% co-financing of the activities undertaken by the territorial pacts. A total of 21 Catalonian pacts, including the well-established Vallès Occidental pact, are now operating. The available funds are to be allocated to local areas according to the following criteria: the population of the area; its unemployment rate and business activity in relation to that of its province and that of Catalonia, giving priority to the zones most in need; equal treatment of women; and the objectives of the National Action Plan for Employment.

The level of funding allocated is relatively small, on average around EUR 1.4 million per pact or only EUR 230 000 per pact per annum in matching funds. Assuming a 50% matching grant by local authorities, the base funding level of the pacts is on average circa EUR 450 000 per year. This is enough to fund co-ordination costs and smaller innovative programmes. The modest funding level is not regarded by the Catalonian authorities as a shortcoming but a design feature. Like the territorial employment pacts under the original EU programme, the Catalonian pacts are seen largely as innovative governance at the territorial level. The pacts are expected to be a major channel for ESF and regional government funds, as well as for the activities of the local authorities. The pacts must also attempt to leverage additional resources from the private sector, local and regional authorities, and national and EU sources. It is unlikely, however, that the new pacts will succeed in leveraging additional funding to the same extent as did the Vallès Occidental pact in the initial EU-funded pilot period since 21 pact organisations now compete for EU funding in Catalonia.

The pacts may use their funds for a number of specified purposes: the development and co-ordination of the pact organisation, including analysis of the regional situation as well as for the implementation of the programmes developed. The pacts have a broad focus, with emphasis on programmes that are supplementary and innovative with a focus on labour market and employment goals.

The Catalonian pacts are voluntary local partnerships that do not conform to a uniform territorial pattern. Thus while in most cases they correspond to county jurisdictions not all of the 41 Catalonian counties have their own pact organisation. In a number of cases the new pacts are organised at the municipal level, for example, the long established pact organisation in Mataró but also the Sabadell and Terrassa pacts in the two largest cities in Vallès Occidental. Moreover, the territory of three pacts (Girona, Lleida and

Tarragona) comprises entire provinces, whereas the other eighteen pacts are situated in the province of Barcelona. Evidently, political criteria as well as economic logic played a strong role in the formation of the pacts.

Experiences in sector-based co-operation: Almería

Almería is a unique Mediterranean costal and mountainous province in southeastern Spain, within the large autonomous community of Andalusia. In the last decade the province has experienced rapid economic and employment growth and a marked improvement in its labour market situation. Currently at 8.5% Almería has one of the lowest unemployment rates of all Spanish provinces and a per capita GDP of over EUR 11 000 in 1998, which is still only 82% of the Spanish average but the highest in the region of Andalusia (Cámara Almería, 2002). Two major growth sectors in the local economy are agriculture, primarily green house production of winter vegetables for North European markets, and tourism. The costal areas have also experienced a real estate boom as a consequence of the influx of foreigners establishing vacation or retirement homes there. For both tourism and agriculture water is key resource in an extremely dry climate and thus water management issues play a central role. There is thus a particularly close relationship between the regional water agency (*Aguas de la Cuenca del Sur*, ACUSUR), local authorities, and water users. The province is also home to a relatively large university with 15 000 students in the provincial capital of Almería.

Except for the relatively lower unemployment rate, the labour market has the typical characteristics of that of Spain as a whole: low activity rate, especially among women; very high female unemployment rates; an even higher rate of temporary employment contracts (around 50%) and high turnover (Cámara Almería, 2002).

A special feature of the local labour market in Almería is the presence of a large population of legal and illegal immigrants employed largely in agriculture, a majority of whom are of Moroccan origin (Cámara Almería, 2002). Especially the geographical proximity of Morocco together with the pull-effect of the prevailing large differences in income levels has lead to a high number of illegal immigrants and social tensions.[15] Anti-foreign riots directed above all at Moroccans erupted in Almería in 2000 (OECD, 2003a). In El Ejido, where the violence was centered, an estimated 10 000 of the 45 000 residents are foreign workers, most of whom live in slum conditions. For several days in a number of south-eastern towns Spanish residents harassed and attacked African immigrants (*New York Times*, 2 December 2000). The subsequent five-day strike by farm workers caused serious disruption and economic loss to the green house vegetable farms.

While immigration policy is the responsibility of the central government, labour market and social integration fall primarily under the responsibility of the regional and local authorities who are responsible for active labour market policies, education, health, social assistance, housing and social services.

The basic structure of the territorial administration in Andalusia is similar to that in Catalonia described above, with one major exception: The county and county council, which play a central role in local administration Catalonia (see Section 2.2) do not exist in Andalusia. In the province of Almería it is the Provincial Cortes (council) that plays the most important role in supra-municipal territorial governance.

Another important difference is that, at the time of our interviews in late 2003, the national public employment service (INEM) was still responsible for active as well as passive labour market policies in Andalusia. The regional employment service under the Junta of Andalusia (regional government) did not take over responsibility for active policies until January of 2004. In addition to its labour market programmes, INEM supported local development projects and business start-ups through various programmes. Examples are employment programmes in which the unemployed restore local monuments and heritage sites and support for rural development in smaller municipalities as well as funding for additional personnel and training for the Almería Council and Tourist Board. INEM also entered into a number of *ad hoc* agreements with municipalities to provide integrated local employment services.

Co-operation in tourism

The year-round warm, dry climate, many miles of coast and scenic mountain areas within national parks make Almería attractive for tourists. The tourism sector, which is concentrated on the Mediterranean coastal areas of the province, includes both vacationers and a large and growing colony of Northern European permanent residents (predominantly from Great Britain, France, Germany) with second or retirement homes in the province. With over 40 000 hotel beds, 864 000 accommodated travelers, and more than 4 million overnight stays, tourism is a major source of economic activity and employment. About one half the tourists are from outside Spain. The growing attractiveness of the Almería coast as a location for second and retirement homes has engendered a strong real estate boom in recent years in the province, which has seen the construction of entire self-contained beach front urban developments (*i.e.* at Almerimar).

The Provincial Tourism Board is the principal agency for the co-ordination of local activities and support of enterprises in the tourism sector. It is an independent agency of the Provincial Cortes with a broad spectrum of activities in the tourism sector. It seeks to enhance the attractiveness of the area for tourist through traditional actions such as promotion of the "Almería Coast" image; represents Almería tourism at national and international events and preparation of publications, brochures, posters, videos, etc., to this end. The Board is also aims to increase the attractiveness of local tourism assets and of the quality of enterprises in the sector, for example, through study and development of the tourism potential of towns within the province[16] as well as through quality promotion measures, training, innovation and modernisation in the tourism sector.

The Tourism Board's governing body is a General Assembly, whose president is the President of the Almería Provincial Cortes. Its members are representatives of the town councils that belong to the Board, business associations of the tourism sector, the provincial delegations of the government of Andalusia, the trade unions among others. Its principal task is the approval of the annual work plan and special initiatives and approval of the budget. The Executive Council, whose president is the president of the Almería Provincial Cortes, is mainly responsible for the organisation of the Provincial Tourism Board, preparation of its budget and of the action report and work plan for approval by the General Assembly. Its members include various county councilors as well as members of the town councils, enterprises linked to the tourism sector, travel agencies, banks and other enterprises belonging to the Board, the government of Andalusia and the central government. A professional manager conducts the day-to day business of the board in consultation with the Board's president. The Provincial Cortes exercises supervision over the Board's finances and organisational structure. The Tourism Board is financed by an annual levy on its members and by grants and aid from other public and private bodies.

INEM co-operates closely with the Tourism Board and has substantially augmented the Board's resources through programmes designed to promote local development, training for employees, and consulting to entrepreneurs. For example, through its programme for agents for employment and local development it financed 11 additional staff positions in 2003 as well as a labour market diagnostic study for the province.

Joint management of water resources

In Almería, one of the most arid areas in Europe, water is a scarce resource and the management of water resources is a principal focus of planning and co-operative activity. The heavy use of water for agriculture and tourism as well as to meet the needs of residents greatly exceeds the sustainable supply. Over exploitation of aquifers for irrigation is depleting ground water resulting in deteriorating water quality. Forecasts of future demand predict an even worsening situation. The Southern Basin Hydrological Plan, or Almería plan, was developed and approved by the

Ministry of Environment through the Hydrographic Confederation of the South of Spain. Given the centrality of water resources for the region, it is regarded as a master plan to meet water needs, guarantee water quality, promote development and protect the environment. Infrastructure and water management improvements include water transfers to the costal regions through the establishment of an integrated water management system (Negratin-Almanzora connection, Almanzora-Western connection) and the construction of a large desalination facility for converting sea water, which at full capacity can supply the water needs of a city of 500 000. The total investment costs exceed ESP 24 000 million, financed through European and state funds as well as private financing from water users. Other measures are designed to control and correct water losses in the distribution system and to promote efficiency by metering actual consumption.[17]

The principal actors are public agencies, the Ministry of Environment and the Hydrographic Confederation of the South of Spain, the public corporation ACUSUR as well as the *Junta de Usuarios de Agua del Valle del Almanzora* and over 60 local water user associations in the area. The water users bear part of the capital costs of the infrastructure investments as well paying water use fees.

The Users Communities (or Irrigators Communities) of which there are over 6 000 in Spain, are public authorities regulated by Water Law, relatively autonomous, there statutes and ordinances have to be approved by their respective *Confederación Hidrográfica* for the water basin to which they belong. The landowners with water rights are obligatory members of their local Irrigation Community. They jointly allocate and regulate use of the water rights allotted to the Users Community and share the common costs of maintaining and improving the water distribution system. It is the regional Hydrographical Confederation (*Confederación Hidrográfica del Sur* in the case of Almería) that has overall responsibility for water management. In contrast to the self-governing Users Communities, users have a more limited role in the regional public water authority, in which they constitute only of the members the governing board (Del Campo, 1999).

Principal national issues in water management relate to the continuation of the traditional policy of water transfers to meet rising demand (instead of conservation through demand management), pricing of water to users and the share of capital costs they are required to pay, and depletion of ground water through over-exploitation and illegal irrigation. Water resource management and the National Water Plan have become increasingly the focus of controversy in Spain. Spanish water policy has historically relied on dams and large-scale water transfers between water basins to increase supply. The National Water Plan announced in 2000 proposed as its centre piece the diversion of a billion cubic meters of water per year from the Ebro River to arid regions on coast; approximately 90 million cubic meters would be allocated to the province Spain's Mediterranean of Almería. The project foresees building 118 dams and more than 1 000 km of canals and pipelines costing an estimated EUR 18 billion, one third of which is to be financed through EU funding. The Almería plan described above is one component in this master plan.

Public criticism in Spain culminated in mass protests in the region from which water is being diverted (Zaragoza) and from environmentalists. The economic critic of the planned Ebro river diversion is that sustainable development and economic efficiency would be better served by demand management through higher water prices. Particular singled out for criticism are enormous wastage in the distribution system, which has been estimated to amount to about th of the water flow,[18] and the highly subsidised pricing of water for agricultural, which leads to inefficient usage and waste (Arrrojo, 2003; Marti, 2000).[19]

Critics argue that water prices are currently too low or fail to reflect actual water use;[20] and that demand management is a superior alternative to water transfers. They favor balancing supply and demand by moderate increase in prices to encourage economical use as well as increased use of desalination plants, which even at a cost of around 0.50 EUR/m^3 is cheaper than transferring water in many regions of Almería (Albio et al., 2002; Garrido, 2002).

Greenhouse miracle: the plastic sea

The plastic-sheet roofs of green houses cover more than 30 000 hectares of arid Almería. Concentrated in lowlands and costal plains, from a distance the shimmer of sunlight reflected from the plastic gives the appearance of a vast inland sea. Intensive vegetable production (mainly tomatoes, zucchini, peppers, cucumbers) in low-cost plastic greenhouses has been enormously economically successful in Almería in the last 30 years. With a total production of 2.5 million tons and a value of over EUR 1.5 billion in 2002. The bulk of the vegetables produced are exported to EU countries, mainly to Germany, France, the United Kingdom and the Netherlands. In 2002, 18% of the 200 000 persons in employment was in agriculture, compared to 10.2% for Andalusia and 8.2% for Spain as a whole. Suppliers and business services related to agriculture are an additional related source of business activity and employment in the region (Cámara Almería, 2002).

Starting initially with field-grown crops under plastic tunnels and simple covered fields under wooden structures, there is now a strong trend toward fixed metal-frame structures and more sophisticated production methods. Commercial agriculture and especially greenhouse production is technology intensive, requiring the adaptation of greenhouse design and climate management and crop techniques and practices to local conditions. The most modern Almería greenhouses now have completely computer-controlled systems for climate control and supply of water and nutrients to plants using soil-less (hydroponic) production techniques. The new generation of greenhouses represents, however, a markedly higher capital investment and higher costs for maintaining technical equipment. Furthermore, marketing and the logistics of transporting products to distant and highly competitive European markets require a high degree of business know-how.

The simply constructed plastic greenhouses in a mild Mediterranean climate have the advantage of low construction and heating costs in comparison with glass greenhouses in northern climates, but also the disadvantage of more limited climate control, for example regulation of humidity or the balance of CO_2, which may result in a higher incidence of plant disease or slower growth. Almería producers also have the disadvantage of greater distance to markets and higher transportation costs. Both types of factors may have detrimental effects on product quality. Another important factor contribution to Almería's low production costs is the ready availability of cheap North African labour.

Almería's innovative strategy of using simple plastic greenhouses under its favorable climatic conditions (annual average temperature of 20 degrees and over 3 000 hours of sunshine) to supply fruit and vegetables to European markets appears to have developed from local experiments, initially the use of plastic covering to induce early ripening of table grapes. Eventual vegetable production, which is of higher value, has supplanted grapes and citrus fruits and accounts for 90% of the province's agricultural production. The initial low capital costs made it possible for production to be developed by local farmers and the structure of ownership is still predominantly that of small (around 1 hectare) family-owned businesses, which join together in co-operatives for marketing purposes. Co-operation with Dutch agricultural enterprises, which provided technical assistance and marketing know-how, initially played an important role. A key prerequisite for the success of this strategy was access to European markets through Spain's membership in the EU after 1986 and an increase in vegetable consumption in European diets. The future of vegetable farming requires continuous innovation in products, techniques, and marketing. Although Almería enjoys a climatic advantage and lower costs for labour and land in comparison, for example, with the Netherlands, this is offset in part by higher productivity in the latter.[21] The small and medium-sized entrepreneurs in the greenhouse agricultural sector, apart from marketing co-operatives, do not appear to be well organised to assist their members in the increasingly complex tasks of financing and operating more sophisticated greenhouse technology nor is there strong public support from the provincial or regional authorities.

The University of Almería has an agricultural faculty that gives particular attention to the problems of greenhouse agriculture; moreover, there are several public and private research stations. However, there appears to be no systematic effort to link and transfer academic research to the greenhouse entrepreneurs, comparable, for example, to the agricultural extension services in the United States (Canatliffe and Vamsockle, 2000). Moreover, few of the greenhouse entrepreneurs from a farming background appear to have any systematic training that would be of assistance in the increasingly technically sophisticated farming methods being used. The greenhouse success story appears to have developed in a largely unplanned and uncoordinated way and little organised effort appears to be devoted to addressing the industry's problems and ensuring its continued success.

Finally, the greenhouse vegetable industry in Almería is particularly dependent on the future development of EU agricultural policy, in particular market access for Southern Mediterranean countries. Currently North African olives, fruits and vegetables are subject to high tariffs and import quotas that limit their ability to compete with Spanish products. EU policy aims, however, at the gradual elimination of trade barriers. For example, in its Association Agreement with Morocco the EU has committed itself in principle to the gradual dismantling of trade barriers by 2012.[22] The long-term prospect is for a continued gradual reduction in existing trade barriers, which makes the development of a strategy of innovation and diversification a top priority for the industry.

What impact on local governance?

This section seeks to assess the impact on governance of the various experiments surveyed in this chapter. In addition to the capacity and potential of partnerships in co-ordinating policies and taking an integrated approach to local development, the following aspects of their functioning will be used in the analysis: a) the level at which the partnership is organised; b) the scope of its programmatic focus; c) the inclusiveness of the partnership; and d) the adequacy of its management framework and accountability standards.

Local partnership in Vallès Occidental

The Vallès Occidental employment pact is a local partnership at the county level including trade unions, business associations as well as representatives of the provincial council of Barcelona and NGOs. It is thus a formal, broad-based partnership with a markedly bottom-up approach and a clear employment focus.

The pact serves both as an instrument of governance – i.e. to co-ordinate policies, adapt them to local conditions and involve other partners in the orientation of measures – as well as implementing projects at the county level. The contribution of the pact has been primarily in developing joint innovative activities at the county level rather than rationalising existing programmes.

For this purpose the pact has not only pooled existing resources but, especially in its initial period, been successful in attracting additional resources to the county. The pact has been successful, in particular, in establishing itself as a manager for European Social Fund programmes.

The pact's management framework is a strong formal organisation with clear goals and a well articulated division of labour. An integrated diagnosis and strategy, with a strong labour market focus based on the Catalonia Employment Plan, is set forth in the pact's agreed "framework document". This and other "co-ordination tools" provide a high degree of transparency and accountability. The pact documents and monitors its own activities for the benefit of pact actors and the general public in an exemplary fashion, as seen earlier.

The programmatic focus of the Vallès Occidental pact's activities is on the labour market and social integration of women, immigrants, and the handicapped. Some programmes also address the concerns of the employed and enterprises (e.g. "awareness campaign" on work health and safety, a study of training needs, but also support services for collective bargaining), which is a reflection of the prominent role of the social partners in the local pact. Surprisingly little attention is given to local economic development, except for local urban and rural environmental projects, although Vallès Occidental is a former textile centre now undergoing restructuring. Development issues are addressed primarily at the municipal and regional levels (see discussion of CIDEM) with no linkage to the county level pact. This narrow focus does not reflect a shortcoming in pact performance but a design feature: the pacts function primarily as an instrument for the implementation of regional labour market programmes, which is their principal source of funding.

The Vallès Occidental pact, which has existed continuously since 1997, has been the subject of a number of evaluations. There is clear evidence that it has had an important impact both on local governance and implementation. In its initial 1998-99 phase many of these issues were discussed at the county level for the first time. Moreover, the pact provided unions and employers with a forum in which they could address broader community issues on an equal basis, playing an important role in institutionalising social partnership at the territorial level. Important to the pacts success was that it was able to achieve and sustain a consensus on goals (ECOTEC, 2002).

Horizontally, the Vallès Occidental pact contributed to local governance by developing joint activities based on a common perspective between local actors that did not normally participate (social partners, NGOs) and between territories that did not normally co-operate (the municipalities). Participation in the partnership is relatively traditional in that employers' organisations and trade unions play a dominant role in comparison with other NGOs.

In the complex structure of Catalonian territorial administration the Vallès Occidental pact also plays an important role in facilitating vertical ties: the pact links the municipalities with the county and both with the Department of Employment of the regional government of Catalonia, whose representative jointly chairs meetings of pact bodies together with a representative of the county council. The Barcelona provincial council is represented in the executive committee. Notably absent are representatives of the state administration, which is probably a reflection of the relative low territorial level of the activity of this pact. Moreover, the regional (Catalonian) employment service has to our knowledge no direct link to the pact's activities, which seems inconsistent with the pacts focus on employment issues.[23]

The mainstreaming of the pact model within Catalonia is a tribute to the success of the Vallès Occidental pact and of the potential for partnerships in local governance in Spain. It is unlikely, however, that the new pacts will succeed in leveraging additional funding to the same extent as did the Vallès Occidental pact in the initial EU-funded pilot period since 21 pact organisations now compete for EU funding in Catalonia.

Co-operation in Almería

Almería is – in comparison with the rest of Andalusia – a success story based on its two major industries: tourism and greenhouse agriculture. The downside is that the economic base in Almería is much less diversified and hence more vulnerable than that in province of Barcelona, where Vallès Occidental is located. Almería is particularly dependent on the future development of EU agricultural policy regarding market access for North African countries.

Moreover, the social infrastructure of co-operation and partnerships appears less well-developed in Almería. There is no broad local partnership but a more traditional, sector-based pattern of co-operation in tourism and water resource management. Trade unions and employers' organisations are less prominent actors.

The Provincial Tourism Board, which is a specialised body attached to the Provincial Council, is organised at a higher level in the Spanish territorial administration than the Vallès Occidental pact (province vs. county). It is concerned with a broader range of issues (not only employment but also economic development) and involves a broad spectrum of relevant actors. Its industry-based focus on tourism, however, is relatively narrow.

Based on documentation, interviews and visits, the Board is a well organised and highly professional operation, closely integrated with the provincial authority, which also engages in broader local economic development activities in towns and rural areas of the province. Horizontally the Board links and provides services to municipal and other local actors including business associations, local enterprises and unions. Vertically, it links these actors to the provincial and regional levels in Andalusia, and even the state administration.

In contrast to the Vallès Occidental pact in Catalonia, the public employment service (INEM), although not a member of the Board, co-operates closely with it. INEM has substantially augmented the Board's resources through programmes designed to promote rural development, training for employees, and advice to entrepreneurs.

Accountability is based on the standards of legal and fiscal accountability traditionally found in the public service. In contrast to the Vallès Occidental pact, there was no indication of the use of goal-oriented and multi-year planning and monitoring of results or of regular evaluation.

The success of tourism is dependent in the long run on a number of broader issues that face the province that cannot be addressed within the sector-based framework of the Tourism Board. For example, adequate road, airport, and rail connections, which are the responsibilities of regional or state agencies. There are moreover potential conflicts with the agricultural sector; for example, tourists tend to regard the "plastic sea" of makeshift greenhouses as an eyesore (some rural tourist areas have banned them). There is also a potential conflict between tourism and agriculture over scarce water resources. For example, in the extremely dry climate of Almería it has been estimated that a golf course requires 3 million liters of water per day.

In Spain, the management of water resources and provision of the necessary infrastructure are of the utmost important for regional development and entail extensive co-operation and planning. This is not, however, a policy area in which local partnerships can play a significant role.

- Policy-making in water resource management is dominated by the national authorities (National Water Plan, Ministry of Environment), regional authorities and specialised agencies (Hydrographic Confederation of Southern Spain, ACUSUR) in an integrated regional and national planning context. Local interests are best articulated though regional authorities working within the framework of regional and national institutions.

- Moreover, there is no lack of local participation in water management: the local actors affected are already well-organised in Users Communities to articulate their interests to decision-makers at the regional and national levels.

The greenhouse agricultural sector, which is the most important and most vulnerable element in the Almería success story, appears – in comparison with tourism –, to be only weakly organised and to lack supportive links to provincial and regional governments. The small and medium-sized entrepreneurs in this sector, apart from marketing co-operatives, do not appear to have any well-organised business associations to assist their members in the increasingly complex tasks of financing and operating more sophisticated greenhouse technology, disseminating know-how, improving marketing and product quality.

Nor is there a great deal of lateral support from other local institutions: There are no technical assistance or marketing services available to the greenhouse agricultural sector comparable to the well-developed support provided by the Provincial Cortes of Almería to tourism and, to a lesser extent, rural development.

Although the Junta of Andalusia (regional government) is primarily responsible for agriculture and regional development policy, the greenhouse vegetable industry does not appear to be a priority concern, perhaps because it is strongly concentrated within Andalusia in the province of Almería.

The Spanish governance context and partnerships

The formerly highly-centralised Spanish state is undergoing a major process of devolution of powers to the 17 autonomous communities. In the past local economic development, employment and social policies were the responsibility of central state agencies and their territorial organisations at the provincial level. Primarily responsible for co-ordination across different policy domains was the office of the provincial civil governor, the highest representative of the state in the province. In that hierarchical administrative structure, for which the French prefect system was the model, there was no place for inter-governmental partnerships with active participation of civil society in local governance. In the new Spanish constitution adopted in 1978 and implemented stepwise over the past twenty-five years, employment and economic development are "shared powers" and primary responsibility for implementation rests with the regional authorities. Understandably, the relationship between central government and regional authorities has dominated the political agenda in Spain to such an extent that the problems of local authorities and co-operation in local governance and implementation have been relatively neglected: the overlapping division of labour between central and regional government agencies in exercising "shared powers", the need to better link local actors to the newly empowered regional authorities, the need for horizontal co-operation between the overlapping jurisdictions of the local authorities (municipalities, cities, counties, provinces), and the need to better integrate the social partners and other NGOs in local governance. There is an urgent need to consider the implications of the ongoing restructuring of the Spanish state for the modernisation of local governance, in which partnerships could potentially play an important role.

Unlike many other countries, Spain has no national programme to promote local partnerships in employment and economic development. This is in part a reflection of the fact that local governance, *i.e.* the governmental structure of the autonomous communities and their territorial organisation, is an exclusive power of the regions. In fact the two case studies examined in this chapter are very diverse. In Vallès Occidental in Catalonia earlier experience with partnerships in the implementation of specific programmes culminating after 1997/98 in the Vallès Occidental pilot EU territorial employment pact, an exemplary local partnership model that has now been adopted throughout Catalonia. In the case of Almería in Andalusia, which also was home to a EU pilot pact in Cádiz, there is no broadly-based local partnership but only a more traditional sector-based co-operation in tourism and water resource management.

Moreover, the decentralisation process in Spain is asymmetrical: The Spanish Constitution merely enumerates a list of powers that may be assumed through legislation by the autonomous communities. Whether, how, and when they do so differs greatly. Catalonia was quick to assume a maximum of autonomy under the new Constitution and established, for example its own regional employment service, whereas at the time our interviews employment policy in Andalusia was still being implemented by the INEM.[24]

Conclusions and issues for consideration

The Catalonian pact model is a positive and innovative response to the special problems of local governance in Spain and merits careful observation and evaluation. Based on the experience of the Vallès Occidental pact, we can identify the following possible shortcomings in the Catalonian partnership model that should be carefully monitored and, if need be, addressed through appropriate programme changes:

● The Catalonian pacts are strongly focused on labour market and social projects but do not address strategically local economic development issues. Consideration should be given to establishing stronger links with agencies concerned with local development, for example, the Catalonian Centre for Innovation and Business Development (CIDEM).

● Despite their labour-market focus, the Catalonian employment service, the most important local labour market actor, is not integrated in pact activities. We recommend that the regional employment service be involved in governance or at least at the technical level of projects.

● The rationale for the very different territorial coverage of the Catalonian pacts remains unclear. Most are organised at the county level but several include only a single larger town and three others outside the province of

Barcelona cover entire provinces. Our favorable assessment of the county-level pacts' contribution to vertical and horizontal co-operation may not be applicable to these pacts.

● There is no evidence of a regular exchange of information and dissemination of good practice among the Catalonian pacts. This end might be promoted, for example, through a common web page for the programme, recognition of successful innovative projects. In this respect the former EU pilot programme for territorial employment pacts might serve as a model.

● Finally, the Catalonian pacts appear to be primarily 'policy-takers' with little collective impact on the policies of the Catalonian regional government, although participation in the development of the regional employment plan was part of their original mission. One reason for this is their, in most cases, relatively small scale and local orientation but another is the still relatively-centralised style of regional administration in Catalonia.

In Almería, in comparison with the well-organised partnership in tourism, the greenhouse success story in agriculture appears to have developed in a largely unplanned and fortuitous manner with too little organised effort being devoted to addressing the industry's special problems and ensuring its continued success. A first step in this regard should be to strengthen sector-specific institutions at the provincial level. This might include:

● A publicly-sponsored board or agency for the agricultural sector – analogous to the Tourism Board – that links provincial and especially the responsible regional authorities with local business associations and co-operatives in the agricultural sector.

● In addition to interest representation *vis-à-vis* regional and national authorities, a principal service task would be to bundle resources to provide training, technical and financial advice to the predominantly small and medium-sized entrepreneurs in this sector, and establishes strong links to local university-based agricultural research and teaching.

From the perspective of local economic development, the principal shortcoming of the Tourism Board is the narrow scope of its mandate. In Almería there is an urgent need for a broadly-based forum for addressing development, employment, and social issues that transcend particular sectors (*i.e.* environmental issues, the integration of immigrant workers, diversification of the economic base).

Finally, we recommend that the Spanish government and the governments of the autonomous communities consider the potential of partnerships to address better the challenges of decentralisation for local governance in Spain. This might take the form, for example, of financing or co-financing further pilot local partnerships, providing technical support, monitoring, evaluating and disseminating information on partnership experiences.

Notes

1. According to data from the Municipal Census, the proportion of immigrants in the total population has grown from 1.6% in 1998 to 4.7% in 2002.

2. There are a series of basic principles to which the regional employment services must adhere (Ruiz, 2003).

3. Participants are the national Minister for Labour and Social Affairs together with the representatives of the ministries of the autonomous communities.

4. Registered unemployment in 2002.

5. Data for 1998.

6. There are in addition special provisions for the organisation of public services in the Barcelona metropolitan area that are not relevant here.

7. The municipality is called a town if it has more than five thousand inhabitants and a city if the population exceeds twenty thousand.

8. The number of councillors varies from 19 to 39, depending on the population of the municipality.

9. Some services which come under the jurisdiction of the municipal government can be transferred by agreement to the county authorities and agreements between counties may also be concluded. There is, therefore, considerable room for manœuvre for territorial co-operation and a variety of forms are found in praxis.

10. *www.diba.es/promocio_economica/bones_practiques/welcome.htm*.

11. An additional feature of the complicated structure of territorial administration is the position of Delegate of the central government, who is charged with the direction of the state administration within the territory of the autonomous community and co-ordination with the government of the region.

12. The other Spanish pacts were located in Cádiz, Asturias, Palencia, León, Ceuta and Melilla.

13. In the EU, Objective 1 regions are those with less than 75% of the average EU GDP. Objective 2 regions, which receive the second highest level of support from the EU regional funds, are regions with structural difficulties undergoing social and economic change.

14. See *www.ccvoc.org/pacteocupaciovalles*.

15. In 2000 Spanish GDP per capita was more than 5 times that of Morocco (OECD, 2003a). See also Hoggart and Mendoza (2000) on African immigrant workers in Spain.

16. The provincial tourist board is responsible in particular for tourism in smaller towns and rural areas; the city of Almería has its own tourist organisation.

17. See *www.planalmeria.com/presentacion.html* for details of the Almería plan.

18. Arrojo (2003) reports, for example, that the Zaragoza water network is so leaky that there is no difference between daytime and nighttime consumption.

19. Economists argue that subsidised water prices to agriculture lead to a misallocation of resources: the average income per cubic meter of water in the agricultural sector is, for example, lowest for cereals (EUR $0.13/m^2$), higher for fruit trees (EUR $0.84/m^2$) and highest for vegetables (EUR $1.64/m^2$), even higher in green

house vegetable farms with micro irrigation and 50 to 1 000 times higher in industry and services.

20. Pricing in agriculture – ca. 70% of water use – is often based on acreage irrigated instead of actual use.

21. For example, greenhouse production of tomatoes averaged 10-12 kg/m^2 in Almería compared with 42 kg/m^2 in the Netherlands. A more detailed breakdown for the year 1998 estimates that production costs are twice as high in the Netherlands for tomatoes but marketing costs are only half those of the Spanish competition, with a net cost advantage of about 25% for the Spanish product (USD 0.26 vs. USD 0.32 per pound in 1997-98; Canatliffe and Vamsockle, 2000).

22. Currently Morocco is subject to a tomato quota of 150 000 tons per year, rising to 175 000 tons in 2004 and increasing by 15 000 tons per year in the following four years (OECD, 2003a).

23. According to regional authorities, this shortcoming in vertical co-operation is currently being addressed.

24. Interviews in Almería were conducted in the fall of 2003. Only after January 2004 was responsibility for active labour market measures transferred to the regional authorities in Andalusia.

Bibliography

Aguado, R. (2002), "Public Policies for Supporting SMEs: A Comparision of the Spanish and Chilean Models", paper presented at the 7th International Post-Keynesian Workshop, June 22-July 3, Kansas City.

Albio, J., Tapia J., Meyer A. and Uche J. (2002), "Water Demand Alternatives to the Spanish National Hydrologic Plan", Unidad de Economía Agraria Working Paper, Zaragoza.

Arrojo, P. (2003), Interview in Sierra Magazine, September/October 2003.

Cámara Almería (2002), "Almería en Cifras 2002", Almería: Cámara oficial de comercio.

Canatliffe, D. and Vamsockle J. (2000), "Competitiveness of the Spanish and Dutch Greenhouse Industries with the Florida Fresh Vegetable Industry", University of Florida Cooperative Extension Service Working Paper.

Catalonia Department of Labour, Industry and Commerce (2003), "Plan General de Empleo de Cataluna", Barcelona.

Del Campo, Garcia A. (1999), "Spanish Irrigators Communities and Their National Federations", Madrid: Federation of the Spanish Irrigators Communities.

ECOTEC (2002), "Thematic Evaluation of the Territorial Employment Pacts. Final Report to the Directorate General Regional Policy", ECOTEC Research and Consulting, Brussels.

European Commission (2003), "Employment in Europe", Luxembourg: Office of Official Publications.

Garrido, A. (2002), "Transition to Full-Cost Pricing of Irrigation Water for Agriculture in OECD Countries," OECD document, Paris.

Generalitat de Catalunya (2003), "Pactos Territoriales Para El Empleo", Departament de Treball, Barcelona, May 2003.

Hoggart, K. and Mendoza, K. (2000), "African Immigrant Workers in Spanish Agriculture," Centre for Comparative Immigation Studies, University of California-San Diego Working Paper No. 2ai.

Kingdom of Spain (2003), "National Action Plan for Employment 2003", Madrid.

Marti, O. (2000), "When the Rain in Spain is not Enough", UNESCO Courier, December.

Ministry of Labour and Social Affairs (2002), "2002 Guide to Labour and Social Affairs". Madrid: Ministry of Labour and Social Affairs.

OECD (2003a), *OECD Economic Surveys: Spain*, OECD, Paris.

OECD (2003b), *Managing Decentralisation. A New Role for Labour Market Policy*, OECD, Paris.

OECD (2001), *Local Partnerships for Better Governance*, OECD, Paris.

Pacte per l'Ocupació del Vallès Occidental (2000), "Results of the Pact: Final Report". Barcelona: Generalitat de Catalunya. *www.ccvoc.org/pacteocupaciovalles/*.

Ruiz, D. (2003), "Spain: Modernisation through Regionalisation", in OECD (2001), *Managing Decentralisation: A New Role for Labour Market Policy*, OECD, Paris.

ISBN 92-64-01530-2
New Forms of Governance for Economic Development
© OECD 2004

Chapter 8

Wallonia: Stimulating the Emergence of Agents of Change

by

Xavier Greffe,
University of Paris I (Panthéon-Sorbonne), France

High structural unemployment, distressed urban areas and the need to modernise the public employment service have prompted the regional authorities to provide a solid impetus to local development in Wallonia. An array of measures have been put in place to foster a partnership approach at local level, combine services to job-seekers and promote economic development initiatives, within the framework of an encompassing region-wide strategy for economic and social development. While the impact on local governance from narrowly-focused organisations remains limited, these agents of change may well provide a key contribution to revitalising the local economy.

Better governance – the process whereby society identifies its problems and meets its needs – is central to employment strategies.* To enhance governance, public services and local authorities are working together, and with the private sector and civil society, to identify needs relating to the labour market and refine the mechanisms required to meet those needs. So partnerships are not just a broad aspiration but a prerequisite for good governance. They are not the only component, as other factors such as decentralisation and accountability are equally important. But in complex societies, where identifying and resolving the problems of target groups involves a growing number of players, partnerships can create much-needed links between economic and social issues, for instance, or between government, enterprises and civil society, and they should be assessed in that light. Partnerships should make an impact at several levels. Close to job-market players, for instance, they can develop paths into the labour market and ensure sound human-resource management; and by building special training and skills initiatives into those paths, they can assert the region's strengths and make it more competitive in the global economy.

So partnerships should seek to promote co-operation within and between all sections of society; draw up problem-solving strategies; fulfil every aspect of their remit – be it project execution or service provision – and jointly assess the outcomes, thereby strengthening the region's collective learning capacity.

A region undergoing economic and institutional change

Belgium's Walloon Region – with just over 3.3 million inhabitants spread across five provinces and 262 communes (259 French-speaking and 9 German-speaking) – is characterised by its numerous institutions. Advocating labour-management dialogue, the Region has for over thirty years now been in the throes of a considerable restructuring crisis that has shaken the traditional pillars of its economy, as well as its social structures. In spite of a noticeable improvement in the macro-economic situation since 1995, the Walloon economy is still structurally fragile: it no longer declines as sharply with each downturn, but makes very little headway in the event of an upturn. In 1999 the

---

* The author wishes to thank Alberto Melo, University of Algarve, Portugal, for his contribution.

Walloon Government, prompted by the need to mobilise the region's social partners and collectively tackle these challenges, proposed a ten-year Contract for the Future of Wallonia, or CAWA as the current version is known. The aim was to shape behaviour patterns with a collective project that initially consisted in drawing up 8 goals, 52 projects and 800 initiatives. Some of the initiatives involved re-organising the labour market by giving it a more local focus and putting greater emphasis on partnerships. The project was thought-provoking and attractive but not always backed up by macroeconomic-type forecasts, although this was intentional. The Contract soon became a benchmark for management and opinion leaders, and instilled confidence where there had previously been pessimism and a lack of motivation.

The initial exercise was then evaluated and revamped. Both the external and internal evaluations showed that having a large number of broad goals rather than numerical targets meant that priorities could not always be set, and that individual preferences might be passed off as collective priorities. Some players were also under the misapprehension that the Contract was likely to bring an injection of government funds to support the long list of initiatives, whereas the very fact that it was a contract hinted at a very different strategy, i.e. mobilising a few who then go on to mobilise others. The revamped project placed the emphasis on partnership-based approaches to achieve the critical mass required for success, hence the focus on co-ordinated economic and social activities, particularly at local level. Numerical targets were also set to ensure that the challenge was clear and the necessary resources were available. So the CAWA is based on a new form of governance that mobilizes players and their partnerships, makes decision-making transparent and objective, and ensures that initiatives are properly planned and evaluated.

One of the driving forces behind this new governance is the determination to make the most of economic opportunities and transform them into work for the region's 200 000 jobseekers (including 40 000 subsidised jobs), bringing down an unemployment rate that is higher than the European average and that of neighbouring countries. Unemployment based on the national definition stands at 14%, although it is lower according to the ILO definition (9.9%). This figure of 14% should be set against 8.8% in Germany, 11% in France and 3.3% in the Netherlands. The figure is practically the same as in 1990, after peaking in 1996 and subsequently declining. Unemployment is high, but other features are worth noting:

- Youth unemployment was higher in 2001 (28.3%) than in 1990 (23.5%).

- Long-term unemployment rates among young people (11.9%) and women (7%) are still higher than average long-term unemployment (5.8%), although the gaps have narrowed markedly since 2000.

- 25% of the long-term unemployed have been out of work for over five years.

- 80% of the unemployed have a level of education corresponding to lower secondary level.

- Some employment areas have not only second-generation but even third-generation unemployed, as the first major structural crises date back to the 1960s. There, work is an abstract concept that some find alien, hence the need to reinforce employment initiatives targeting that group.

- Wallonia also has a lower rate of employment (almost 60%) than many European countries, in any case lower than neighbouring countries and below the EU average (63-64%). One reason is low employment among three target groups: workers over the age of 55, young people, and women over the age of 40. This really is what might be called "inhibited employment".

So while Belgium's macroeconomic performance has been looking more satisfactory in recent years, the situation on the job market is still giving cause for concern, particularly in the Walloon Region. This has been put down to factors such as wage structure rigidities; high non-wage labour costs; insufficient incentives to work; and some skill disadjustment (OECD, 2001). In 1999, Belgium decided to introduce an active welfare state to promote the long-term integration of individuals and target groups into the labour market, as a whole segment of its employment policy had for a long time been delegated to the social partners in some 170 institutions. But here it is basically the responsibility of the regions that is brought to the fore, in this case the Walloon Region.

Throughout the 1990s and in accordance with Belgium's institutional set-up, plans were launched to improve the employment situation. They included efforts to reduce the cost of labour (by lowering social insurance contributions and linking wages to the "health index"); ease certain institutional rigidities on the labour market; redistribute available work (voluntary part-time work, shorter working hours; early retirement on a half-time basis); and encourage the recruitment of young people (*Plan d'embauche des jeunes*, subsidised jobs, provision of services that were barely, or not at all, part of the normal economic process). Compared with the rest of Belgium, the Walloon Region has focused more on subsidising non-market activities, creating jobs in SMEs, and developing *entreprises de formation par le travail* (firms providing in-work training).

These new policies are based on a division of responsibility between federal and regional government. The federal tier deals with unemployment benefits, working conditions, early retirement, special schemes or activities to ease the long-term unemployed back into the labour market, and some subsidised employment in the public sector. Much of this is done through the National Employment Office (ONEM) and at local level through the communes and local employment agencies (ALEs). Like the communal offices that handle this work, the ALEs establish benefit entitlements and check the status of the unemployed, but they also manage some of the programmes for the long-term unemployed. One key feature of the ALE remit is to provide jobs which those unemployed for over two years must accept if they are to continue receiving benefits. In this case the ALEs have sole responsibility for conducting checks, whereas for other jobseekers and depending on local circumstances, the communal authorities are authorised to carry out controls and run checkpoints for benefit recipients. As the ALEs are not in contact with all of the unemployed, who claim their benefits through welfare centres and apply for work through job centres, they have a fairly poor image which, as this report will show, complicates the introduction of certain reforms and partnerships. The social partners may also play a role here, as they are authorised or "delegated" by law to pay out unemployment benefits, subject to prior agreement.

The regional tier of government (in this case the Walloon Ministry of Employment which allocates some 14% of the federal budget) is in charge of job placement policies, job creation policies, employment subsidies and vocational training. In the Walloon Region, the institution that formerly implemented these policies, once they had been devised and drawn up by the regional Walloon Government, was FOREM (the Community and Regional Agency for Employment and Vocational Training). It would do so via three structures: sub-regional employment directorates, local employment offices or local employment registration and information centres (SLAIE), and training centres. Another institution involved was the IFPME, specialising in training for SMEs.

Consequently there is a fairly dense system of institutions, with regional as well as federal initiatives in many cases. As an OECD study has shown, Belgium is the European country with the largest ratio of public employment service (PES) staff to the labour force (OECD, 1997). It moves down to third place if the staff administering benefits are excluded. As for private sector involvement in job broking, this has been slow to develop in Wallonia, particularly because of ILO Convention No. 96 and the monopoly held by public employment services.

Within this system, the social partners play an important role, far more than in other European or OECD countries. Belgium has unfailingly enforced ILO Convention No. 88 which in 1950 required that arrangements be made for the "co-operation of representatives of employers and workers in the organisation and operation of the employment service". The management boards of both ONEM and FOREM are essentially bipartite, and the social partners play a key role in introducing and administering unemployment benefits. At a lower level, the social partners meet on sub-regional committees to discuss and formulate proposals and projects for employment, training and education. But a noteworthy feature specific to the Walloon Region and Belgium as a whole is that partnerships are traditionally more common at the management level of major institutions than at local level, whereas other countries have introduced them at a local rather than more centralised level.

When the Walloon Region was faced with an employment situation that continued to give cause for concern and required increasingly refined solutions to meet the needs of the unemployed, it was obliged to develop new institutions closely geared to these problems, and also look closely into the functioning of FOREM, its employment and training agency. Over the past few years a number of factors have emerged, requiring at best some adjustment:

- FOREM's fairly limited role in terms of job placements, accounting for only 7.2% of the total (compared with the Belgian average of 10.3% for public employment service placements) (Denolf and Denis, 1996; OECD, 1997). The figure probably needs to be put into perspective as this is FOREM's direct role, but its indirect role also includes information-gathering for all the players, and supporting jobseekers during all or part of their search for work. Some put this weak performance down to the fact that the public employment service has lost touch with what is happening on the ground, or that changes in job descriptions may have de-mobilised staff and made service provision less efficient (see below).

- The development of fee-charging services, which has created problems of competition and conflict of interest with enterprises and temporary employment agencies.

- The complex management of integration paths, which makes co-ordination teams at every level dependent on interpersonal relationships. The impact of this lack of co-ordination has been magnified by differences in beneficiary status or the skill concepts used. All of this argues in favour of more clearly defined roles, beginning with those of the policymakers who define the concepts.

- The ILO Convention, which has been ratified by Belgium and redefines the role of the public employment service.

- The position of the European Commission which, like the ILO, stresses the key role that private placement agencies can play.

- Lower expectations of bipartite management, particularly in terms of innovation.

- A general need for more finely tuned approaches, more in touch with what is happening on the ground, and requiring closer involvement by all of the players in the labour and training market. As we shall see, key measures such as the introduction of human resource advisers or *Missions régionales pour l'emploi* (regional employment units) have come about through pilot initiatives at local level.

There were several possible options for development or even reform, starting with a drastic change in the number and role of the many structures tackling employment problems. But the rules of the Belgian constitution made such a strategy difficult. Another option would have been to avoid fundamental changes to the design of all these structures but institute very strict delegation or concession systems to clarify responsibilities, which tend to become diluted in a public employment service. But the option now being put in place is different again. The idea is a bottom-up arrangement, moving up through the system or even bringing into general use the innovations that emerge on the ground and are distinctive in that they bring players closer together, pool their information and even pool their projects. The current system seeks to enhance its own efficiency by acknowledging partnerships at every level so that needs are better perceived and stakeholder synergy increased – an environment in line with FOREM's basic goal of achieving "client focus". The aim of these partnerships is to set up platforms or networks to enhance diagnosis (network partnerships), work differently by introducing new approaches (process partnerships) and produce new services (product partnerships). Another more informal goal may be to create unstable situations with the potential to alter behaviour patterns. Working in partnership like this means anticipating procedural improvements but also running the risk of high transaction costs.

The expected repercussions are twofold: a widespread improvement in integration paths and adjustment processes in employment at the local level; and heightened competitiveness for the Walloon Region in the global economy, owing to more closely geared preferences and training systems. This widespread use of bottom-up innovation is bound to foster economic and social development provided that two inseparable components – the management of economic activities and of employment/training – are as closely integrated as possible. Otherwise the system will have to strike a balance between two unstable situations, *i.e.* growth without employment, and employment that is economically unwarranted and hence unsustainable.

This redefinition of roles and adjustment mechanisms is taking place in synergy with FOREM's determination for some years now to change the way it functions. The opportunity arose with the advent of an external constraint (the ILO Convention) that had to be tackled, but there were also other more urgent concerns to be addressed, arising from shortcomings in the way FOREM operated.

Employment partnerships: innovating from the bottom up and redefining basic functions

Over the past five years, the Walloon Region has had to make pronounced changes in the institutional design of its labour market. Formerly the system was organised around the services delivered by FOREM, which dealt simultaneously and directly with information, personal services, business services and training, but the Walloon Region has taken up a number of spontaneous local initiatives and turned them into organisational features in their own right. The decision to bring these partnership-based initiatives into wider use has done much to revamp FOREM, which was in any case facing a re-organisation of its *modus operandi* following the signature of the ILO Conventions. So the public employment service is largely a network of partnership platforms bringing together a wide range of players, with FOREM playing a visible but not necessarily direct role.

Bringing spontaneous innovations into wider use

Today the employment system in the Walloon Region comprises a host of institutions, the oldest of them dating back fewer than ten years. This report looks at some of the more important ones amongst them to see why they were set up, how they became institutionalised or more widespread, and what problems remain.

Les Maisons de l'emploi (employment centres)

On the initiative of the communes, local structures were set up to help jobseekers and the unemployed to find useful information on job opportunities and gain access to integration paths or the actual labour market.

In 1996 one such commune, La Chapelle Lez Herlaimont, took the spontaneous initiative of setting up a *Maison de l'emploi*, which became part of the Walloon Region's experimental programme in 1999 and subsequently joined the regional network co-ordinated by FOREM. In 1999, it set up a local Employment Information Office, run by a social worker from the premises of the ALE, which also housed the commune-run unemployment checkpoint. The centre had already taken the name *Maison de l'emploi* when the Walloon Region decided to introduce the idea on a wider scale. This early version of the *Maison de l'emploi* would organise job fairs, working in co-operation with FOREM which was helping to run it, and so the commune naturally decided to join the experimental scheme. Negotiations were then held with FOREM to pool both partners' resources, as stipulated in the regulations.

In another commune, Wanze, the authorities realised that most jobseekers lacked skills, were under the age of 25, had difficulty finding information and required support during their job search. They accordingly decided to set up a centre bringing together all of the partners involved in getting people back to work, including the public and private sectors, economic development units, enterprise clubs and associations. The local trade-unions had reacted very positively to the municipality's initiative, as they felt FOREM services were not meeting expectations when it came to practical support for job-seekers. The system was set up gradually from 1988 onwards, as a more or less formal partnership of stakeholders linked with the ALE. In 1993, as the first local employment information services were coming on stream, the Wanze authorities set up a non-profit organisation (NPO) to back up its employment service; this organised numerous activities but ran up against a problem, in that its solutions were more suited to skilled applicants than other jobseekers. Unable to see through its plans for a Local development agency (ADL), it learned about the forthcoming *Maison de l'emploi* project and immediately applied to take part.

From 1999 onwards, the Walloon Region began envisaging the possibility of turning these communal structures with no real legal status into the "nerve endings" of its public employment service. In partnership with communes and *Centres publics d'aide sociale* (CPAS), or social assistance centres, which ran communal, regional or federal social assistance schemes and services, the Region's aim was to set up structures where the public would have access to information and counselling on how to find work. The Contract for the Future of Wallonia makes this quite clear: "The government will bring together information and support structures, which are currently too dispersed, in a centre giving the public access to full information on occupations, entry requirements, training courses, job offers and opportunities to practise older, more traditional crafts." From the earliest drafts it was clear that these centres, bringing together several of the employment system's partners, would not only provide services for jobseekers and employers but also enhance the quality of those services by involving institutional partners who had until then been working alone.

A procedure was drawn up to guarantee the quality and professionalism of service delivery and individual partner inputs. It ensures that any applications to FOREM come from both players, *i.e.* municipalities and the CPAS, so that the two make a clear commitment, with the communes providing suitable premises for instance. While the commune's role is obvious, that of the CPAS is less so. The presence of its staff in the *Maisons de l'emploi* provides specific jobseekers with information on possible solutions to their problems. It also provides the staff of both the *Maison de l'emploi* and the CPAS with opportunities for information exchange and capacity building. The partnership may also help to put certain jobseekers in contact with the *Maisons de l'emploi*. Here the Ministry of Employment has clearly sought to promote regular co-operation between CPAS and FOREM at local level. As for

FOREM, it provides computers and software to assist jobseekers in their search. It also covers 50% of the communication costs, and makes three members of the FOREM staff available to work in the *Maison* (or more in exceptional cases). Further staff may join them if partner funding is available. For this joint initiative by the communes and the CPAS, FOREM checks that service provision complies with the specifications on quality and professionalism. By early 2002, five of these *Maisons de l'emploi* had been set up and 86 applications submitted. By the end of 2004, 102 *Maisons* should be up and running in individual communes or groups of communes, giving an average of one *Maison* for every 2.5 communes.

Initially at least, the services provided by the *Maisons de l'emploi* remained physically separate from ALE services and the checkpoint function, whereas many of the earlier innovations of this kind had combined them. This was done on space management grounds but also to draw a line between the administration of unemployment benefits, job broking in the strict sense of the term, and job search. In fact the distinction stems from Belgium's institutional structure: as workers' rights must be the same throughout the country, the payment of unemployment benefits is a federal responsibility. While the distinction may be contested on somewhat narrow grounds, as we shall see below, its purpose is to ensure that *Maisons de l'emploi* remain open, user-friendly places without a bureaucratic image, centres where those seeking work or a change of job can find the information and advice they require. Although communes are in favour of closer physical links between the ALEs and the *Maisons de l'emploi*, in order to improve information flows and foster co-operation (and also because they are providing the premises in both cases), the two should remain separate so that the *Maisons de l'emploi* do not become synonymous with unemployment. Regular signing-in checkpoints for the unemployed will therefore remain functionally if not physically separate while job broking functions, now shifting to the private sector, are expected to be phased out altogether.

The *Maisons de l'emploi* are essentially run by two bodies, a restricted local management board and an extended local "support" or partnership committee. The board is the operational body and has three members: the commune or group of communes, one or more CPAS, and FOREM. The extended committee is a forum for any partners interested in helping to run the *Maison de l'emploi*, using it to enrich and develop their own activities, and willing to sign a membership agreement with the key partners. It is therefore via the extended committee that the partnership takes form, varying in shape and size depending on the commune and individual needs. Both bodies are chaired by the burgomaster. A point worth noting is that a *Maison de l'emploi* does not plan its strategy in advance but acts in response to initiatives taken or suggested by local players.

Several partners play key roles here. The trade unions, for instance, take the view that they add value to the *Maison de l'emploi* with the skills and competencies they have acquired in the field of social legislation. The training centres known as *Carrefours de la formation* (which do similar work to the *Maisons de l'emploi* but at a higher territorial level, as we shall see below) view the *Maisons* as a change of venue that brings them into closer contact with jobseekers but it also provides a substantial amount of information. For the firms providing in-work training, it is also an opportunity to reach out to a number of young people who would otherwise be in contact solely with the CPAS. The non-profit organisations working in the field of integration can visit these *Maisons* to meet the employment institutions they might not encounter elsewhere. In the local *Maison de l'emploi,* trade and professional associations such as those in Wanze can find the information their members need on tax or financial incentives to overcome their apprehension about hiring staff. According to some burgomasters, these "employment centres" are becoming "enterprise centres", such is the demand from smaller businesses and the self-employed for information on support. These combinations can lead to quite exemplary partnerships. In La Chapelle Lez Herlaimont, for instance, the original three institutional partners (commune, FOREM, CPAS) have been joined by the Local development agency, the Local employment agency and a non-profit organisation, *Symbiose*, which provides psycho-sociological counselling for jobseekers. And so the *Maisons de l'emploi* are achieving their second goal, which is to build up a network of partnerships to enhance individual diagnoses and projects while providing mutual support.

The main role of the *Maisons de l'emploi* is to provide jobseekers with information and advice. Their aim is to offer initial guidance, and if necessary refer jobseekers to FOREM services or, in what should be rarer cases, the CPAS. But they are not one-stop shops, owing to the intentional dividing-line between the *Maisons* and other services dealing with the rights and obligations of the unemployed. They can also call in human resource advisers to inform or advise employers. Other activities and events include information sessions by key job-market players; job fairs; user surveys (in Braine-le-Compte, for instance, a suggestion box was used to collect "100 ideas on employment", which were then edited by the partnership committee and presented on a joint basis); group interviews; and "employment lunches". But their most innovative achievement has probably been the work of individual *Maisons de l'emploi* which have promoted new business incubators and actually impacted on the volume of job offers.

So the *Maisons de l'emploi* are not only local facilities but act as "nerve endings" for the public employment service. However, their work is based largely on data files containing information about job opportunities but giving virtually no details of the type of skills, competencies or occupations involved.

The *Maisons* also form a network run at regional level by a Steering Committee, which is co-ordinated by the Employment Minister's private staff and includes representatives of five other ministries. Other information centres for jobseekers looking for guidance do exist and are logically more centralised. They include the job resource centres known as *Espaces resource emplois* (ERE), located in or near FOREM's regional directorates and the *Carrefours de la formation* skills centres; these provide broad-based expertise (*e.g.* personal counselling and follow-up, job search techniques, advice on skill acquisition, integration advisers) and serve as resource centres for the *Maisons de l'emploi*, under the aegis of the FOREM advisory branch *FOREM-Conseil*. Larger and better equipped, there are also the *Cités des métiers*, located in the bigger towns and cities, which are to take on the mandate of the ERE networks and offer specialist advice, including information and guidance on careers, international mobility and other topics. They will be receiving a European seal of quality and forming partnerships with universities.

These three structures – *Maison de l'emploi, Espace resources emplois* and *Cité des métiers* – are strengthening FOREM's determination to be seen as a distribution network, with the first developing an individual approach, the second a labour-market approach, and the third a working-life approach.

Missions régionales pour l'emploi (regional employment units)

Initiatives to improve the integration of problem groups, in particular young people, were first launched several years ago. The earliest legislation dates back to 1994, when the first *Mission* was set up in Charleroi. But it was the Decree of 14 May 1998 that brought them into general use and made them a key feature of the employment system.

The purpose of these *Missions régionales* is to develop social support and integration initiatives for target groups in the job market. By and large, a target group comprises those without upper secondary qualifications who are determined to find work. To achieve its goal the *Missions*:

● keep in regular touch with communal, sectoral and other bodies;
● introduce support facilities for players in the field specialising in local work with problem groups;
● draw up action plans in liaison with the target groups;
● sign agreements with employers willing to play an active role in finding employment for such groups; and
● find the necessary funds and training operators.

It does all this in close collaboration with FOREM. There are currently ten *Missions*, an eleventh having been closed down (on the grounds that its work was not effective), and these roughly match FOREM's eleven sub-regional directorates.

To receive official approval these *Missions*, each one with its own partnership, must be supervised by a Sub-regional Committee for Employment and Training, include a specific number of members (see below), and submit mandatory annual planning and activity reports. They must have NPO status in order to facilitate the appointment of a large number of potential partners to their governing board, whose members represent: the Sub-regional Committee; FOREM, to deliver services and provide information on the state of the labour and training market; the trade unions (FGTB, CSC); management (*Union wallonne des enterprises, Union des classes moyennes*); the local CPAS; and the Walloon Agency for the Integration of the Disabled.

In many cases this network of partners has links with the network formed around its Sub-regional Committee, which contributes to the *Mission's* work by informing it about job shortages, for instance, or giving it access to databases. However, the partnership with the *Carrefours de formation* seems to be more tenuous: these skills centres contact the *Missions* mostly when they are setting up training courses and have failed to find the requisite number of applicants. The governing board has a large membership (over 20), but the management committee is much smaller.

The work of these *Missions régionales* covers several fields. The first is alternating school-workplace training, which produces trainees who are ready for the world of work. This implies a close partnership with businesses, as they are both working towards the same goal. Firms will only make jobs available if they have been effectively involved at every stage in the process. In spite of this fundamental constraint, a *Mission* such as the *Mission du Centre*, located in Roeulx and covering the commune of La Louvière, has a success rate of around 66-70% for trainees going straight into jobs upon completion of their courses.

The second category is transition to employment. In partnership with operators specialising in integration, the *Missions* organise training courses, try to solve mobility problems and arrange for employers to meet jobseekers. For want of applicants, much of this work is carried out under the PTP job subsidy scheme.

But there is also a third category of activities, linked to networking and very different from the first two, with the broad aim of raising awareness among job-market operators about the demands of integration. The *Mission du Centre*, for instance, has tried to have social clauses inserted into public procurement contracts, obliging successful bidders to recruit locally, particularly among problem groups. These initiatives are limited in scope as public procurement law falls within the competence of the federal government. What is more, the insertion of social clauses into public procurement contracts is currently prohibited under European regulations. Until the European Commission decides otherwise, and under an agreement between the federal and regional governments a few experimental public procurement contracts containing social clauses have recently been opened for bidding in Wallonia.

This partnership should be easier to manage than that of the *Maisons de l'emploi* as the aims are clearly specified, although on a case-by-case basis. This is a form of product partnership, whereas the *Maisons de l'emploi* have a process partnership. Yet a closer look at how the *Missions* work reveals two possible weaknesses.

The first, seldom highlighted, relates to the substantial amount of public funding awarded at regional and European level. Although the *Missions* are set up at the instigation of local players, they are funded via the regional government, which thus retains considerable powers to monitor their affairs. An important share of the funding also comes from the European Social Fund (ESF), and this complicates the partnership by introducing new stakeholders.

The second weakness, acknowledged by many of those who run the *Missions*, is the difficulty they have in assuming their overarching role, which is to bring together and match up four components: employers, jobseekers, training, and jobs. They have a multifaceted and complex remit, which many units have to perform with few staff on sometimes fairly insecure posts. It is striking to see how a unit such as the *Mission du Centre* superimposes multiple duties on the same staff, making it harder for them to take an overarching or even managerial role. But these are probably a source of strain rather than a real weakness.

Agences de développement local (Local development agencies)

Local development agencies (ADLs) were set up at the instigation of the Walloon Government on 24 July 1997, and they too were based on earlier experiments in just a few communes, well before the concept of local development had been properly grasped in municipal circles. In Aiseau-Presles, for instance, the commune would hold annual job fairs bringing together employers, employees, jobseekers and potential entrepreneurs. In response to corporate demand voiced in seminars at the fifth job fair, the commune decided to set up an agency to handle contacts between the private, public and voluntary sectors on a permanent basis. Sufficient resources were obtained at regional level to create one post and a local initiative centre, subsequently converted into a non-profit organisation which applied to become the local development agency as soon as the Walloon Government decided to institutionalise this type of arrangement.

The project was part of a drive to create local jobs, the principle being that a local partnership would help to identify and carry out projects promoting local job creation. The ADL was established on the town council's initiative and reports to three separate ministries (Employment, Economy and Local Authorities). Its remit is to set up:

- A strategic local development platform: bringing together all the partners, the platform draws up an action plan as part of a specific goal to promote economic development and create/maintain jobs. At least half of its members must be private citizens and local community players, and it is chaired by the burgomaster or his/her representative. It meets for half a day, on average once a month. So the platform is the driving force behind local development, a forum for debate, reflection and communication.

- A liaison and co-ordination committee: at executive level, it implements the platform's policy and oversees the performance of the operational unit.

- An operational unit: comprising one Grade 1 and several Grade 2 officials for every 10 000 inhabitants over and above the first 10 000. These officials are pre-selected by FOREM. They are trained by the *Université Libre de Bruxelles* (Brussels Free University) on either a *DES* or short administration course. A 2-year subsidy from the Ministry of Employment covers the pay of the Grade 1 official and one of the Grade 2 staff, in line with the local authority pay scale. But other staff may be taken on, provided that partners cover the relevant costs. In Aiseau-Presles, for instance, the Agency has three posts: one financed by the region, one jointly by the region and the commune, and one by the ESF.

While these agencies do have a clear mandate, their work may vary substantially from one ADL to another, and a study of the 57 existing agencies, out of the 100 planned in all, gives quite an uneven picture. The three ADLs visited for the purposes of this report cover a wide spectrum; one was endeavouring to fulfil its development role by setting up a strategic platform on welfare issues; the second turned out to be acting largely as an interface between local traders or entrepreneurs and the municipal services; and the third was providing services on demand, fairly unimaginatively with the exception of an early initiative to improve tourism facilities. All three maintained that there was corporate demand, but each one appeared to be meeting that demand in its own way.

The Aiseau-Presles ADL operates rather like a intelligence and support service for development projects. With its strategic platform it can analyse projects, assist in their formulation and execution, and even take action itself. The first and foremost example was a welfare platform, but others have since focused on the environment or housing. The initial platform led to the creation of a welfare catering service, a community library, and plans to convert a former abbey incorporating some low-cost housing in liaison with a social housing company. Other projects worth noting include plans to set up employer groups (which did not materialise), and the creation of new service jobs such as "home hairdressers". This particular ADL also participates in job creation schemes such as PACE and the "4 x 4" Programme (run by the Ministry of the Economy), and the EU Community Initiative EQUAL.

Many players or would-be entrepreneurs contact the ADL because their applications to other institutions have failed, but a major constraint on the Agency's efficiency is that many jobseekers are victims of structural unemployment, a situation that the ADL is not well equipped to handle. In any event, unemployment there has declined faster than in neighbouring communes, in spite of a perverse effect whereby the commune loses its subsidies and entitlement to priority schemes if the local unemployment rate falls below a certain threshold.

The ADL in Waremme has a different view and takes another approach. Besides a clearly stated objective to develop business in the town centre, its policy includes establishing relations with employers, welcoming and assisting new firms, resolving common surveillance and security problems, and promoting jobs for the community's youth through training initiatives. In practice the Agency's work consists largely in referring firms to other schemes such as business parks, or to other communal services, and providing support where appropriate. The ADL is in fact acting as a chamber of commerce in the narrower sense, *i.e.* working solely on behalf of firms already in the area; further evidence of this came from the staff interviewed for this study, who confirmed that the local Chamber of Commerce confines its work to outreach initiatives promoting local firms further afield, without addressing corporate links with the local environment. The ADL's role here might be questioned if this were to become a more permanent arrangement. It does provide the Agency with recognition by the local community, but one wonders whether such work – joint business arrangements – stands to gain from being conducted by this kind of agency.

The ADL in Durbuy takes a more empirical approach, operating as it does in a rural environment that sets great store by tourism and is now experiencing neo-urban problems as a result. The ADL's rationale is to support any factors conducive to the development of quality tourism and it accordingly brings together potential partners and gives them all the assistance they need to resolve any problems they may be encountering. There is equal emphasis on welcoming tourists (language solutions), maintaining a vibrant network of smaller shops to compete with larger outlets (loyalty cards) and providing infrastructure. However, when it comes to more specifically economic activities (zoning, a new craft park, relations with farmers and their development strategies), the links are more tenuous. It is striking, for instance, that the emphasis should be on tourism and yet no rural development plan has been drawn up with the Walloon Rural Foundation,

Map of Belgium

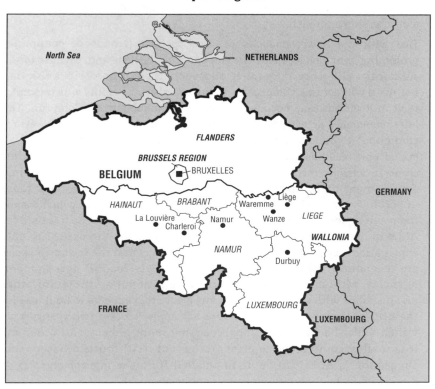

farmers or other rural stakeholders. This highlights the sometimes marginal role of these agencies (which are incidentally very recent) in actually developing economic activity, and raises questions about their place in the Walloon system.

These examples, along with developments in other agencies, call for a number of comments. Without questioning the usefulness of these ADLs, there is evidence that their action has its limits:

- Some approaches to mandate-setting can be fairly vague and may well reflect a lack of co-ordination between ministries. As a result, some agencies explore a range of different issues – social, cultural, vocational training, economic, crafts – at the same time but somewhat inconsistently, raising questions as to the real significance of the term "local development project", which is used quite systematically.

- While ADLs are capable of responding to specific requests and helping initiatives to get off the ground, they are less able to go beyond the reactive stage and become more proactive, for example by incorporating one-off requests or initiatives into an overarching local development plan based on a partnership approach.

- Ties with the *Intercommunales de développement* (groups of communes promoting joint development) are not particularly close and, because of the substantial difference in resource allocation, there is an obvious risk that the ADLs will confine themselves to the social sector alone, which is not a fault in itself but may not necessarily be sustainable in the long run. The *Intercommunales de développement* are designed and managed by several communes to build and operate economic infrastructure of benefit to all (*e.g.* airport facilities, business parks, business incubators, networks). They come in various forms, but are an essential feature of local economic development today: they carry out research, conduct studies and, more importantly, make choices as to how the area will develop, which makes them sub-regional development agencies in their own right. So it is hard for ADLs to live in their shadow, yet this appears to be the case. The only explanation – and we shall return to this later – is that the *Intercommunales* are "economic" development agencies and ADLs "social" development agencies, although this would hardly be rational as there are other organisations with a social remit. In any event, this appears to hold true for the ADL in Aiseau-Presles. But it does not apply to other two agencies we visited, which have a clearly stated economic remit, although for Waremme it is mainly commercial and for Durbuy (at best) tourism-based. One suggestion is ADLs can be distinguished from the *Intercommunales de développement* by their more microeconomic approach.

Les Missions centre-ville (town-centre management units)

In the wake of crises, business closures and rising unemployment, the revitalisation of town centres and inner cities is high on the agenda, and the structures currently in place date back to the mid-1990s, when some municipalities began looking into possible solutions. The earliest initiatives were developed jointly by town councils and traders' associations, for it was in their mutual interest to resolve problems such as crime, lifeless town centres and even urban flight. There was soon a need to go beyond these often informal contacts and choose between one of two options. One was an agreement to award financial support to local traders willing to liven up town centres, but the drawback here was that the system became subsidy-driven.

The second option was to set up an ongoing partnership as a basis for launching individually funded projects. This was adopted and systematically proposed by the Walloon Regional Government, but only to communes with over 30 000 inhabitants. The idea was that smaller centres had fewer problems but, more importantly, that it was necessary to avoid duplication by two types of institution which might end up competing: after all, what difference is there between a local development agency supporting traders who move to or open stores in the town centre, and a *Mission Centre-ville* promoting its town centre by attracting stores there? But the link between the two structures is the scope they both have to benefit from subsidised employment, hence the importance of their supervision by the Ministry of Employment, essentially warranted by their contribution to direct employment ("*stewards*") and indirect employment (developing economic activities). This initiative, stemming from pilot projects by the Town-centre Management Association (AMCV), was brought into widespread use under the "Integrated Action Plan for Town-centre Management and New Occupations" in 1998, when it took the form it still has today. The purpose of the *Missions centre-ville* is therefore to prevent the deterioration of town centres and inner cities and make them more competitive as part of a policy to promote job creation.

If these units were to be a success, they had to meet four conditions: have their own legal foundation; be transparent; be open to new partners; and be reactive to the various tiers of government liable to impact on the organisation and vitality of town centres. But there was another, more subtle constraint: the units also had to be able to operate as a network throughout the Walloon Region, as experience had soon shown that some of the larger private operators would only become involved in region-wide projects.

There are now 16 *Missions centre-ville*, mostly in towns with over 30 000 inhabitants, although this regulatory threshold is not always clearly respected: it was devised largely to channel applications to either the *Missions centre-ville* for communes with a population of over 30 000, or to local development agencies for towns with fewer inhabitants. The *Missions* are usually non-profit organisations, and employ three categories of staff, *i.e.* a manager, administrative staff (one or more), and a team of what are known as urban or environmental operatives (*stewards, ouvriers urbains* or *éco-cantonniers*). Staffing costs are usually covered by the Walloon Government, but in some cases extra staff have been taken on using other sources of funding.

The Walloon Region also has an agency (AMCV) which, under an agreement with the Ministry of Employment, helps the units to manage and run their network. The AMCV provides technical support for all of the *Missions centre-ville*. It delivers services geared to their management needs, including management software, training, and experience-sharing. Towns intending to set up a *Mission centre-ville* can also commission a feasibility study.

The most striking feature of the work undertaken by these units is its diversity. Rather than listing all their initiatives (marketing and promotion, information stands, vacant property initiatives, mobility planning, enhancement of the urban environment), we shall highlight the wide range of strategies these units deploy, some apparently more warranted than others.

The approach adopted by the Mission centre-ville in Liège is based on close collaboration with commercial operators. Ten members of its governing board represent the commune, while the other ten represent the private and semi-public sectors, including Le Commerce Liégois (an umbrella association for the city's traders), car-park and public transport operators, and the Chamber of Commerce and Industry (CCI). It is firmly focused on providing services for city-centre users, be they customers, local inhabitants or storekeepers, and generally employs stewards or citadiers. These pass information from the council to local traders and vice versa, as well as checking street furniture for repairs and thus playing a monitoring role. They even help to keep the streets clean by clearing some of the litter, a duty that some Missions in other towns are not prepared to ask of their stewards. Part of their job is to take notes for mobility planning purposes, and by their very presence and rounds they would appear to play a passive security role. A recognition indicator has shown that 70% of the city centre's traders and visitors are familiar with these stewards and some aspects of their work. But a closer look reveals that the stewards are just go-betweens, liaising between the town council and its traders, and that the Mission is not attempting to boost business at all, taking the view that this should be done by traders' associations, although it does back individual projects such as the Christmas Cité de Noël.

The Mission centre-ville in La Louvière takes quite another approach. It too is concerned with revitalising the city centre, but this is now part of a broader set of equally important objectives: promoting culture (helping to organise an urban opera "Décrocher la lune"), managing derelict land in the town centre, and liaising between the local community and municipal departments. So its partners hail from a variety of backgrounds, with a high proportion of cultural services. The Mission has become a kind of mediator and, to highlight its importance, local businesses were asked to make a financial contribution initially levied by the traders' association. The idea was subsequently dropped, however, probably because it proved too complicated for the amount of financial support it provided. In this case, NPO status is not a problem, as the commune has chosen to rely on a network of such associations working in a range of fields (e.g. culture, sport) and in liaison with its municipal services. But some features of the La Louvière experience are found in the other Missions centre-ville, including the complex management of its staff funding systemsand the unsatisfactory nature of some types of job, beginning with those subsidised under the PTP scheme.

In 2002, there were so many different initiatives that the Walloon Region asked the Missions centre-ville to draw up a policy plan, setting managers some key goals.

Centres de compétences (skills centres)

Today these *Centres de compétences* or skills centres are viewed as modern technical platforms open to jobseekers, training institutions and enterprises alike. They have accordingly been set up as multi-user resource centres and run on a partnership basis. These too can be traced back to local partnership-based initiatives.

The first of these *Centres de compétences* appeared in the early 1990s, some of them under different names. The most commonly cited example is the Transport and Logistics Centre set up in Liège at the instigation of FOREM and a number of local development advocates, mobilised by the European-wide association *LEDA Partenariat*, when plans were announced to redevelop the Bierset airport zone, but ongoing plans to provide training in logistics were a further factor. The Centre was to train people for the jobs that were hoped for (but not guaranteed) with the new development, unlike FOREM's existing training centres, which were for jobseekers or the training needs of existing firms only. Another skills centre set up at around the same time was *Technifutur*, specializing in computer-integrated manufacturing, assembly, ICTs, mechatronics and hydraulics. The success of these early initiatives prompted the Walloon Region to encourage potential training operators and employers' unions to set up similar structures, hence the emergence of other projects such as the Industrial Maintenance Centre in Le Hainaut, the Timber Centre in Libramont, and the Logistics Centre in La Louvière.

The Region then decided to create the quality label "*Centre de compétences*", awarded to training structures meeting the following four requirements:

- A *Centre de compétences* should reflect a development rationale that suits the surrounding area, or development plans for that area. The Timber Centre in the Belgian province of Luxembourg is a striking example: its challenge is to enable local firms to go beyond the primary processing of timber, which adds very little value, and invest in secondary processing, which is far more worthwhile in terms of value-added but previously took place abroad, using the timber exported there.

- A *Centre de compétences* should be designed and run on a partnership basis. Most public structures – starting with FOREM – contact (or are contacted by) social partners, for instance at industry-specific meetings to draw up collective agreements (*e.g.* the graphics industry trade association whose headquarters are located next to the local *Centre de compétences*). But there are other partners too, such as employers' associations, scientific or technical centres, and universities. There are three approaches to setting up partnerships. The first is when specific partners take responsibility for an operation – *e.g.* monitoring developments in a particular occupation – and then pass on the relevant information to the centre and all the other members. The second is when partners sign an agreement defining their individual roles and contributions. In the third, the partners join a non-profit organisation which then runs the *Centre de compétences*.

- A *Centre de compétences* should be accessible to all, with four potential user groups: jobseekers; workers (including risk groups), some of them on further training schemes; teaching and training staff, in particular for their further training needs; and students.

- A *Centre de compétences* should not be confined to training in the strict sense of the term but should also launch new skills awareness campaigns and monitoring activities (in liaison with the Walloon Employment Monitoring Unit), conduct audits to identify corporate needs, assist with labour-market integration, support groups of SMEs, and produce distance-learning software for use both in the Centre and on the web. The Cepegra Centre, for instance, is now publishing software programmes to train computer graphics specialists and web-page designers.

There are now twelve of these Centres (the latest one, on new materials, was inaugurated in October 2002), but plans for eight more are under discussion (*e.g.* industrial painting, environmental protection techniques, water-based skills, motor sports and automobile mechanics). New themes have already been suggested for future development (arts and crafts). The centres form a network, with a steering committee to collect and share information, organise events and address quality issues. The network publishes a quarterly operating report giving details of its performance in terms of the number of training courses, awareness campaigns, new distance-training products, enrolment rates for each centre (a crucial factor given the quantity and quality of the training resources available) and corporate coverage, as well as giving a list of potential contacts. This initiative is all the more remarkable in that it has as many public as private partners, and the selection of skills it has developed shows how determined the Walloon Region is to adapt, develop and redeploy its know-how to leverage competitiveness in a global economy.

Reforming FOREM

FOREM is in a full re-structuring phase, as reflected in its 2001/2006 management contract, involving major changes to its statutes. Before moving on to see how this reform will boost partnerships and make for better governance of employment and training systems, let us first recall certain aspects of its performance to date and the circumstances that led to its reform:

- There is fairly wide agreement – although the question is still open to debate – that FOREM was finding it increasingly hard to live up to expectations as a benchmark institution managing the labour market and matching job supply and demand. Several reasons have been put forward: difficulties in matching supply and demand; services too cut off from employers and, more importantly, jobseekers; insufficiently detailed information on job vacancies which is of little use; confusing links between integration mechanisms and training mechanisms. The ratio of vacancies notified to vacancies filled has hardly changed over the past five years, for instance, and yet this should be one of FOREM's basic management indicators, at least under its previous remit, assuming that all notified vacancies are sent to FOREM which may not be the case (Table 8.1). These shortcomings, however, are not at all specific to the Walloon Region and are found in many other public employment services facing major quantitative and qualitative disadjustments in the labour market. But this kind of situation could not continue indefinitely, regardless of any external constraints.

● Within such a large organisation (with its headquarters in Charleroi and eleven sub-regional directorates), the inevitable identity problems have arisen and these must now be solved. To summarise the issue, much of the work was formerly done by "placement officers", who registered and assisted jobseekers in their search, followed up and solved administrative problems relating to status, and liaised with firms to provide the services they required. This gave a heavy burden of responsibility to placement officers, and so an initial reform replaced each one with three different members of staff, i.e. a counsellor to perform the first set of duties; an administrative official; and an enterprise adviser who was subsequently to become a human resource adviser. This division caused further problems, as those taking over from the placement officer no longer had an overview of the work, and so the first two sets of duties were eventually combined into the post of *animateur* or "facilitator". The enterprise advisers encountered a number of problems, compounded by the decision to charge fees for their services. Yet a drive to re-mobilise all of an institution's resources means clarifying its role and the roles of each member of staff.

Table 8.1. **Percentage of vacancies filled, FOREM, 1997-2001**

Year	Vacancies filled (%)
1997	82.4
1998	73.4
1999	82.7
2000	80.5
2001	82.1

Source: FOREM Statistical Report, 2001.

- ILO Convention C181 (1997) concerning private employment agencies, together with Recommendation 188 on the same subject, highlighted the role that private placement services should play, at a time when FOREM had virtually a monopoly in the field. The Convention was a reversal of the trend underpinning ILO policy up to that point, *i.e.* a gradual shift away from private fee-charging employment agencies and towards public employment services. Private agencies were now to play a role, but not systematically to the detriment of public services. Co-operation and information exchange between the various placement services were to characterise the way the labour market functioned. The Walloon Region therefore moved in that direction and adopted some basic principles: co-operation and information exchange between the PES and approved private operators; compulsory registration with the PES confined to jobseekers applying for training or integration schemes for which the PES received funding from the Region; and the regrouping of all FOREM's fee-charging business services into one market-based entity.

- There has been a noticeable change in the functioning of the labour market over the past few years, as economic players have altered their behaviour with the advent of internationalised markets, the service economy and the knowledge society. Consequently, paths are now more individual but also less uniform than they were said to be. There are various reasons for this. For some people already in the labour market, it is a question of anticipating constantly changing skill requirements and finding the right trajectory. For the long-term unemployed, it is more about simultaneously resolving a number of problems relating not only to skills and competencies but to others issues such as housing, health and mobility. This means interfacing with several different players or in different fields, and personal circumstances will systematically be addressed individually. It is precisely in response to the constraints of individualisation that integration paths were originally devised. But this often led to complex systems with overlapping responsibilities, hence the need for longitudinal follow-up within the framework of specific responsibilities. Because the conditions under which people seek and find work are becoming increasingly complex, the public employment service is having to diversify its approaches substantially, draw on increasing sources of expertise to tackle employment and, more importantly, work in partnership with all of the institutions in the job market, many of which already have their own approaches. The partnerships that FOREM must strike up with these institutions have accordingly been given a clear remit, namely to restore the overall efficiency of the system by providing all of its stakeholders with technical benchmarks and skills.

A new architecture

Faced with these new challenges (allowing for a changing labour market; enhancing the quality of service provision; complying with international conventions redefining the role of public services as placement agencies), FOREM has significantly altered its structure and made partnerships a vehicle for its work in the field of employment. It began by taking on three clearly separate roles, one as overarching manager in the labour market; another as a training institution; and the third as a fee-charging service provider, particularly for temporary work.

In terms of adjusting job supply and demand or regulating the labour market, FOREM's role has undergone radical change. To comply with international conventions it has given up any direct job-placement work, a decision that has had considerable impact. The announcement that the function was to be privatised proved to be a catalyst for applications to open private job-placement agencies, and prompted a reallocation of responsibilities within FOREM. The traditional profile of the placement officer has had to evolve to cater for three basic competencies, and there are now personal counsellors for individual jobseekers; human resource advisers for employers; and a labour supply manager for enterprises.

But as a public employment service, FOREM still regulates the action of all those involved in placement and integration. It must ensure optimal information flows to help those seeking or offering jobs, and provide everyone, directly or indirectly, with the services they may need to take that information on board. To do so it must rely fully on local institutions, or institutions specialising in working with target groups or special circumstances, and put in place partnership-based approaches.

Its overarching management role consists in analysing regional labour-market needs, assisting jobseekers in their search, and co-ordinating labour-market operators to optimise responses to their needs. To enhance availability and accessibility, three of the structures described above act as FOREM's "nerve-endings", each one corresponding to urban centres of a particular size. First there are the *Maisons de l'emploi*; then the *Espaces ressources emploi* or ERE (10 in all by early 2002) which play a similar role to the *Maisons de l'emploi* but target a larger group and focus on specialist jobs and skills; and finally, in the larger cities, the *Cités des métiers* which give out occupation-specific information and share their premises with the ERE and the training centres known as *Carrefours de la formation*. Integration paths, the subject of reservations in recent years as to their effectiveness, will have to be re-organised within this overarching management function.

In the training field, FOREM is present on competitive markets but is asked to develop training services to upgrade the skills of a whole series of low-skilled groups, the long-term unemployed and people in subsidised jobs. FOREM owes its role as a public training operator to its status as the largest training operator in Wallonia, with almost 700 vocational training staff, and to the size of its own centres and those of its partners, *e.g.* the *Centres de compétences*. The reform has been less of a break with the past for FOREM's training branch than for *FOREM-Conseil*, but the training branch still has some ambitious goals in its latest strategic plan, including a client satisfaction rate of 78%, a maximum of 30 days for access to training courses, and a minimum of two weeks' staff training per year.

Two further functions are to feature on the organisation chart. The first concerns the management of temporary-work activities or paid job-broking services. This will raise problems in terms of competition with the private sector. So the function will be performed by a new limited public company, *T-Intérim* (80% of its capital owned by public shareholders). The second concerns general administration or services common to both the overarching management and public training functions, and will therefore be organised accordingly.

A wide-ranging partnership policy

As the Walloon Government is seeking "to enhance and co-ordinate the existing system without introducing new measures or arrangements", it is normal that FOREM should manage and co-ordinate, rather than adding to the complexity of the current institutional set-up.

In all of the functions under consideration, partnerships are increasingly important and FOREM intends to make them a vehicle for its initiatives. As well as being the basis on which FOREM is managed – co-management by social partners – partnerships are found at every level in a variety of forms including *Maisons de l'emploi, Missions régionales* and *Centres de compétences.* From a more functional standpoint, these partnerships fall into two categories, which in FOREM's own terms are:

- Development partnerships, which seek to combine academic types of modelling/scientific expertise with more operational know-how in order to foster strategic development. This pooling of knowledge and know-how is aimed at achieving anticipatory outcomes of benefit to all concerned.

- Structural partnerships, which combine complementary approaches in order to add significant value to the resources available in the Walloon Region.

This new approach is based on the objective data mentioned above but also on the Walloon Government's determination to give FOREM a different *modus operandi:* "New forms of regulation and co-ordination should accordingly be developed to promote policy coherence and networking, giving users transparent service provision geared to their needs." The draft decree is fully in line with Wallonia's employment policy which, in the Contract for the Future of Wallonia, includes the following two goals:

● Further modernisation of FOREM, enabling it to fulfil its remit as a public employment service.

● Closer collaboration between FOREM and other players in the regional labour market.[1]

The recent Decree on the Employment and Vocational Training Agency (FOREM) specifies that "the Service, in its role as overarching manager, is responsible for co-ordinating regional labour market operators for the purposes of integration, providing individuals and enterprises with advice and guidance on the regional labour market, implementing government measures, allocating and supervising grants and subsidies, granting and maintaining welfare entitlements, and managing and circulating information" (Section 2). FOREM is accordingly asked to devote its efforts to increasingly cross-cutting initiatives, remain upstream from the initiatives and institutions structuring the job market, and refrain from competing with other institutions but instead devote its energy to bringing players together and exercising leadership. As FOREM is now being asked to take responsibility for pooling and supporting expertise, partnerships are central to its new approach.

This will alter FOREM's traditional relations with players in the labour market. Where jobseekers are concerned, partnerships have already been introduced at the vocational guidance stage, but they will now spread to areas such as information and initial counselling, integration and basic training, and skill acquisition courses.

With regard to relations with enterprises and industries, the partnership approach is also a longstanding tradition, recently bolstered by the need to find work for the victims of mass redundancies or corporate restructuring programmes; and the need to identify job shortages, with the commissioning of joint industry-specific studies (e.g. transport, food-processing, white-collar work, metal goods, the non-market sector). This partnership approach will now extend to the publication of job offers under special agreements, and the establishment of skills centres.

But it is with operators specialising in integration and training that stronger and more permanent partnerships will be emerging. They will cover the publication of information on training provision, the development of expertise among employment staff, and the reception of jobseekers and the unemployed.

This is going to affect FOREM working methods, and some comments are called for at this point. First, FOREM has launched a major internal reform to ensure that its staff is trained in this partnership-based approach, regardless of their post, profile or management methods. They have also been given a chance to choose their position on the new organisation chart. As a number of jobs at FOREM will necessarily shift away from technical execution towards co-ordination, development and counselling, there will be greater investment in staff training, coaching and skill development.

The second set of changes will affect performance measurement at FOREM. Traditionally based on integration rates and the number of vacancies notified or filled, for instance, measurement will now focus on network performance, partnership development and quality, and the level of partner mobilisation.

What will become of the Sub-regional Employment and Training Committees?

One crucial problem is whether or not there is dialogue between the job-market partners linked with FOREM. Successful job initiatives and employment policies depend on sound co-ordination at local level, and so there should be ongoing dialogue between players who are the instruments of those policies and players who make decisions relating directly or indirectly to employment.

The Sub-regional Employment and Training Committees (CSEF) have traditionally been responsible for leading the employment debate and devising or supporting initiatives to promote improvements in this field, particularly because of their membership which includes representatives of both management and labour, as well as other potential partners such as the *Intercommunales de développement*. Established by the Decree of 22 December 1989, these CSEFs were given a threefold mandate:

- to monitor the situation and trends on their local labour markets (act as micro-monitoring units);
- to devise, propose and recommend measures to promote social and professional integration, labour policy and training; and
- to provide opinions on any issues relating to employment or training at the request of the regional or federal minister for employment and training, including the approval of in-work training enterprises or regional schemes to promote labour market integration.

Since April 2000 a further key aspect of their work, under the Rosetta Plan, has been to identify specific job shortages by category and inform those concerned.

There are now nine of these committees, and their number is soon to rise to eleven. Some have launched numerous initiatives and left their mark on the development of local employment policies; one example is the Charleroi CSEF, which was behind the setting up of a *Mission régionale* and the appointment of human resource specialists to advise employers. Other committees have not always gone this far, one reason being that the social partners are represented by public service staff, without much authority or influence.

The decision has recently been taken to link these committees to FOREM and even incorporate their technical units into the institution, turning them into real "nerve-endings" that can pinpoint and resolve employment and training problems, and to strengthen partnerships in the field. In return, FOREM will put resources and other means of leverage at their disposal, whereas the committees previously had to struggle to put their decisions into practice. This apparently means that the social partners will be involved in basic work at regional level, whereas they were previously only co-managers of FOREM's core institution. The outcome is accordingly expected to be positive for FOREM, which will now see the benefits of dialogue between social partners at every possible level. In return, the likelihood is that the committees' own discussions, opinions and initiatives will be more successful and their potential maximised thanks to the extra resources at their disposal. To strike this balance, the teams (5 to 6 people at most) will remain separate, and the Committee Chairs will remain in charge of each team but quite separate from FOREM; a framework agreement drawn up by the Walloon Region between FOREM and the Chair of each Sub-regional Committee will make these links clear on a case-by-case basis.

One aim is to achieve harmonised goals and more efficient initiatives. It is also hoped that bringing together partners and information (in particular from the Walloon Employment Monitoring Unit) on the same premises will turn what is often just a scientific picture of the job market into a policy strategy for that market. A further aim is to improve the financial regime of these committees, whose role has never been well defined; the subsidies they receive from the regional authorities will no longer be automatically deducted from the funding received from other partners, a practice that formerly narrowed their scope and was ultimately a disincentive.

This is actually a fairly ambitious gamble, for several reasons. Membership of these committees is essentially confined to the social partners and even then to varying degrees, given the imbalance between trade unions and management. A survey by the Charleroi Committee revealed a marked difference in the average number of members, with 4.09 for labour compared with only 2.63 for management, whereas the ideal average would be 7.[2] At the moment, these committees are far from representative of all the partners dependent on the job market. Were that to be the rationale, they could be extended and full membership – rather than just membership of subsidiary bodies consulted on an *ad hoc* basis – could be offered to communes and voluntary bodies, for instance. Their links with the *Intercommunales de développement* also need to be defined. They are usually invited to participate in the work of the committees, but follow-up is far from systematic, and the question is whether FOREM's "absorption" of the committees, as some see it, will facilitate matters. For one final problem is that the decision to place the committees within FOREM's sphere of influence makes them look reliant on the key partner, which is not perhaps the best way of describing a forum that is intended to unite and serve as a common denominator.

The complex interface between economic, employment and social issues

Are the partnerships set up by the Walloon Region improving the governance of employment systems? Better governance can be measured with two criteria:

- Objectives relating to governance *per se*, i.e. closer integration of public and private activities, and closer links between the various aspects of their work.

- Employment-related objectives for the Walloon Region: improving integration paths regardless of educational attainment at the outset; enabling enterprises to improve their human resource management in an increasingly knowledge-based economy; and setting a standard for human resources that will make the region competitive in the global economy.

The previous system – built around the social partners – was fully in line with one or both of these objectives. But in what had become a highly problematic structural setting, it was not always able (or willing) to alter the way the employment and training markets functioned. Wallonia has experienced an exceptionally serious restructuring crisis, and will only fully emerge by becoming a knowledge economy that distributes planning and enterprise capacity at every level and in a variety of forms. Faced with challenges on the training, placement, integration and other fronts, the regional government has taken a number of local initiatives which more closely reflect those challenges and brought them into wider use, with the intention of putting a partnership stamp on the employment system as a whole. But the system is a work in progress and a number of problems persist.

To shed light on these problems, we shall first look at the goals of the planned partnerships to identify their impact and limitations. Two criteria can be used here. First and foremost are differences in how the partnership functions, i.e. whether it is supposed to formulate strategy (strategic partnership) or validate decisions (validating partnership). Then there is the purpose of the partnership, i.e. to put into place information, processes or products.

The next step is to discuss a number of problems that are found in any partnership but to differing degrees. We shall then draw our conclusions and set out some recommendations. The main issue we address regarding this partnership-driven policy relates to the complex interface between the two inextricably linked areas of economics and employment, and the lesser difficulty of building up an employment system that is relatively disconnected from social concerns.

Types of partnership and specific outcomes

Strategic partnerships or validating partnerships

A decisive factor when analysing and assessing partnerships is the distinction between strategic partnerships and validating partnerships. Partnerships can take one of two approaches. The first genuinely seeks to change the nature of decision-making processes by ensuring that decisions are based on a multiplicity of information systems and objective functions. This is a strategic partnership, aimed at mapping out a route through a large number of options and assuming from the outset that information sources are relative and preferences are of equal merit, regardless of the player implementing or co-ordinating the process. The term strategic here is not based on the time factor (short- versus long-term) but on that multiplicity of values, which is precisely what is missing from the long-term approach. The second approach is when a partnership is run by a policy centre seeking to enhance the validity of its decisions by gathering as much information as possible and hence consulting as many players as possible. Without playing a minor role, the partnership is there mainly to gear decisions to the preferences of a key player. So the difference between the two approaches lies mainly in how the partners are viewed, and whether or not there is key player.

It is clear, as stated at the outset, that the partnerships required to enhance local governance in the field of employment are first and foremost strategic partnerships, with validating partnerships playing a secondary role. As employment problems are by their very nature multi-dimensional, the assumption from the outset must be that all of the players are on a par when it comes to roles and value systems, even if this means setting up other more technical partnerships later. This multiplicity combines the economic and the social dimensions, employment and unemployment, activity and sustainability.

Yet, perhaps because of co-ordination difficulties, all of the initiatives described earlier feature a series of validating partnerships and few opportunities for strategic ones. An area in which partnerships ought to be strategic is, as we have seen, the Sub-regional Employment and Training Committee, but this report includes a number of comments on the forthcoming system, which certainly does not guarantee that the right type of partnership will emerge. On the other hand, the Maisons de l'emploi, the

Missions régionales, the ADLs and the *Missions centre-ville* definitely feature validating partnerships, which are usually linked to the presence of a key player or group of players but will struggle to achieve the right strategic focus.

To highlight this lack of strategic policy focus, we should take a closer look at the relative importance of strategic policies in the partnerships under consideration. The need for a strategic policy focus must be expressed if projects are to be defined coherently, take as long as their briefs require and be mutually reinforcing. Yet many employment-related partnerships put together projects and initiatives without sufficient coherence to ensure that their execution will benefit others, even indirectly. Below are two examples.

In its survey of local development agencies, the Free University of Brussels reveals a host of somewhat disparate initiatives and projects (ULB, 2002). A study carried out by SEGEFA for research and training purposes draws the same conclusions, emphasising how hard it was for ADLs even to set up their strategic platforms and how, in the end, the only initiatives that counted were launched by the operational unit (SEGEFA, 2001). And when economic issues were addressed, the initiatives usually involved ADLs acting as intermediaries rather than playing a pioneering or exploratory role. Most of their work consists in providing support and the strategic platform is, with few exceptions, a body that registers rather than streamlines development projects within the area concerned. ADL operational units prove to be more incisive, although there is no less emphasis on support initiatives and no increase in pro-active behaviour. This would explain why ADLs lag behind on environmental issues, a theme that emerges as soon as territorial thinking become strategic. It is worth noting, although this is not the rule, that some *Intercommunales de développement* work more readily in strategic mode than others, which only goes to highlight the ambiguity of separating economic issues from employment.

In the specific case of ADLs, another possible explanation for the lack of a strategic policy focus is that operational units eventually prevail over strategic platforms, either because the second are too recent, or because their function is merely registration. In fact, many key players in the local development arena barely have the time for any real involvement in ADLs, which have to compete with the *Intercommunales de développement* and the considerable financial resources at their disposal.

It is striking that the draft decree on ADLs now requires them to be assessed on their capacity to act as real socio-economic intermediaries at the communal level, in other words to be an integral feature of local development. This makes it crucial to have a strategic agenda, which will only have any real content if the platform's membership includes the most relevant players, rather than just those with an *ad hoc* interest in a specific project. Only then will there be any chance of accomplishing each item on the agenda as set out in the draft decree (Section 1, paragraph 3), i.e. diagnosing the situation in a locality; identifying a policy focus for the ADL; capitalising on good practice; and comparing ideas on local development.

The same is true of the *Missions* or town-centre management units, but on a somewhat different basis. The *Missions* perform a whole range of activities and many even have their own clear policy focus. The problem is that they focus on different things. While some are confined almost exclusively to relations with local traders, other focus solely on mobility plans. Even when their stated policy focus is forward-looking and well defined, their activities are still relatively dispersed. The Walloon Region acknowledges this implicitly in the draft decree, which stresses the need to clarify, set out and take responsibility for strategy. The SEGEFA-Liège study on *Missions centre-ville* puts this lack of strategy down to competition between the *Missions* and communal or other bodies, particularly in the field of security, housing and tourism. So questions are inevitably raised about the purpose of such units, which depend to a large extent on efficient communal services. But there is another possible reason: initially the Region wanted to revitalise its city centres, which implied real estate and commercial town planning initiatives calling for a substantial amount of special skills and resources. As neither were available, the *Missions* had to launch fairly superficial development and communication initiatives, without being able to tackle the issue in any depth.

This does not call into question the need for basic partnership structures, which offer scope to bring in independent experts but do not feature any one partner in too dominant a position.

Apart from the specific cases mentioned above, the fact that these employment partnerships have trouble defining their policy focus may well stem from the difficulty of reasoning in terms of the commune. Neither SME projects, nor the job market, nor even business networks are necessarily local in that they could be called typical features of a commune. Obviously the *Maisons de l'emploi* and the *Missions régionales* escape such a narrow definition, but their remit is less strategic than that of the ADLs and the *Missions centre-ville*. Probably the best counterexample is that of the skills centres (*Centres de compétences*): these develop skills specific to the Walloon Region or reflect a feature of local life specific to a sub-region or province rather than the just the commune, and can therefore adopt a genuine strategy when analysing and devising training courses geared to changes in technology, skills and the economic fabric.

Network, process and product partnerships

The current reforms have introduced on a wider scale three types of partnership, not including the co-management practices of FOREM's social partners:

- The first type of partnership seeks to set up networks as a basis for diagnosis and assessment built on trust. The Sub-regional Committees are one example, but the steps being taken to redefine many of the governing boards and committees could also be said to concern this category.

- The second type of partnership seeks to introduce new working methods among players who are necessarily interdependent or performing the same tasks together. These are process partnerships, and the *Maisons de l'emploi* seem a good example. The same concern is found in other institutions.

- The third type of partnership seeks to enhance the production of specific goods or services. This is a more operational aim, well illustrated by the *Missions régionales*.

As the *raison d'être* for Sub-regional Employment and Training Committees, network partnerships are behind the establishment of a growing number of institutions, as reflected in the membership of their administrative and managerial bodies. The aim of this kind of partnership is clear, i.e. to bring together players with specialist information and skills on shared diagnoses and thus build on their respective assets. If these partnerships are to work, they must meet a number of conditions. They must be open and not sideline any potentially useful players; they must also encourage players to go ahead and exchange information, which would hardly be likely if there were a lack of trust or too much distance between players within the partnership.

Two phenomena are worth mentioning at this point. The decision-making procedures governing membership of these bodies are often fairly strict, at least where basic structures are concerned, and may even go so far as to refer the participation of potential partners to more minor *ad hoc* committees. Such procedures are understandable, given the declining frequency or relevance of relations with some players, and the highly specific responsibilities that public finance confers on others. But apparently the pendulum has not swung far enough here, as the following two examples show:

- There is little participation by voluntary-sector institutions, yet they are often behind initiatives to create many new services and jobs; they also give diagnostic studies a longer-term focus than the immediate concerns of partners with economic and social commitments. Their recognition by the Walloon Government, in the form of an annual Social Economy Award, remains fairly symbolic.

● There is fairly little participation by economic organisations, starting with the *Intercommunales de développement*. Such bodies are to feature in some ADL strategic platforms, but this is only too rare.

Where information exchange is concerned, procedures are less institutionalised and we have to rely on evidence in the field rather than actual systems. It is important to stress, however, that FOREM's role as secretariat to the CSEF is double-edged. On the one hand it should step up efficiency. On the other, it means that some fully fledged and other members may not forward all of the information available to them and this will undermine efficiency. Great care should be taken in running such secretariats, once the initial enthusiasm for new resources has died down.

Process partnerships seek to create interaction between potential players in the job market and help them make the most of the information available. The partnership will then encourage players to meet and interact, while leaving them enough flexibility to draw up their own objectives or projects, which is logical given that their responsibilities remain separate. This is the case with the *Maisons de l'emploi*, for instance, which clearly promotes close co-operation, so that each player can enhance both its own action and the overall effectiveness of integration paths. But it can also be the case with the *Missions centre-ville*, whose aim is precisely to create the right synergy between players involved in the rehabilitation or revitalisation of local town centres.

Here too successful partnerships must meet a number of conditions: stakeholders with a role to play should all be involved; the partnership must be strategically managed, *i.e.* genuine efforts should be made to ensure that each partner's views are given full consideration by the others, which means more than just exchanging information; there should be a minimum amount of interdependence between players, to prevent them from keeping their distance, especially over time; finally, areas of agreement should be sought to foster closer co-operation and revive interest in such partnerships.

The initiatives and systems launched in Wallonia provide numerous scenarios, and comments may apply to some institutions more than others. It should also be borne in mind that some of the *Maisons de l'emploi* have only just been opened whereas others have been up and running for some time, and this complicates evaluation. If the analysis were confined to the *Maison de l'emploi* in Wanze, for instance, it would conclude that most of the conditions for a successful process partnership had been met, be it a wide range of stakeholders or evidence of genuine strategic management.

That said, a number of comments are called for:

● Merely grouping players on the same premises will definitely not guarantee the success of such partnerships, and it would be better not to have too many illusions about this.

- An uneven balance of power between the governing board and the "support" or partnership committee will inevitably backfire in a process partnership. It is inevitable, given the financial arrangements and the type of basic work done by the *Maisons de l'emploi*, that the governing board should play a key role in the organisation, but partnership committee members may also take the view that the management bears no relevance to the goals to be met and can no longer maintain their interest in the partnership. It should be stressed that the type of strategic management described above should not be conducted by the governing board but by the somewhat inappropriately named support committee; only then can a better balance be struck between the long and the short term view.

- A partnership-based structure that centres on a single goal may undermine the structure's potential. Some *Missions centre-ville* that have systematically taken the commercial option (openly or not) or preferred one type of player over the others have, in our view, completely lost sight of the strategic dimension and can no longer play their expected role, which could easily go to an existing communal service or another institution.

- Partners cannot merely be spectators or clients yet, in our view, some strategic platforms in the ADLs have apparently been unable to avoid this.

- To provide strategic management, development staff and managers should not spend virtually all of their time managing jobs, as status and financial problems can make day-to-day management so hard that this in itself eventually becomes strategic. A frequent management problem in non-profit organisations, this can take a variety of forms depending on the system in each country.

Product or service partnerships are set up to provide these as efficiently and effectively as possible. Any players who can help to identify needs or define a service and its provision are brought together around a project manager. The best illustration of this type of partnership is the *Mission régionale* but other examples include, once again, ADLs and *Missions centre-ville*.

For these partnerships, the keys to success are usually more readily identifiable than for the previous types, since their purpose is defined on a case-by-case basis and in some detail. This kind of partnership calls for players with relevant information on service users, or potential modes of provision; specifications on production design and the role of each participant; and finally a balance between producer inputs in terms of costs and benefits.

While this type of partnership raises fewer problems than those described above because its purpose is clearer, it does call for certain comments:

- Roles are not always clearly distributed and in practice responsibilities may be blurred, if only because so many people are involved. The introduction of alternating school-workplace training in some *Missions régionales* is a logical step, but its main outcome has been to create a host of players and hence blurred responsibilities.

- The notion of service user requires clarification, as there can be one or more direct users and one or more indirect users. In that case, service design and production should be enriched, and the distinction between economic and social issues should be dropped, although this is not always the case.

- With some services, partnership-based provision may catalyse the search for windfall effects: the solution here is to clarify information and evaluate, rather than imposing a whole range of access conditions, which may only serve to redeploy the many forms that this windfall search can take.

Questionable conditions for setting up partnerships

Fragile financial management

In partnership-based institutions, financial management is rarely straightforward. It involves managing a variety of more or less regular inputs and the problems are bound to increase as more partners join, or if there is no real financial integration of their respective inputs. Consequently, simplicity should never be an evaluation criterion, regardless of the country concerned. But two phenomena are worth mentioning here.

The first relates to the heavy and systematic use that such partnerships make of the subsidised job schemes run by the Ministry of Employment. Without debating the quality of such jobs, the sheer task of managing them is a major source of financial insecurity for partnership-based institutions. What is more, some staff in the *Missions centre-ville* maintain that funds do not always arrive as regularly as they should, particularly when subject to re-approval, and this obliges institutions to cover their cash flow requirements with bank loans. Apparently partial solutions are being developed.

The second is the major role played by European Union Structural Funds, in particular the Social Fund. While it was logical for the earliest initiatives to be funded in this way, nothing changed when the system was brought into widespread use, and it is striking to see how many references there are to European funding. There is some doubt as to the duration of this funding, and it is highly likely that alternative resources will have to be found in 2006. But another consequence of the system is a further loosening of what should be very close links between economic partnerships and employment partnerships. Funding for employment partnerships comes from the ESF and, under the Belgian constitution, must be channelled through the French-speaking Community, which is rather complicated given the number of players and rationales involved in the final allocation. Funding for economic partnerships, on the other hand, comes from another Structural Fund, the ERDF, directly to the Walloon Region and by-passes the French-speaking Community. So the methods of accessing European funds here actually alter the goals and behaviour of partnership-based institutions, whereas of course the reverse should be true. Only partnerships such as *Centres de compétences* that see a strong link between economic and employment issues manage to avoid this risk. It would therefore be advisable for all structural funding to go directly to the Walloon Region, with an agency there to adjust allocation and ensure that goals are in line with specifications, which is in any case a pre-requisite for development.

Complex personnel management

Employment partnerships make use of several types of "protected" or subsidised job. This requires complex financial management owing to abundant regulations and delayed payments; uncertainty about training, as mandatory provision is far from common; variable prospects of a return to work, and varying degrees of protection for job-leavers. But perhaps the greatest problem is that the low skill requirements for some of these posts do not match the demands of the job. Let us look at some of these job categories and how well they match partnership needs:

- Often intended for non-profit organisations or *Missions centre-ville*, public-sector jobs for "subsidised contractual employees" are available under both federal and regional schemes. They are reserved for the unemployed in receipt of benefits for at least one day, and are open to candidates with upper secondary qualifications or graduates. Initially for two years, the contracts may now be for longer periods, and wages are deemed adequate (around EUR 16 000 per annum). They are accordingly suitable for assistant or even managerial posts in some cases. As the subsidy can vary, non-profit organisations may have to shoulder part of the cost. The managers appointed to run these agencies may seem underpaid by job market standards (but these posts are a springboard to unsubsidised jobs). There is indeed evidence of a fairly high turnover among city-centre unit managers, and low pay or – more likely – poor career prospects could well be the reason.

- Relatively similar to the previous category, "Royal Decree 258" jobs are more advantageous: wages and subsidies are higher if there are two or more such posts in the same institution.

- The third category of jobs are available under the *Programme de transition professionnelle* (PTP), a transitional job scheme set up by the Federal government in co-operation with the Walloon Region and municipal authorities. They target the long-term unemployed (out of work for at least two years) without upper secondary or higher qualifications. The contracts are for two to three years, and 20% of the corresponding "time credit" should normally be given over to training. Wages may vary but are usually based on public-service or collectively agreed pay-scales for similar jobs. They should normally be the same for everyone working in the same unit. Funding is complex, as it comes from three sources: a federal subsidy; a subsidy from Wallonia's regional Ministry of Employment; and a possible subsidy from the regional Ministry of the Economy depending on the type of institution. As the federal subsidy depends on the local unemployment rate, the employer's contribution is variable and may not even be required in the hardest hit communes but increase sharply in the opposite case.

- The final category of subsidised jobs are what are known as "Rosetta jobs", or "First Job" contracts. They are normally confined to communes with over 30 000 inhabitants, which should exclude ADLs but include the non-profit organisations running town-centre management units. They target young people under the age of 25 who have completed their compulsory schooling, regardless of attainment. They are full-time one-year contracts, but in this case there is no provision for one-fifth of working time to be set aside for training. The jobs are supposed to be for work of a general nature but the regional Ministry of Employment has decided to let the *Missions centre-ville* and ADLs benefit from this provision, given their high-priority mission. "Rosetta" workers retain their unemployed status and the corresponding entitlements upon completion of their first job contract. The Walloon Region covers all the necessary funding, including a number of job-related costs. These jobs command low wages.

Some fairly small structures can accordingly choose from a whole range of jobs, each with its costs and benefits. The hardest choice is between the last two job categories: PTP workers will have longer contracts but lose their entitlement to unemployment benefits, and they are not given any "time credit" for the training they require to return to the labour market. "Rosetta" or first-job holders are employed under better conditions, but on short contracts with no provision for training unless the main employer is willing to make an effort.

Choice of management structure

Many of the partnerships in our study are based on structures with their advantages and disadvantages, although some types of partnership are particularly flexible since they have no specific structure but pool their operations, like some of the *Centres de compétences*. When these partnerships become institutionalised, they usually function either as an autonomous legal structure with the status of para-communal non-profit organisation; or as a management service within the commune, perhaps even a *régie communale* (commune-run enterprise). ADLs can fall into either of these two categories, as can *Missions centre-ville*. However, the *Missions régionales* are for the most part non-profit organisations (NPOs).

NPOs are advantageous in this case, for several reasons. They can make some partners less apprehensive about working with local authorities or government departments. They can mobilise partners' funds. They enjoy some autonomy and can thus distance themselves from politics. They generally have access to employment subsidies, enabling them to reduce their labour costs. But they are also fragile, depending inevitably on the participation and genuine commitment of their partners. Their fairly ready access to subsidised employment schemes may turn out to be a real trap when these jobs not only cause management problems but prevent them from delivering with the necessary professionalism, if not dedication. A further problem may be partner overload, when many partners are found in a variety of associations playing roughly the same role. A final point worth noting about para-communal NPOs is that the authorities retain a majority on their governing boards, since two-thirds of their membership must be government appointees. This requirement distorts the situation, quite apart from the fact that it is not really necessary.

The alternative, *i.e.* a management service within the commune, offers the advantages of simplicity and usually permanency. There may be improvements in terms of status (but not systematically) and the service concerned may find it easier to work with other municipal departments, in spite of some incomprehension or rivalry at the outset. However, its proximity to political circles and government may make potential partners somewhat apprehensive, and reactions may range from clientelism to lobbying. Some of the rigidities specific to an NPO environment disappear, but others inevitably accompany public management and finance.

The ideal structure may therefore be mid-way between the two cases described above, combining the flexibility and neutrality of the first with the solidity and permanency of the second. Hence the idea of an autonomous commune-run enterprise (*régie*), which does seem to hold out potential benefits. The draft decree on ADLs, for instance, envisages two options: a para-communal non-profit organisation, with two-thirds of its committee members appointed by the authorities; or an autonomous *régie communale* with a majority of town councillors on its governing board. Furthermore, the requirement concerning the number of inhabitants when establishing an ADL as an NPO or *régie communale* is apparently being removed from the draft decree.

Perhaps the real solution would be to give NPOs more responsibility by providing their resources as a package, tied to a "cost plus incentive fee" contract, as they are after all basically partnership-based structures, open to a wide range of participants. Another solution might be to set up a non-profit undertaking but ensure that there are sufficient private players to make financial commitments.

Dichotomies to be overcome

As well as featuring the drive launched by the Contract for the Future of Wallonia, employment partnerships are an attempt to enhance employment governance for both institutional and individual stakeholders by producing information, helping to devise plans and projects, and offering support. Now widespread, employment partnerships can often be traced back to innovations in the field, and many are still too new to be properly assessed. But many of these employment partnerships are disorganised and disconnected from economic players and the economic situation. They are validating rather than strategic partnerships, in that they accept rather than challenge the distinction between economic and social issues, and to a lesser extent the distinction between unemployment and social issues.

The distinction between economic issues and employment is very clear but far from rational, and only in the case of skill centres is there an integrated approach, precisely because of the need to anticipate skill requirements. But throughout this report we have shown that employment partnerships are set up first and foremost between institutions in the job market, without going sufficiently far upstream in the job creation process. When efforts have been made to do this, they tend to target "new service jobs", which are not devoid of interest but still relatively rare.

Many of these partnerships intentionally distinguish between employment and unemployment, partly because of the institutional set-up in Belgium. While it is normal to take the view that information or job-entry mechanisms should be systematically based on more than just unemployment and integration problems, it is then a case of deciding not so much on what they should be based but to what extent. The interface between the *Maisons de l'emploi* and the ALEs is a case in point. This distinction between unemployment and employment makes sense to employers and workers, but should not be taken too far when organising a public employment service or its "nerve-endings". There is a risk that government will create a duality that fails to reflect the real nature of the employment problems facing an economy in the throes of profound restructuring, where a skills shortage is compounded by jobseekers taking work for which they are overqualified. This inordinate separation between employment and unemployment has already been highlighted by the 1997 OECD report on the Public Employment Service in Belgium, which put it down to the distribution of responsibilities, i.e. passive programmes at federal government level (with its local centres) and active programmes in the regions. In many cases the distinction is justified on the grounds of labour mobility, to ensure that workers' rights are fully respected, regardless of where they live. But this does not rule out a better interface, especially as jobseekers are more often unemployed people looking for work than people in work applying to move.

The resources available to these partnerships are not geared to their needs. The missions they take on, directly or even indirectly, via the initiatives they launch require finely honed professional skills, in areas such as the joint management of business projects and the implementation of commercial urban planning schemes. Yet the staff available at a cost acceptable to them cannot provide them with those skills.

While it is logical and advisable that FOREM should help to run and support these partnerships, it should not completely alter them. Mechanisms that strictly regulate membership of the management bodies involved in FOREM, or even impose co-ordination structures on them, might seriously undermine their capacity to be effective and thus achieve good governance.

What recommendations can be made, on the understanding that there is no question of overloading these already heavy structures?

Some follow on from the analysis set out in this report:

- Bring the *Maisons de l'emploi* and the ALEs closer together, since too many players make do with – at best – geographical proximity.
- To achieve this, integrate passive and active labour-market policies more closely, as suggested in the 1997 OECD report.
- Bring the ALEs, the CPAS and the *Maisons de l'émploi* closer together.
- Improve the ties between Local development agencies and the *Intercommunales de développement*.
- Pool employment partnership resources and allocate them via a "cost plus incentive fee" contract, which requires an autonomous structure and is aimed mainly at ADLs and *Missions centre-ville*; these resources could take the form of a contract-based special fund set up within the framework of a Plan Contract.
- Ensure that the human resources available to the partnerships match the objectives they have been set, particularly in the case of the *Missions centre-ville*.

Apart from these specific recommendations, however, there is also the question of whether the proliferation of these relatively disparate partnerships will improve governance on the jobs front. That can only be achieved with strategic partnerships that address the economic, employment and social issues together, because the players here are all different and the three functions are so separate in Wallonia's institutional system. Otherwise, it will merely be a case of assembling several different layers without any positive synergy: an economic layer that is really the employment layer; an employment layer that is in fact the organisational layer; and a social layer that is confined to integration. Such a system would of course be untenable.

The problem with the proposed system is that the committees in charge of the partnership side are above all "support" committees which are there to back up governing boards. And the players on those partnership committees appear to wield less influence than those on the governing board. A proliferation of validating partnerships does not necessarily make for a genuine strategic partnership approach.

Two institutions need to be singled out here. One is the *Centre de compétences* (skills centre) which appears to have grasped how to build a strategic partnership but is not actually at the centre of the process. The other, which ought to be at the centre of the process, is the Sub-regional Employment and Training Committee. It should at least open up more to issues such as land-use planning, the social economy and housing if it is to play its intended role as a forum for dialogue. But that will be far from easy, as the opposite perception of it is as an institution mainly for civil servants and social partners, and it could be viewed as a mere offshoot of FOREM. This would reduce it to a validating partnership.

In any case this type of institution should act as an interface, at a fairly broad territorial level, and foster dialogue between a wide range of structures, including the *Maisons de l'emploi*, the *Intercommunales de développement*, ADLs, the *Missions Centre-ville*, INVEST, and groups of communes.

Such an interface would make these employment partnerships integral features of a strategic vision in which their work would be systematically geared to the demands of economic and social development in their own areas. This is crucial if the reforms undertaken by the Walloon Region to stimulate its employment system and modernise its policy tool FOREM are effectively to improve governance in the field of employment. For the moment, this responsibility appears to be split between the Sub-regional Committees, the *Intercommunales de développement* and the skills centres, and to a lesser extent the *Maisons de l'emploi* and the ADLs.

Notes

1. Note to the Walloon Government on the draft decree on the Walloon Regional Employment and Vocational Training Agency.

2. Activity report by the Sub-regional Employment and Training Committee in Charleroi.

Bibliography

Denolf, L. and Denys, J. (1996), "Les entreprises et le recrutement en Belgique", HIVA, Katholieke Universiteit Leuven, Louvain, Belgium.

OECD (2001), *OECD Economic Surveys: Belgium*, OECD, Paris.

OECD (1997), *The Public Employment Service in Belgium*, OECD, Paris.

Segefa (2001), "Accompagnement des Agences de développement local dont les résultats de leur évaluation sont insatisfaisants", University of Liège, Belgium.

ULB (Université Libre de Bruxelles) (2002), *Évaluation globale du dispositif des Agences de développement local.*

ISBN 92-64-01530-2
New Forms of Governance for Economic Development
© OECD 2004

Annex

Expert team

The OECD recruited a multidisciplinary team of experts for this study, with expertise in economics, labour market policy, political science, public administration, sociology and geography. According to their specialisation, the experts were assigned to the various countries: Filip de Rynck (Czech Republic), Mike Geddes (Norway), Xavier Greffe (Belgium, Spain), Michael J. Keane (Mexico), Neil McInroy (Czech Republic), Alberto Melo (Belgium), Brian Morgan (Slovenia, Sweden), Hugh Mosley (Spain), Micheál Ó Cinnéide (Mexico, Norway), Anders Östhol (Czech Republic), Els Sol (Sweden), Murray Stewart (Slovenia). Sylvain Giguère directed the work of the team and supervised fieldwork in each country.

Below are biographical notes on the authors of the chapters of this publication.

Filip De Rynck is professor in public administration at Hogeschool Ghent and the University of Antwerp, in Belgium. His main areas of specialisation are regional development, local government, management of networks, intergovernmental relations and urban policy. He recently prepared a white paper on urban policy in the Flemish region.

Michael Geddes is in the Local Government Centre, Warwick Business School, in the United Kingdom. His research interests are in the fields of local governance, partnership and local economic development. He is currently undertaking major evaluation studies for the UK government in these areas, and previously led a substantial study of local partnership in the EU for the European Foundation for Living and Working Conditions.

Sylvain Giguère is the Deputy Head of the LEED Programme of OECD. A Canadian economist, he joined the OECD in 1995 and established a new field of work on local governance, addressing the issues of decentralisation, partnerships and policy co-ordination. He directs research on labour market policy, employment and skills and has been responsible for several OECD publications. Prior to joining the OECD, Sylvain worked in government on structural reform and policy.

Xavier Greffe is Professor at the Université de Paris I (Panthéon-Sorbonne) and Director of the Doctoral Studies in Economics. He is an expert for the European Commission and the OECD on issues related to decentralisation, local development, the social economy and the economic impact of culture. He chaired a European association for local development (LEDA Partenariat) and is currently the co-ordinator of the OECD LEED Scientific Advisory Group on Local Governance, based in Trento.

Michael J. Keane works at the Department of Economics of the National University of Ireland, Galway. His areas of research include regional and local economics, tourism development and social entrepreneurship. Current research projects include policies for integrated tourism development, territorial economic dynamics and the contribution of social entrepreneurship to local development.

Brian Morgan is Director of the Small Firms Unit at Cardiff Business School, University of Cardiff. Prior to this he was Chief Economist at the Welsh Development Agency. During the last fifteen years he has worked as a senior policy adviser in Wales and in Whitehall and has worked extensively across Europe. He is a director of a number of businesses in Wales, and is Chairman of the Welsh Whisky Company.

Hugh Mosley is Senior Research Fellow in the Labour Market and Employment Research Unit at the Social Research Centre (WZB) in Berlin where he has worked since 1986. His recent work has been on implementation issues, especially on public employment service reforms and on policy evaluation. Hugh has published extensively in specialised journals and advises the European Commission and the OECD on labour market policy.

Micheál Ó Cinnéide is Professor of Geography at the National University of Ireland, Galway. Strategies that are effective in empowering local communities to pursue self-reliant approaches to development are of particular interest to him. He has worked with various organisations throughout Europe and has published extensively on matters germane to local and regional development.

Els Sol, a sociologist and geographer, is associated professor at the Hugo Sinzheimer Institute at the University of Amsterdam, the Netherlands. Her research focuses on labour market policy, regional governance and the use of private instruments like contracts for public labour market policy. Els is leading a major research on "Contractualism in Employment Services. A Comparative Study of Eight Countries", to be published in 2005.

Murray Stewart is Professor of Urban and Regional Governance in the Cities Research Centre, University of the West of England, Bristol. Murray's research interests are in collaboration, partnership and leadership in relation to urban and rural regeneration. He has been the leader of a recent project of the European Commission on Participation, Leadership and Urban Sustainability (PLUS), which involved nine countries and eighteen cities.

OECD PUBLICATIONS, 2, rue André-Pascal, 75775 PARIS CEDEX 16
PRINTED IN FRANCE
(84 2004 02 1 P) ISBN 92-64-01530-2 – No. 53711 2004